Fictions of Reality
in the
Age of Hume and Johnson

Louis Carrogis de Carmontelle, *David Hume*, ca. 1765. Reproduced by permission of the Scottish National Portrait Gallery

Fictions of Reality
in the
Age of Hume and Johnson

Leo Damrosch

The University of Wisconsin Press

The University of Wisconsin Press
114 North Murray Street
Madison, Wisconsin 53715

3 Henrietta Street
London WC2E 8LU, England

5   4   3   2   1

Printed in the United States of America

Library of Congress Cataloging-in-Publication Data
Damrosch, Leopold.
Fictions of reality in the age of Hume and Johnson/Leo Damrosch.
280 pp.   cm.
Includes bibliographical references.
1. English prose literature—18th century—History and criticism.
2. Great Britain—Intellectual life—18th century.   3. Hume, David,
1711–1776—Literary art.   4. Johnson, Samuel, 1709–1784—Criticism
and interpretation.   5. Fictions, Theory of.   6. Reality.
I. Title.
PR769.D3   1989
820'.9'91209033—dc20   89-16619
ISBN 0-299-12380-4   CIP
ISBN 0-299-12384-7 (pbk.)

Contents

Acknowledgments

THE IDEAS in this book were developed in a series of seminars, to whose members I am deeply grateful, at the Universities of Virginia and Maryland and at the Folger Institute in Washington. Helpful suggestions also came from lecture audiences at the University of California at Santa Barbara, the California Institute of Technology, the CUNY Graduate Center, the University of Delaware, and Harvard, Princeton, and Vanderbilt Universities.

What turned out to be the penultimate version of the manuscript was read for the Press by W. B. Carnochan and John Richetti, both of whom offered trenchant critiques that were crucial to revision. In addition, the final version received invaluable criticism from David Damrosch, William Dowling, and Joyce Van Dyke—to the last of whom, as always, books are but one of my many debts.

Chapter 5 incorporates material, now greatly revised, that originally appeared in *Studies in Burke and His Time* (later renamed *The Eighteenth Century*). I thank the editors for permission to reprint.

Note on References

In the hope of lightening the exposition I have renounced all footnotes, which means that fine points of agreement or disagreement with other scholars are not documented, and also that some debts are rather elliptically indicated. There is a list of works cited at the end of the book, omitting only those such as *Paradise Lost* and Locke's *Essay* that can be conveniently cited by line or section number. For reasons of space the list is not a comprehensive bibliography; it does not include the many works that I have consulted but have not drawn upon directly.

Typographical conventions are modernized throughout. In a book that treats a wide range of writers, it makes little sense to juxtapose standard texts that use modern conventions with others that are conscientiously archaic. In addition, I have slightly altered punctuation when the original forms would be needlessly confusing.

Fictions of Reality
in the
Age of Hume and Johnson

Introduction
Texts and Their Realities

I N AT LEAST five major kinds of writing, on the border between imaginative literature and so-called nonfiction, the later eighteenth century produced some of the highest achievements in our language: Hume, Gibbon, Burke, Johnson, and Boswell are arguably the greatest British philosopher, historian, political philosopher, critic-moralist, and biographer. Every one of these writers was deeply influenced by imaginative modes, and many able critics have explored the "literary" effects in such works as Boswell's *Life of Johnson* and Burke's *Reflections on the Revolution in France*. While recognizing the importance of this theme, I want to consider also the ways in which these writers insisted on the primacy of reality—of lived experience as shared by a culture—in a way that separates them from the Renaissance before and Romanticism after. My subject is the fertile tension between writing as necessarily fictive, whether it is nominally fiction or not, and the reality which these kinds of writing claim to reproduce or recreate.

It is a modern truism that "fact" and "fiction" interpenetrate at every level of experience, so that even the most abstract and logical modes of thought are inseparable from invention. Gian-Carlo Rota writes memorably, "Mathematics, like theology and all free creations of the mind, obeys the inexorable laws of the imaginary" (xviii). Recent studies of eighteenth-century nonfictional writing have (rather belatedly) begun to exploit this insight; to take a single example, David Marshall has convincingly shown that in Adam Smith's thought, "whether we are confronted with a person or a text, we must face a fiction" (595). This recognition of the ubiquity and necessity of fictions is central to my study. But so is a complementary recognition that there is a significant difference between texts that point

3

to potentially verifiable external data and texts whose inner worlds are self-defining and self-guaranteeing—"autotelic," as the New Critics used to say.

By a familiar convention, a fictional writer pretends to describe events that really took place, but only the most inexperienced reader would be taken in. (Swift loved the story of the bishop who read *Gulliver's Travels* and hardly believed a word of it.) A historian, very differently, "affirms that the events entextualized did indeed occur prior to the entextualization. Thus it is quite proper to bring extra-textual information to bear on those events when interpreting and evaluating a historical narrative" (Scholes 207). Such a recognition is uncongenial to the Romantics and their postmodern heirs, for whom *il n'y a pas de hors-texte,* but it is fundamental to the writing of the later eighteenth century. An appreciation of the literary aspects of nonfiction need not entail the notion that there is no such thing as nonfiction, which can lead to such extraordinary assertions, even from relatively traditionalist critics, as that when Boswell writes the *London Journal* "external reality hardly exists for him" (Spacks 235). I think it makes better sense to try to see the continuity between the poles of imagination and fact.

My thesis, briefly stated, is that the writers I discuss regarded reality as stable *and also* as relative. They lived in an age of epistemological crisis or destabilization, but they were still close enough to a tradition of stable ontology—a "real" reality that was supposed to be independent of human minds and grounded in the order of the universe—to try to salvage the coherence and reassurance of that older view. They were well aware that a more or less skeptical empiricism had become the intellectual norm, casting doubt on philosophical abstractions and on the assumptions of established religion, and they were at least partly aware that the notion of "reality" is always relative to some community (cultural community, interpretive community, community of believers, and so on). But instead of being baffled or silenced by this crisis, they sought to resolve it through writing.

The forms of writing in which they sought resolution are extremely varied, but they all operate in an ambiguous zone between absolute reality and reality as perceived. Either explicitly or implicitly they assert that the intuition of a stable and enduring reality had always been a sound one, but not in a naive or context-free way; reality becomes—indeed *is*— stable and enduring to the community that perceives it as such. But since a shared sense of order was precisely what was breaking down, these writers all strove, in varying ways, to redefine and reestablish the com-

4

munity for which their preferred version of reality could seem stable and enduring. Their texts seek both to elicit and to create the consensus to which they appeal: *this* world will exist as a determinate reality so long as *this* community exists, and the existence of world and community are inferrable from *this* text which you are reading and (the author hopes) concurring with. By offering themselves to readers who can read their way into the community they posit, they offer access to their version of reality as well. The communal reality rests on shared fictions, but fictions of a different order than the self-consciously invented fictions of art. Reflection reveals the fictive quality of these "nonfictional" texts and of the interior fictions to which they appeal, but unlike novels and poems they are *felt to be true* by most people all of the time, and by philosophers most of the time (whenever they are not consciously analyzing as philosophers).

I have called this book *Fictions of Reality in the Age of Hume and Johnson* because I shall try to show that these two writers, despite their obvious and deep points of disagreement, both accept the notion of consensus as the basis for an intelligible reality. Hume, to be sure, regards all moral and even epistemological notions as artifices that "nature" inspires in order to make life livable, whereas Johnson believes that they are securely founded on divinely sanctioned laws. Their differences in this respect are as deep as they and their contemporaries believed. But at a still deeper level they inhabit a common intellectual world, and throughout this book I shall invoke them as choric voices in dialogue with each other and with the age.

Each of the other writers is treated within this general context. Boswell, for instance, explores the relation (or tension) between community and reality from the inside, using the autobiographical journal as his form; Gibbon attempts to speak for the culture from an Olympian standpoint, inviting readers to join him in a community of irony. Gilbert White, by contrast, assumes a reality independent of human perception, but quite unconsciously projects it through cultural categories—in his case, categories that already seemed old-fashioned to most of his contemporaries. Burke's writings reflect the hinge upon which a massive cultural shift turns, as the old consensus gives way irrevocably. And finally, Godwin affords a look ahead into the new age, whether one calls it "Romantic" or something else, in which the imaginative status of private and social fictions was to be fundamentally reconceived.

The present academic moment is a propitious one for this kind of study, since scholars have been increasingly interested in cultural criticism, for which the nonfictional texts I consider are particularly relevant.

Much academic writing, however, has continued to be preoccupied with traditional generic categories, even when these are translated into cultural terms. At a modest level, this produces close scrutiny of "the ode" or of "sentimental fiction"; at a more ambitious level, it produces large claims, at a level of explanatory theorizing that many nonliterary historians would regard as illusory, of the reasons why "the novel" developed or "satire" declined.

Such writers as Johnson, Gibbon, and Burke have certainly not been neglected in recent scholarship, but many of the most impressive studies—for instance, John Sitter's *Literary Loneliness in Mid-Eighteenth-Century England*, Fredric Bogel's *Literature and Insubstantiality in Later Eighteenth-Century England*, and Jerome Christensen's *Practicing Enlightenment: Hume and the Formation of a Literary Career*—have stressed anomie, indeterminacy, or ideological duplicity rather than the shared fictions that make social life possible. Christensen, for example, detects a confidence in the existing order that lies beneath Hume's supposedly corrosive skepticism, but whereas he regards this affirmation of norms as an unacknowledged (perhaps even illicit) subtext, I see it as Hume's central purpose. It should be added that philosophical studies like David Norton's *David Hume: Common-Sense Moralist, Sceptical Metaphysician* and Donald Livingston's *Hume's Philosophy of Common Life* take an approach much closer to my own.

One gets the impression, moreover, that the poets are still allowed to set the tone for the age, which generates a picture of frustrated and disappointed talents marooned between the confident Augustans and the confident Romantics. One reason for this emphasis, no doubt, is the century-long fallout from Arnold's claim that poets in the eighteenth century were trapped in an age of prose. Specialists in the field have been laboring to correct this "misconception" ever since the 1930s, but in ways that were bound to fail because they accepted the premises of the hated position: since an age of prose would be a bad thing, the eighteenth century must somehow have been an age of poetry. Pope's brilliance has made such an assumption just barely tenable, but Collins, Gray, and Cowper seem not quite equal to representing the entire half century that followed Pope. Perhaps Arnold's assessment is not so wrong after all, if one regards the eighteenth century not as a hiatus between Renaissance and Romanticism but as the beginning of the modern age. In this context prose might be seen as, in Erich Heller's words, "not merely a manner of writing, but a style of comprehension" (3), against which poetry from the 1740s onward defines itself in explicit reaction. Poetry and prose, from this point of view, are not just different rhetorical techniques, but "different coinages of the mind, different currencies by which we pay for our attempts to understand the world" (Heller 4).

The challenge to literary history, it seems to me, is to deal effectively with the situation that William R. Keast defined thirty years ago, in an essay that appeared side by side in *ELH* with Northrop Frye's influential "Towards Defining an Age of Sensibility": "During the second half of the eighteenth century the impulse to create finished literary works was embodied—perhaps to a greater extent than ever before in English literature—in histories, biographies, orations, and philosophic treatises of many kinds; . . . it was embodied, in short, not in projections of the poetic imagination but in great works of the intellect" (153). Three decades later, this distinction may look naive, since all forms of discourse are in a sense equally imaginative. But only in a sense. The forms dominant in the later eighteenth century were ones in which "the literary imagination appears to disguise itself and to submit to significant constraints—literary criticism, historiography, scholarship and erudition, natural history" (Gossman, *Empire* xiii).

To some extent the neglect of these writings is due to the fact that ever since the Romantics, the term *literature* has implied, as Raymond Williams puts it, "an ever firmer separation between imagination and reality, fiction and fact," whereas in the eighteenth century it meant "a group of written works of a certain level of seriousness, capable of sustaining an attention that others could not" (*Politics and Letters* 325–26). When the Romantic bias against nonfiction (indeed against nonpoetry) was supplemented by New Critical formalism, these works were bound to be pushed to the margin. Yet the gains of the New Criticism should not be carelessly abandoned: all texts are finally individual, and the movement of thought and language within them is what defines the realities they assume and recommend. My own ideal remains a historically informed New Criticism.

There are other reasons besides formalist ones to concentrate on individual and well-known texts. C. S. Lewis warns memorably, at the outset of his magisterial history of sixteenth-century literature, that we can never really know "the actual content of the past or (less plausibly) of some artificially isolated period in the past," and that "spirits" or "qualities" attributed to historical periods "are always most visible in the periods we have studied least. The 'canals' on Mars vanished when we got stronger lenses" (64). I do not claim an epistemic shift for the whole culture, along the lines of a theory like that of Michel Foucault. My argument is confined to certain intellectual texts that were highly visible in their own time and have continued to seem significant to later generations. And while I am sympathetic to attempts to enlarge the canon, I agree with Eric Rothstein (5) that we should heed Edgar Wind's injunction: "The commonplace may be understood as a reduction of the exceptional. . . . Both logically and causally the exceptional is crucial, because it introduces (however strange it may sound) the more comprehensive category" (238). Or to cite Dominick LaCapra's recent critique of *mentalité* historians, "Certain artifacts are exceptional products of cultural activity, and it is ill-advised, even self-defeating, to deny their critical power or uncanny ability to play uncommon variations on commonplace themes" (*History* 93).

It needs to be emphasized also that although Johnson and Hume and Burke are certainly canonical writers, few of their writings resemble the traditional "masterworks" that the canon was once supposed to enshrine. With the exception of Hume in his youthful *Treatise* and Gibbon in his neoclassically ordered *Decline and Fall*, the texts we will consider all have a miscellaneous and occasional quality; they represent ever-renewed attempts to locate some kind of order in the welter of experience, and are not programmatic structures of explanation. Thus Johnson's writings are distributed through "an imperfect edition of Shakespeare, a dictionary, a set of uneven poetic biographies, a number of occasional essays, a few imitative poems, an oriental moral tale, and various prefaces and critical writings" (Kernan 203—and Johnson's sermons, travel book, and political tracts should be mentioned too). Burke's writings are similarly distributed through "letters of advice and instruction, political memoranda, motions and resolutions, practical works of political economy, committee reports, articles of charge, parliamentary orations and addresses, platform speeches, and so on" (C. Reid 5—and Burke's philosophical treatise should be added). These forms of writing, which are essayistic in the deepest sense of that term, reflect a conviction that readers must be tempted into collusion with the author over a wide range of topics of shared interest, not presented with fully formed and self-contained artifacts (*Tom Jones* was in this sense the last Augustan work). Burke wrote in his youth that "most books prove, affirm, demonstrate; they come with settled notions to us, and make us settle ours too early" (*Notebook* 88). His own writings and those of his contemporaries offer readers the inquiry as well as, and sometimes even instead of, the result. Johnson's *Rasselas* ends with a "Conclusion, in which Nothing is Concluded."

Something more should also be said about the paradoxical status of fictions of nonfiction. It is quite true that every piece of writing, whether

8

it presents itself as fictional or not, is committed to a version of reality, whether it is the familiar Dublin milieu of Joyce's *Ulysses* or the Berke-leyan anti-world of Borges' *Tlön, Uqbar, Orbis Tertius*. What is striking in the works we shall examine is that their nonfictional assertion is so self-reflexively overt: they *represent the difficulty of representing* a world independent of themselves, a heterogeneous order of reality which is stub-bornly independent of the mind, and of which they are trying to make sense. The first generations of empiricists had tried out two possible ex-tremes. Locke held that reality was external to the self but comfortably congruent with the "impressions" that the self perceives; Berkeley held that reality is wholly mental but that private realities are not solipsistic be-cause God thinks everything, including us (Berkeleyan epistemology is in fact a covert theodicy). By mid-century empiricism found itself in a much less secure position, asserting at once the reliability and the unprovability of perceived reality. This struggle to make sense—to establish a depend-able congruity between *the* world and *one's own* world—is my subject in this book.

This approach has a good deal in common with the "new pragmatism" that has been much discussed in recent years. Stanley Fish, for instance, quotes the philosopher John Searle on "brute facts" and comments, "What I am saying is that the facts Searle would cite as 'brute,' the facts stipu-lated by the standard story, are also institutional, and that the power of the law to declare a man and woman husband and wife is on a par with the (institutional) power of the standard story to declare that Richard Nixon exists" (240). As we shall see in the next chapter, such a position has much in common with Hume's, in which skepticism is held at bay only by the inescapable immersion of individuals in the thought patterns of their culture. Hume, Johnson, Gibbon, and Burke might all agree with Fish that "what we know is not the world but stories about the world" (243). But they would also assert, as Fish presumably would not, that a world about which stories are told is not merely a cultural invention. A culturally specific language game allows us to see Nixon as an American president rather than as a neolithic hunter-gatherer, but it is hard to imag-ine any human language game (though Fish could doubtless invent one) in which Nixon could be a mollusc. A totemic system might identify him *with* molluscs; a poetic metaphor might see him *as* a mollusc; but no sane person would mistake him *for* a mollusc.

As contrasted with a total relativism, the Hume tradition points for-ward to something like Hilary Putnam's "conceptual relativity," which is not "just a name for what a bunch of people can agree on" (17–

18) but an attempt to hold two assumptions simultaneously: "There are 'external facts,' and we can *say what they are*. What we cannot say—because it makes no sense—is what the facts are *independent of all conceptual choices*" (33). On the question of the truth status of reality, these eighteenth-century writers have more in common with modern historians than with modern literary theorists. To put it another way, at a time when advanced literary theory has rendered problematic all questions of a reality external to texts, we are in danger of losing the coordinates that are needed for reading works that take the problem of reality as central. This is why, in recovering a sense of the epistemological stakes that Hume, Johnson, and Gibbon saw as fundamental to their work, it is often helpful to turn not to literary theory but to current arguments about the nature of historical writing, for which the problem of a reality independent of the text remains inescapable.

It may well be true that no "objective" account of the past is possible, but that is because human understanding is subjective and symbolic, not because the past never happened. And I would add that the ideal of objectivity, though finally unrealizable, is entirely intelligible and defensible. Peter Gay expresses it very well in *Style in History*: "This pressure toward objectivity is realistic because the objects of the historian's inquiry are precisely that, objects, out there in a real and single past. . . . The tree in the woods of the past fell in only one way, no matter how fragmentary or contradictory the reports of its fall" (210). Marc Bloch, co-founder of the *Annales* school, was deeply aware of the riddling complexity of the past, but he was prepared to speak of "the true order of reality" (146) and to distinguish between reality and its interpretations: "The past is, by definition, a datum which nothing in the future will change. But the knowledge of the past is something progressive which is constantly transforming and perfecting itself" (58). Bloch's investment in this notion of the past, and in its meaning for the present, was much more than merely theoretical or academic. He wrote these words during the Second World War, in which he was active in the Resistance, and soon afterward the Germans tortured and executed him.

Even in literary-critical terms, a distinction between history and fiction, or between imagination and invention, continues to have value. In a penetrating essay entitled "Narrative Form as a Cognitive Instrument," Louis Mink argues that although historians increasingly recognize the impossibility of "objectivity," since facts have no meaning until they are selected and presented from some individual perspective, it remains equally impossible to relinquish the belief that "everything that has happened belongs to a single and determinate realm of unchanging actuality" (141). We may never be able to prove that a particular event has happened; we may even come to recognize that the very notion of an "event" presupposes a story that has conferred that status upon it, so that "an event is an abstraction from a narrative" (147). All the same, "history" and "fiction" continue to refer to different things, even if they turn out to be poles at either end of a continuum. So Mink concludes, "Our understanding of fiction needs the contrast with history as much as our understanding of history needs the contrast with fiction" (148–49). The tension between history and fiction is unresolvable because the two terms work as dialectical opposites rather than as logical coordinates.

From the point of view of the history of ideas, our own moment represents a later stage along the same road that Hume and Johnson were traveling. A recent theorist of history identifies the following "paradoxical characteristics" in historical explanations:

They make frequent use of the terminology of cause and effect but constantly frustrate causal analysis. They claim a kind of scientific status but are cast in narrative form and embellished with imagery, irony, and inference. They seem to imply the existence of laws, norms, and levels of probability which are seldom stated and hard to abstract from the particular terms of descriptive accounts. (D. Porter 25)

These are problems that were first clearly formulated in the eighteenth century, and if they remain unresolved today, the main lines of thinking about them continue to be the ones that were developed at that time.

From a quite different angle, moreover, students of literature are increasingly interested in historical contexts. Literary scholarship has become aware of politics in ways that were once hardly noticed at all: not the parochial quarrels of Whigs and Tories, but the ideological assumptions that hold society together. My approach has obvious affinities with the new historicism, and no doubt would never have been conceived without the inspiration of that highly imaginative intellectual movement. But it differs from most versions of new historicism in an important respect: I am principally interested in the ways in which an individual imagination shapes its world, rather than the ways in which the world shapes all the imaginations that reside in it. My objection to the latter approach is not so much that it is mistaken as that it is impossible; scholarship that attempts it tends to work from the critic's imaginative invention of a Renaissance or eighteenth-century world, rather than from the full density of information that inhibits most historians from grand cultural generalizations.

Nevertheless, the story I shall try to tell is political in the deepest sense: it centers upon the deep conservatism that characterizes the social views of every "major" writer, and nearly every "minor" one, between the 1680s and the 1780s. Until lately this conservatism has been surprisingly little discussed, no doubt because it is uncongenial to the assumptions of twentieth-century liberalism, and the most recent critiques have tended to be programmatic and unsympathetic. My hope is to try to see the eighteenth-century consensus from the inside, rather than to focus on its mystifications as *marxisant* critics do, or to claim affinities with modern "conservatism" as, for instance, some Burkeans have done. Rather than exposing the rationalizations of eighteenth-century ideology from a position of superiority—an all too simple procedure when one has the advantage of two centuries of hindsight—I shall try to explore the ideology as it understands itself.

The fact that so many writers held conservative views suggests that their conservatism reflected deep-seated cultural needs—granting, of course, that most members of the society, whether or not they accepted its dominant ideology, were in no position either to criticize or to replace it. The 1790s seem genuinely revolutionary to me, and I have deep sympathy with the radical program of Godwin, Blake, and their intellectual and political circle. But something may be learned from a study that ends rather than begins with that program, and tries to understand how its hopes were compromised not just by unconscious complicity with the old order—as they certainly were—but also by profound constants in human experience that resist all attempts at radical change.

At any event, little is gained by treating these writers as if they had willfully overlooked truths that should have been obvious to them. As Hannah Arendt says of the American founding fathers, "Whether these men were 'conservative' or 'revolutionary' is impossible to decide if one uses these words outside their historical context as generic terms, forgetting that conservatism as a political creed and an ideology owes its existence to a reaction to the French Revolution and is meaningful only for the history of the nineteenth and twentieth centuries" (44). G. M. Trevelyan wrote long ago that "to ask 'What was Shakespeare's attitude to Democracy?' . . . no more admits of an answer than the inquiry, 'What was Dante's attitude to Protestantism?' or, 'What was Archimedes' attitude to the steam engine?'" (153). Of course no one can avoid drawing upon his or her own assumptions. Trevelyan himself was an exponent of the "Whig" view of historical development and of a certain kind of social history. Still the attempt to imagine what the past felt like *at the time* continues to have value, even if that understanding is necessarily shaped by one's own values and assumptions. Trevelyan also says, "Every true history must, by its human and vital presentation of events, force us to remember that the past was once as real as the present and as uncertain as the future" (150).

In defense of emphasizing ideas rather than their social context, I cannot do better than to invoke J. G. A. Pocock's trenchant remarks in the first chapter of *Politics, Language and Time*. What he said in 1973 is even truer today: a scholar who studies the ways in which language embodies ideas, even when these are seen as existing under social conditions, is likely to be accused of "idealism," "false consciousness," "abstractness," and "unreality" (35). Lying behind such accusations is a too-rigid dichotomy between idealism and realism, with the concomitant "practice of referring to the extra-intellectual or extra-linguistic as 'reality,' and to the intellectual or linguistic equipment, at least by implication, as non-reality" (38). But reality—or more accurately, realities—are mediated through language, and as Pocock decisively says, "We are studying an aspect of reality when we study the ways in which it appeared real to the persons to whom it was more real than to anyone else" (38).

The conservatism shared by these writers is absolutely fundamental, not an accident of personal history or affiliation, and it forms the foundation of their view of reality. One cannot deal with it adequately by pointing to defenses of "the status quo" as if change was self-evidently desirable and the status quo self-evidently corrupt. Every one of these writers, like Pope and Swift before them, despised "corruption" and hoped to see a wide range of specific "abuses" corrected. What is at stake finally is world-maintenance. In a time when the imaginative bases of life seemed under attack, it was felt to be necessary to assert the "natural" rightness of the current organization of things, and even persons who were outspoken against "abuses" were likely to denounce change. "All the business of the world is to be done in a new way," Johnson declared indignantly; "men are to be hanged in a new way; Tyburn itself is not safe from the fury of innovation" (Boswell, *Life* 4:188).

Recent historical studies have helped us to understand what this threatened intellectual and social world felt like to its inhabitants, and an example may be useful. In *English Society, 1688–1832: Ideology, Social Structure and Political Practice during the Ancien Regime*, J. C. D. Clark mounts a richly documented challenge to the "Whig" (often Marxist) orthodoxy that has prevailed in British historiography during the past several decades. According to this orthodoxy, in the eighteenth century rationalist individualism, in alliance with bourgeois commercial culture and the Industrial Revolution, supplanted the hierarchical and patriarchal ideology of the seventeenth century. From a positive point of view, aggressive "new men" fought their way to power in a world of competing entrepreneurs; from a negative point of view, social idealism gave way to a political world of naked competition and exploitation.

This picture has been increasingly adopted, though Clark does not say so, by literary scholars. Their counterpart to the radical individualism of Lockean social theory is the alleged anomie of individuals cast adrift in a world of epistemological skepticism; their counterpart to bourgeois competitiveness is the complex of social and psychological assumptions that are said to underlie, or even to explain, the novel. And even when specifically political ideas are under consideration, it has been all too tempting to rehabilitate conservative writers by translating their ideas into more acceptable categories. Only thus can one explain, for example, the widespread acceptance of Donald J. Greene's claim in *The Politics of Samuel Johnson* (1960) that Johnson's political views were essentially identical with North American liberalism of the 1950s.

Against the orthodox picture, Clark offers abundant evidence that the old hierarchical, patriarchal, religiously grounded ideology had remarkable staying power, not just throughout the eighteenth century but far into the next as well. He shows, for example, that although some parts of Locke's political theory were invoked at certain times (such as the American Revolution, when the doctrine of contractual rights had polemical value), Locke's writings were ignored to a surprising extent throughout the period. He shows also that to name the "Industrial Revolution" in capital letters is to give too decisive a significance to changes that were gradual and, for the majority of persons, all but invisible until well into the nineteenth century.

Clark's polemic has elicited predictable outrage from its intended targets, but more disinterested critics, for instance Joanna Innes in a review article in *Past and Present*, concede that "the social role and ethos of the nobility, popular Anglicanism, social and political philosophy as expounded from orthodox pulpits, and conservative political philosophy more generally, have all—at least until very recently—suffered *relative* neglect" (182). The Whig establishment, Innes agrees, made heavy use of "conservative" themes (184), and although eighteenth-century Britain was more extensively commercial than Clark recognizes (179), it remained an explicitly hierarchical society topped by nobles and gentry, with land the greatest source of wealth and most of the population scattered in small rural communities (195). It is that world whose values are both reflected and perpetuated in the texts we shall now examine, and as Godwin's critique very bitterly shows, those values seemed virtually invulnerable even to people who sought to fight free of them. The old intellectual world may have been in trouble, but it turned out to be able, by a series of increasingly subtle readjustments, to continue affirming the old fictions long after their fictional status was widely acknowledged.

Finally, it may be helpful to situate this book among some others in which I have explored related themes. It takes its place as the fourth in a series, united in theme though not written in chronological sequence, addressing the problems that surround the representation of reality at the beginning of the modern age. *God's Plot and Man's Stories: Studies in the Fictional Imagination from Milton to Fielding* (1985) examines the claim that fiction can mirror, or even embody, a divine structure of meaning, and the implications of fictions that have to invent that structure for themselves. *The Imaginative World of Alexander Pope* (1987) considers a great poet who found himself obliged to abandon Renaissance symbols and to "stoop to truth," as he puts it in the *Epistle to Arbuthnot*. And *Symbol and Truth in Blake's Myth* (1980) explores the Romantic critique of empiricism and the recreation of reality as symbolic myth. The present book considers a period when neither Renaissance microcosm nor Romantic heterocosm—M. H. Abrams' terms in *The Mirror and the Lamp*—seemed a viable alternative, and when literature felt obliged to represent reality directly, with all the paradoxes that such an ambition entails.

1

Johnson and Hume
Fictions of Self and World

AUTHORS AND TEXTS

SAMUEL JOHNSON and David Hume have always been regarded as antagonists if not antitypes, and it may seem eccentric to join them in a single study. The points of difference between them are both obvious and important, and indeed they help to define essential parameters of eighteenth-century thought and experience. But it is at least as important to see—as recent studies of the "common sense" Hume help us to do—that they inhabit the same culture and respond to the same pressures in it. As the historian Marc Bloch points out, "To be excited by the same dispute, even on opposing sides, is still to be alike. This common stamp, deriving from common age, is what makes a generation" (185). Beyond the level of conscious opposition, Hume and Johnson share assumptions of the kind Stanley Fish describes in interpretive communities, at a level so deep that they are "indistinguishable from consciousness itself" (272).

One can accurately say of Johnson what has been said of Hume, that he "saw himself as a moral philosopher, a student of human action in its broadest sense, comprehending aesthetics, ethics, politics, economics, literature, law, religion, and history" (Livingston 1). Countless articles and books survey each of these topics in the two writers and I have gratefully made use of them, but my aim is different: not to establish what Hume and Johnson thought on specific points, but to ponder the implications of their sense of reality and its representation. Rather than examining extended narratives such as the *History of England* and the *Lives of the Poets*, which are readily amenable to "literary" categories, I shall consider their essayistic treatment of the psychological and social fictions of living, and the relationship of these to the fictions of art. At various points extended quotations will be needed; these will be familiar to specialists, but even for them there is good reason to permit Hume and Johnson full expression in the dialogue that modern scholarship conducts with them.

In life no direct contact between Hume and Johnson ever took place, though on one occasion they were apparently guests at the same dinner (Mossner 438). Boswell, who records that Johnson once left the company when Hume came in, was never able to bring them together, and had to omit Hume from an invitation that included all the leading intellectuals of Edinburgh (Mossner 394, 586). Johnson abhorred in Hume what he perceived as a self-promoting and destructive skepticism:

Hume, and other sceptical innovators, are vain men, and will gratify themselves at any expense. Truth will not afford sufficient food to their vanity; so they have betaken themselves to error. Truth, Sir, is a cow that will yield such people no more milk, and so they are gone to milk the bull. If I could have allowed myself to gratify my vanity at the expense of truth, what fame might I have acquired. Every thing which Hume has advanced against Christianity had passed through my mind long before he wrote. (Boswell, *Life* 1:444)

This is to confess an affinity even while repudiating it, an affinity that is felt to be especially unsettling since Johnson interprets "truth" in specifically religious terms.

Moreover, Johnson's famous bull-milking metaphor looks rather peculiar as soon as one inspects it closely. If Christianity were really a bovine that passively yielded nourishment, it might then be hard to resist the very different appeal of the energetic bull. Even in its own terms, Johnson's self-definition depends upon Hume for its (negative) point of departure, while claiming priority in the discovery of doubts whose inventor Hume claims to be. "The wish to affirm one's own existence in the face of others," Fernand Braudel observes, "is necessarily the basis for new knowledge: to deny someone is already to know him" (25). Johnson cannot possibly remain untouched by the Enlightenment, however often he mocks Hume and Rousseau in the conversations that Boswell records, and his sarcasms fail to conceal his deep affinities with it.

In this context, religious doubt has to be seen as a special case, apart from which Hume's doubts are not really so destructive as many have supposed. In his own opinion he was dismantling the extravagances of intellectuals rather than challenging the accumulated common sense of the human race. Hume therefore regularly condemned, just as Johnson did, those who "endeavour to distinguish themselves by ridiculing every thing, that has hitherto appeared sacred and venerable in the eyes of mankind"

(*Of Moral Prejudices, Essays* 538). In his first major work he declared, "Whatever has the air of a paradox, and is contrary to the first and most unprejudiced notions of mankind, is often greedily embraced by philosophers, as showing the superiority of their science, which could discover opinions so remote from vulgar conception" (*Treatise* 26). In fact Hume and Johnson were committed to the same goal: to rehabilitate traditional wisdom in accordance with a conviction that "the true philosophy approaches nearer to the sentiments of the vulgar, than to those of a mistaken knowledge" (*Treatise* 222–23), and that "philosophical decisions are nothing but the reflections of common life, methodized and corrected" (*Inquiry . . . Understanding* 170).

There would be no point in thinking philosophically, of course, if the only result was to ratify truisms. The point, rather, is to try to make better sense of experience than unreflective truisms do, while remaining faithful to the consensus that the truisms reflect. As Hilary Putnam says, "Without the constraint of trying to 'save the appearances,' philosophy becomes a game in which anyone can—and as a rule does—say just about anything. Unless we take our intuitions seriously, we cannot do *hard* philosophy at all" (28).

Hume and Johnson disagree at many points about the scope and content of traditional wisdom, but they do not disagree about its right to final authority. Johnson's assertions of solidarity with the "common reader" are simply the literary version of this position; as he says in the *Life of Pope*, "Of things that terminate in human life the world is the proper judge; to despise its sentence, if it were possible, is not just; and if it were just is not possible" (*Lives* 3:210). It is impossible because the consensus of the group simply *is* the way the world makes sense, and it is not "just" because there is no transcendental standard from which to reject that consensus. Moreover, intellectual ingenuity is more likely to distort the sense-making consensus than to clarify it. "The common voice of the multitude, uninstructed by precept and unprejudiced by authority, . . . in questions that relate to the heart of man is, in my opinion, more decisive than the learning of Lipsius" (*Rambler* No. 52). Very similarly, Hume says decisively in his essay *Of the Original Contract*,

Though an appeal to general opinion may justly, in the speculative sciences of metaphysics, natural philosophy, or astronomy, be deemed unfair and inconclusive, yet in all questions with regard to morals, as well as criticism, there is really no other standard by which any controversy can ever be decided. And nothing is a clearer proof that a theory of this kind is erroneous, than to find that it leads to paradoxes, repugnant to the common sense of mankind, and to the practice and opinion of all nations and all ages. (*Essays* 486)

The fundamental difference between Hume and Johnson flows, in fact, as much from temperament as from doctrine. Interestingly, they both experienced serious breakdowns in early adulthood, marked by similar collapses of will which Hume, in a letter probably intended for Dr. Arbuthnot (Mossner 83 ff.), compared to the acedia of the mystics (*Letters* 1:17), and which rendered Johnson "so languid and inefficient, that he could not distinguish the hour upon the town clock" (*Life* 1:64). But Hume's recovery was more successful by far. Johnson continued to fear an idleness that was at once a product and a cause of obsessive guilt; his friend Arthur Murphy commented that "indolence was the time of danger: it was then that his spirits, not employed abroad, turned with inward hostility against himself" (*Life* 1:269n). Johnson's self-critique was regularly deflected outward in assaults on the threatening forces he perceived on all sides, and as a young man he was converted to a rigorous form of religion that had deep emotional affinities with Puritanism. Hume's self-acceptance led him to assume a posture of classical tranquility—Peter Gay calls him "the complete modern pagan" (*Enlightenment* 401)—and he cultivated an irenic tone. In his own words, he aspired to a "command of temper" and "great moderation in all my passions" (*My Own Life, Essays* xl), while Boswell says of Johnson, "Every thing about his character and manners was forcible and violent; there never was any moderation" (*Life* 4:72).

In *My Own Life* Hume claims never to have been disturbed by attacks upon him, though in fact he is known to have suffered from them greatly. Johnson, very differently, actively invited attacks, and Boswell suggests a reason: "I am as certain as I can be of any man's real sentiments, that he *enjoyed* the perpetual shower of little hostile arrows, as evidences of his fame" (*Life* 4:55). Johnson needed enemies—including Hume, no doubt —in order to define himself, while Hume needed soothing admirers. Thus he wrote to Hugh Blair about a Parisian masquerade,

It is difficult to imagine the caresses, civilities and panegyrics which poured on me from all sides; you would have thought that every one had taken advantage of his mask to speak his mind with impunity. I could observe that the ladies were rather the most liberal on this occasion; but what gave me chief pleasure was to find that most of the elogiums bestowed on me turned on my personal character; my naivety and simplicity of manners, the candour and mildness of my disposition &c. (*Letters* 1:437)

From behind the truth-telling masks comes a stream of delicious flattery, and while Hume is careful to indicate that he's not taken in, he can hardly fail to enjoy this confirmation of his idealized self-image. Meanwhile, as Christensen observes (230), Hume himself wears no mask, presenting an amiable countenance that offers itself as the unmediated sign of interior worth. In a world of overt role-playing, Hume's role is to be himself. But what exactly is that?

As with Franklin in the *Autobiography*, Hume strives to put together a character that will answer to his own best hopes, as well as to those of the people he wants to impress. It is a recurring theme in eighteenth-century writing that social selves are deliberately constructed, and Hume, in the early editions of an essay called *Of the Independency of Parliament*, proposes a political explanation for the modes of behavior that he and Johnson embody: "In all controversies, we find, without regarding the truth or falsehood on either side, that those who defend the established and popular opinions are always the most dogmatical and imperious in their style; while their adversaries affect almost extraordinary gentleness and moderation, in order to soften, as much as possible, any prejudices that may lie against them" (*Essays* 608). Repelling all doubts, both within and without, Johnson becomes an aggressive controversialist who ferociously denounces Whigs, atheists, and a host of other targets. Hume, for whom skeptical doubts are a personal and professional commitment, is committed to an ideal of social harmony that reduces every controversy to the level of friendly debate.

Both Hume and Johnson openly confess their longing for fame, idealized as a wish to confer benefits upon posterity. "I feel an ambition to arise in me," Hume declares, "of contributing to the instruction of mankind, and of acquiring a name by my inventions and discoveries" (*Treatise* 271). Posterity has indeed confirmed this hope, but it is well to remember that success was not inevitable and that both men were well into their thirties before it even seemed likely. Johnson's long period of obscurity is well known; it may be more surprising to find Hume at thirty-six, having served as tutor to a mentally unbalanced young nobleman and as secretary to a failed military expedition, still grappling with the problem of a career: "I consider that I am at a critical season in life; and that if I retire into a solitude at present I am in danger of being left there, and of continuing a poor philosopher for ever" (*New Letters* 25–26). The *Treatise of Human Nature* lay ten years in the past, having received such wounding reviews and sold so few copies that Hume could lament that "it fell *dead-born from the press*" (*Essays* xxxiv). He italicizes the phrase to indicate an ironic allusion to Pope's *Epilogue to the Satires*, where "truth" is distinguished from ephemeral writing:

> All, all but truth, drops dead-born from the press,
> Like the last Gazette, or the last Address.
>
> (2.226–27)

But Hume does not really believe that his book lacked intellectual staying power. Rather, it failed because it misconceived the relationship between author and audience.

To remain "a poor philosopher" would be to quarantine oneself as a professional in a culture for which the newer, specialized professions were neither firmly established nor financially rewarding. If the intellectual is "an expert whose expertise is not wanted by the society at large" (Berger and Luckmann 126), Hume's career may be seen as a determined effort to escape that thankless role by transforming himself into an essayist and historian whom everybody is willing to read. The two *Inquiries* are much more than a strategy of popularization of the *Treatise*: they reflect Hume's decision to give his writing a more explicitly communal basis. His turn to history further extends the turn to society and morals that he had begun to make in the final book of the *Treatise*, "finding in the recalcitrance of historical documents something to resist the mind" (Sitter 49).

In an empiricist age that was suspicious of grandiose literary aspirations, any reaching toward "truth" was almost compelled to be essayistic, working from particular insights rather than aspiring to a self-contained intellectual and aesthetic realm. Wisdom can only be substantiated in the world of experience. That world is a social one; arguments that appeal to it will seem decisive only to persons whose experience is shared with the author. A major goal of the essayist is to simulate or reenact this sharing of experience. Persuasion works by enacting a process rather than by stating a conclusion, tracing the movement of the author's mind in order to encourage a corresponding movement in the reader's. The success of the work depends upon the reader's willingness to trust the authorial voice, which means that an early reviewer of Hume's *Treatise* (possibly Warburton) was missing the point when he pointed to the many "egotisms": "The author would scarcely use that form of speech more frequently, if he had written his own memoirs" (Mossner 122). In a sense that is just what Hume has done, and the *Treatise* can indeed be seen as "a quasi-autobiographical exploration of the mind" (Phillipson 145).

The essayistic mode, then, is much more than a ploy to attract readers; it represents a deliberate reaction to the formalized structures of seventeenth-century rationalism. As Burke says in his *Philosophical Enquiry into the Origin of Our Ideas of the Sublime and Beautiful*, "The method of teaching which approaches most nearly to the method of investigation is incomparably the best. . . . It tends to set the reader himself in the track of invention, and to direct him into those paths in which the author has made his own discoveries" (12–13). Moreover, this method is both an appeal to social consensus and a contribution to it. Near the end of his career

Burke observes, with obvious reference to his many years of service in the House of Commons, "In all bodies, those who will lead must also, in a considerable degree, follow. They must conform their propositions to the taste, talent, and disposition of those whom they wish to conduct" (*Reflections* 128). Johnson in the *Rambler* constantly alludes to the *Spectator* and other predecessors that had influenced the growing reading public by adapting to its interests. When Hume's *Treatise* failed to find an audience, it made perfect sense to recast his thought in a more essayistic mode. This is not an age that honors lonely oracular voices; to lead is also to follow.

Both Hume and Johnson pursue a dialectical path in guiding their readers through the puzzles of experience. Johnson's usual procedure is to announce some commonplace, survey it from all sides until it is thoroughly dismantled, and then reassemble it again. The wisdom of common life is shown to be right, but not until its accretion of clichés has been stripped away—as Bate describes it, "turning a thing upside down and shaking the nonsense out of it" (*Samuel Johnson* 496). Hume does the same thing, and although his skepticism is far more thoroughgoing than Johnson's, it actually works to defuse itself, since ordinary (even if mistaken) assumptions rush in to defend the thinker from the paradoxes his thinking has produced.

This sceptical doubt, both with respect to reason and the senses, is a malady which can never be radically cured, but must return upon us every moment, however we may chase it away. . . . Carelessness and inattention alone can afford us any remedy. For this reason I rely entirely upon them; and take it for granted, whatever may be the reader's opinion at this present moment, that an hour hence he will be persuaded there is both an external and internal world. (*Treatise* 218)

Hume's aim is to push paradoxes as far as they can go in order to show that reason bewilders itself in dead ends, reaching conclusions that are most unacceptable precisely when they are most nearly correct, so that they evaporate whenever the philosopher stops philosophizing. "I dine, I play a game of back-gammon, I converse, and am merry with my friends; and when after three or four hours' amusement, I would return to these speculations, they appear so cold, and strained, and ridiculous, that I cannot find in my heart to enter into them any farther" (*Treatise* 269). Rather than inducing skeptical vertigo as some modern scholars assert, Hume seeks to put together a reliable picture of the world; his epistemology confirms the coherence of life by showing that common wisdom works in practice even if reason is bewildered.

The eighteenth-century philosopher is not an isolated hero giving shape to what would otherwise be unintelligible, but a cultural spokesman who explores the ways in which everybody *already does* make sense of the world. If reality were purely a function of consciousness, and if mental fictions were entirely self-guaranteeing, then any and all attitudes toward experience would be equally valid so long as they gave psychological satisfaction. But the goal of eighteenth-century thought, whether conservative or "enlightened," is to dispel illusions and identify a bedrock of experience that underlies psychology. One unpacks clichés in order to understand where they came from, and it is usually possible to rehabilitate them after they have been duly inspected.

One may well conclude that the result is a feat of language rather than of demonstration. "Hume is not so much conducting an experiment," Christensen observes, "as displaying the *rhetoric* of experimentalism" (81). But in fact Hume would have no reason to object to this description, since language for him is not a site of suspicion but the medium that binds human experience together. Demonstration *is* rhetorical. Not all philosophies regard the procedure of taking commonplaces apart as an exposure of their emptiness. In John Dewey's words, "We cannot permanently divest ourselves of the intellectual habits we take on and wear when we assimilate the culture of our own time and place. But intelligent furthering of culture demands that we take some of them off, that we inspect them critically to see what they are made of and what wearing them does to us" (35). Commenting on this passage, Giles Gunn emphasizes the futility of attacks on philosophy that postulate—in order to demolish—some ideal notion of ontological stability that lies beyond human discourse. The aim of pragmatism is to recover and renew "our relation to the constituents of our experience, not in the primitive immediacy of our first encounter with them but only in the 'artful innocence' of our second" (73). Such a pragmatism is highly congenial to Hume, who could easily concur with Stanley Fish's account of the internal canons of criticism: "What counts as a mistake is a function of the universe of discourse within which one speaks, and does not at all touch on the question of what is ultimately —that is, outside of and independent of any universe of discourse—real" (238).

Here, however, is the essential point of rupture between Hume and Johnson: Johnson does indeed believe in a reality that lies beyond human discourse. If Hume's aim is epistemological, confirming the practical coherence of common life, Johnson's is psychological, showing that common wisdom embodies dilemmas that are inherent in human existence. Johnson is a moralist, not a philosopher. Ultimately, Hume's purpose is to defend "nature" from an Enlightenment standpoint, while Johnson's is to condemn it from an Augustinian standpoint; we shall return to this theme later. But the two writers remain united by their commitment to the empirical world, and by an ultimate appeal to psychology that lies deeper than their points of difference. Hence Hume's "usual policy of resolving epistemological problems by psychological theories" (Noxon 272). It is important to recognize that Johnson does not claim, as a seventeenth-century moralist might, that the dilemmas of mortal life should be renounced in favor of the realm of the spirit. The world we live in may not be the only or final world—Johnson insists that it's not—but it is the only one we presently know, and our concepts and arguments are all structured in its terms.

In a fine essay C. H. Knoblauch identifies in Johnson's essays a doubleness inherent in empiricism. On the one hand, we perceive instantaneously the coherence of natural objects, whereas the coherence of written descriptions is additive and provisional (more can always be said, or said differently). On the other hand, written discourse is built up of self-referential syntactic parts that can be fully coherent, whereas our knowledge of the "real" world—as opposed to linguistic accounts of it—is always conjectural; we surmise rather than know the coherence which we believe it exhibits. This analysis is closely congruent with Hume's account of perception and the always-fictional reality that is built upon it. "Here then we have a propensity to feign the continued existence of all sensible objects; and as this propensity arises from some lively impressions of the memory, it bestows a vivacity on that fiction; or in other words, makes us believe the continued existence of body. . . . This propension to bestow an identity on our resembling perceptions, produces the fiction of a continued existence" (*Treatise* 209). Social reality is understood and communicated through language, in which these fictions are given embodiment in conventional forms that seem so familiar that they are taken for granted.

But language can only achieve its work of coherence making if one knows what it means. Johnson gave years of his life to compiling a dictionary, which seeks to disclose order in language but also (as Knoblauch observes) testifies to its social basis and its endless mutation. "I am not yet so lost in lexicography as to forget that *words are the daughters of earth, and that things are the sons of heaven*" (*Preface to Dictionary* 310). Language does not descend from heaven, and if its constituent elements are disconcertingly arbitrary—"I wish . . . that signs might be permanent, like the things which they denote" (310)—that only underscores the fact that they spring from human imaginations.

Johnson's uneasiness about language and meaning reflects the dilemma that Richard Lanham analyzes in *The Motives of Eloquence*: "The Western self has from the beginning been composed of a shifting and perpetually uneasy combination of *homo rhetoricus* and *homo seriosus,* of a social self and a central self" (6). Rhetorical man, in Lanham's terms, is an actor with "an acute sense of social situation" (2), for whom "reality is what is accepted as reality, what is useful," and who relishes ludic improvisation in which language is simply a weapon with which to persuade. Serious man, on the contrary, believes in an objective reality to which language should reliably refer, and he uses it to communicate his own sincerity, exhibiting "faithfulness to the self who is doing the feeling" (1).

Johnson is very much a serious man, demanding truth-telling sincerity both in life and in art. But he does not entirely conform to Lanham's claim that for *homo seriosus* "the bad style will be the excessive style, the style which shows" (1), since his own style, which contemporaries regarded as a throwback to the seventeenth century, is notoriously artificial and excessive. Johnson is after all the conversationalist who talks for victory as well as the defender of the stability of truth, and his dismissive remarks on Swift's "easy and safe conveyance of meaning" reflect his recognition that most writing aspires to persuasion as well as to referentiality: "For purposes merely didactic, when something is to be told that was not known before, it is the best mode, but against that inattention by which known truths are suffered to lie neglected it makes no provision; it instructs, but does not persuade" (*Lives* 3:52).

One way of understanding this tension is to see in it the tendency of the printed word to absorb and supplant traditional rhetoric. In *Of Eloquence* Hume laments the mediocrity of public speaking in his own time, which he attributes to an abdication of oratory's traditional function: "Now, banish the pathetic from public discourses, and you reduce the speakers merely to modern eloquence; that is, to good sense, delivered in proper expression" (*Essays* 104). Something like Swift's ideal of the plain style does seem to be preempting all others, as Hume confirms in a passage that was deleted from the final version of his essay: "The English are conspicuous for *good sense,* which makes them very jealous of any attempts to deceive them by the flowers of rhetoric and elocution. They are also peculiarly *modest,* which makes them consider it as a piece of arrogance to offer any thing but reason to public assemblies, or attempt to guide them by passion or force" (622). Johnson, like Hume, loved the world of talk that offers, as Alvin Kernan says in his study of Johnson and print culture, "almost an animal contact with other bodies of your own kind" (209). But as many of Johnson's friends noted, his gifts could not have been easily adapted to the public stage, and Kernan suggests a reason why: in a time of enlarged and dispersed accumulations of knowledge, power and authority were attained in small groups of like-minded persons and in "the private, silent reading of books" (217) in which an illusion of personal communication can be conjured up.

Books simulate speech but embody language in forms that can never change, and Johnson's highly patterned style is an expression of this artificial coherence, pairing elements of meaning in reciprocal structures "until the whole is as stable as a line of print, as fully self-verifying in little as a language or a philosophic system on a larger scale" (Kernan 176). The local determinacy of rhetorical structure in effect takes the place of philosophical system. In addition, the distancing effect of printed prose liberates Johnson from the bullying urge to dominate that so many people objected to in his social behavior. The quasi-anonymity of "the Rambler" and "the Idler," as Fredric Bogel shows, permits him "to both claim and disclaim authority so as to exert its power without being crushed by its guilt" ("Johnson and . . . Authority" 198). In fact the very notion of authority is blurred, for the method of common sense carries the implication that any thoughtful person should be able to arrive at the same conclusions.

Print, then, is a substitute for life, but by confirming and clarifying lived experience it is also an indispensable supplement to it. We live by mental fictions, and books represent mental fictions at a further remove, yet it is in books that our grasp of reality is verified and guaranteed. We become wise, Johnson says, by building upon the wisdom of the past, and in this sense books are almost more important than experience itself, since unless you know what to look for you can't understand what you see. "The first task is to search books, the next to contemplate nature" (*Rambler* No. 154). In the Highlands Johnson laments the cultural amnesia of a people who lack writing: "In nations where there is hardly the use of letters, what is once out of sight is lost for ever. They think but little, and of their few thoughts, none are wasted on the past, in which they are neither interested by fear nor hope" (*Journey* 65). Another way of putting this would be to say that although truth is founded upon immediate experience, the experience of an individual makes little sense until it is interpreted through categories provided by society at large. A society that lacks a reliable memory is condemned to endless reinvention of itself in a state of continuous synchronic confusion.

Hume, whose epistemology commits him even more firmly to the view that our only experience is direct perception of "ideas" excited by phenomena, takes a similar position, and it is particularly interesting to see the stratagem by which he deals with phenomena that can only be known from books. It must then be the case that the words themselves—ultimately, the marks on the page—are the stimulant phenomena.

> We believe that CAESAR was killed in the senate-house on the *ides* of *March;* and that [is] because this fact is established on the unanimous testimony of historians, who agree to assign this precise time and place to that event. Here are certain characters and letters present either to our memory or senses; which characters we likewise remember to have been used as the signs of certain ideas; and these ideas were either in the minds of such as were immediately present at that action, and received the ideas directly from its existence; or they were derived from the testimony of others, and that again from another testimony, by a visible gradation, till we arrive at those who were eye-witnesses and spectators of the event. 'Tis obvious all this chain of argument or connexion of causes and effects, is at first founded on those characters or letters, which are seen or remembered, and that without the authority either of the memory or senses our whole reasoning would be chimerical and without foundation. (*Treatise* 83)

Knowledge exists, in short, because of the socially agreed-upon integrity of arbitrary signs that make up a reliable chain of shared experience. Events in which one has personally participated imprint themselves on the mind almost as if they were printed characters; analogously, printed characters, which also imprint themselves on the mind, inscribe the traces of events in which other people have participated. So long as everyone agrees on the meaning of the characters—and Hume seems not to question his ability to interpret a dead language correctly—then there is no reason to doubt the truth-value of the events that are perceived through a long chain of vicarious impressions. "It seems contrary to common sense to think, that if the republic of letters and the art of printing continue on the same footing as at present, our posterity, even after a thousand ages, can ever doubt if there has been such a man as JULIUS CAESAR" (*Treatise* 145).

Hume's confidence here reflects cultural assumptions, so fully internalized that he does not question or even recognize them, about the transmissibility of experience from one mind to another. Christensen rightly points out that the notion of unaltered reproduction is based on the technology of printing rather than on the practice of the countless scribes to whom we actually owe our information about Caesar: "Hume reads back the features of the press onto history in general in order to characterize a history in which nothing changes, in which no discontinuity has occurred or can happen" (139). Poststructuralist thinkers are of course committed to a very different and profoundly skeptical view of the status of linguistic "traces," but Hume's picture resembles that of a historian like Marc Bloch: "What do we really mean by *document* if it is not a 'track,' as it were—the mark, perceptible to the senses, which some phenomenon, in itself inaccessible, has left behind?" (55). Bloch quotes the seventeenth-century skeptic Bayle to confirm his point: "No valid objection will ever be raised to the fact that Caesar defeated Pompey. On whatever grounds we may choose to argue it, there is hardly anything more unshakeable than this proposition: Caesar and Pompey existed. They were not merely in the minds of those who wrote their lives" (103). What Hume adds to this is his empiricist account of how we know what we do about Caesar—an account which, by exposing the length and potential precariousness of the chain of reproduction, might well make us more skeptical than Hume is himself.

Historical persons were once alive and are now texts, and as it happens the literal transition from person to text is embodied in the deathbeds of Hume and Johnson, both of which were managed very deliberately as occasions for symbolic enactment. Hume's manner of dying, as his friend Adam Smith represents it, was expressive of a hero whose "temper . . . seemed to be more happily balanced, if I may be allowed such an expression, than that perhaps of any other man I have ever known" (Hume, *Essays* xlviii). Johnson's, by contrast, was appropriate to a hero whose mind, in Boswell's metaphor, resembled the Roman Colosseum filled with dangerous beasts: "After a conflict, he drove them back into their dens; but not killing them, they were still assailing him" (*Life* 2:106). Smith tells the story of a modern pagan who accepts death without anxiety, Boswell (who was unable to be present) the story of a devout Christian who resists it desperately but finally reposes upon religious consolations. According to William Strahan, "after being in much agitation, Johnson became quite composed, and continued so till his death" (*Life* 4:416), expiring "with so little apparent pain that his attendants hardly perceived when his dissolution took place" (417).

It happens that Boswell visited Hume when he was "just a dying," and left a fascinating account of the philosopher's refusal to exhibit fear:

I had a strong curiosity to be satisfied if he persisted in disbelieving a future state even when he had death before his eyes. I was persuaded from what he now said, and from his manner of saying it, that he did persist. I asked him if it was not possible that there might be a future state. He answered it was possible that a piece of coal put upon the fire would not burn. . . . I however felt a degree of horror, mixed with a sort of wild, strange, hurrying recollection of my excellent mother's pious instructions, of Dr. Johnson's noble lessons, and of my religious sentiments and affections during the course of my life. I was like a man in sudden danger eagerly seeking his defensive arms; and I could not but be assailed by momentary doubts while I had actually before me a man of such strong abilities and extensive inquiry dying in the persuasion of being annihilated. But I maintained my faith. I told him that I believed the Christian religion as I believed history. Said he: "You do not believe it as you believe the Revolution." "Yes," said I; "but the difference is that I am not so much interested in the truth of the Revolution; otherwise I should have anxious doubts concerning it. A man who is in love has doubts of the affection of his mistress, without cause." (*Boswell in Extremes* 11–13)

Following his usual procedure—to which we shall soon return—Hume argues from probabilities: he *may* live forever just as a piece of coal *may not* burn (death no doubt is imaged as a kind of burning), but both possibilities are extremely unlikely.

Boswell is shocked not just by the argument but also by the spectacle of an admirable human being who is able to assert it so calmly. He knows he is in danger, and hastens to recall all the pious lessons he has ever received, whether at his mother's knee or at Johnson's; Hume's example must be refuted by counterexamples stored up in memory. But Hume then further alarms Boswell by raising another favorite point, that people believe more fully in historical events like the Revolution of 1688 than they do in the Christian religion. Boswell in turn is driven into paradox: he doubts Christianity as he would doubt a mistress (but can Christianity be fickle or faithless in the way that a person can?). So Boswell finds himself saying that he believes something securely if it doesn't matter much to him, and that he starts doubting as soon as it becomes important to believe. This may well be psychologically true, but Boswell, like Johnson repudiating bull milking, wants "truth" itself. His fundamental problem is that he is just as committed as Hume to the premise that belief must be founded on empirical evidence; this was, after all, the great age of "evidences" for Christianity. To rest one's faith on an internal spiritual conviction would come too close to "enthusiasm" or fanaticism, and Boswell is therefore vulnerable to Hume's arguments from historical plausibility. One may well suspect, indeed, that Hume is right to assert that most of his contemporaries believe more implicitly in Caesar than in Christ.

Johnson later assured Boswell that Hume's deathbed speech could only be self-dramatizing hypocrisy, shrewdly applying a Humean critique of probabilities to the case.

He had a vanity in being thought easy. It is more probable that he should assume an appearance of ease, than that so very improbable a thing should be, as a man not afraid of going (as, in spite of his delusive theory, he cannot be sure but he may go) into an unknown state, and not being uneasy at leaving all he knew. And you are to consider, that upon his own principle of annihilation he had no motive to speak the truth. (*Life* 3:153)

For Johnson this is no abstract question, as Boswell makes clear: "The horror of death which I had always observed in Dr. Johnson, appeared strong tonight." But Johnson's retort goes past Hume's remarks without ever meeting them. As a human being, Hume might well feel uneasy about annihilation, but he would never agree with Johnson that this uneasiness affords evidence that we will *not* be annihilated. And even if he is pretending to more equanimity than he feels, that psychological fact has no bearing at all on the truth status of the incarnation or of eternal life. At all events, Boswell's discomfort was so great that in 1784, eight years after Hume's death, he received welcome relief from his own unconscious: "Awakened after a very agreeable dream, that I had found a Diary kept by David Hume, from which it appeared that though his vanity made him publish treatises of skepticism and infidelity, he was in reality a Christian and a very pious man" (*Private Papers* 16:20–21).

These questions of evidence and belief, and of the integrity of the self that entertains them, will occupy us throughout this book. Meanwhile, we need to recognize that once their deaths are completed and duly celebrated, Hume and Johnson cease to exist as persons. "As [Johnson] opened a note which his servant brought to him, he said, 'An odd thought strikes me:—we shall receive no letters in the grave'" (*Life* 4:413). The world of physical reality dissolves into two different kinds of textual worlds. One is the re-creation of biographers, in which "the image of Johnson as a dying Christian is a wholly conventional truth, for the image is the creation of a world determined to discover in Johnson's manner of dying a source of conventional comfort" (Dowling, *Boswellian Hero* 173). The other world is continually recreated by the original texts in which the living writer first offered a version of himself to his readers, inventing a public self that eventually justified the recording of his life. Biographers frequently perpetuate the hagiographical impulse of Smith and Boswell, focusing on the exemplary value of their heroes. But the other kind of textual existence survives as well, parallel with biographies but in a sense deeper: the invented voice of the essayist who strives for connections between the reader's experience and his own, a mode of shared truth that can prevail even though the self is mysterious and its world a perpetual flux.

Moreover, these are texts that claim to teach as well as to report.

Very likely they originate in self-therapy, using writing as a form of self-substantiation; Johnson says in a letter to Hill Boothby, a woman he hoped to marry, "You know Des Cartes's argument, 'I think therefore I am.' It is as good a consequence 'I write therefore I am alive'" (*Letters* 1:80). But the essayist, unlike the private letter writer, strives to speak with and for the entire community, knowing (or at least hoping) that "the Rambler" will outlive Samuel Johnson. "It is clear," Christensen says, "that because of its romantic basis and because it does not stake its success on truth claims, Hume's work cannot be confuted by argument. Hume's work can be effectively opposed only if it is regarded not as a series of propositions but as a literary practice aimed at attaining a reputation exempt from contingency" (49). It is conceivable that there is something "romantic" in Hume's professed hope to achieve literary immortality (though in that case, Horace, Jonson, and Milton are romantic too). It is perhaps less fair to interpret Hume's anticipation of impending death—he had stomach cancer and knew it—as "merely a facilitating interruption, as a good career move" (48). In any case, such a hope is logically separate from the truth status of Hume's writings, and although Hume certainly thought he had refuted the absolutist claims of philosophical rationalism, he did believe that arguments have consequences and that his own philosophy should be judged by argument. Opposition requires dismissal of that mode of judgment, and exposure of Hume's writings as "a literary practice" calculated, consciously or unconsciously, to hoodwink the reader. Hume's hope is that it will win assent by showing people why they believe what they believe.

ELABORATING THE SELF

It is a modern convention to speak of "the" self. According to Johnson's *Dictionary* the word is more normally a reflexive adjective ("self-same," etc.) than a noun, but in the seventh definition "it signifies the individual, as subject to his own contemplation or action." Locke is quoted: "Since consciousness always accompanies thinking, and it is that that makes every one to be what he calls *self*, and thereby distinguishes himself from all other thinking things; in this alone consists personal identity, i.e. the sameness of a rational being." The connotative slipperiness of *self* is then illustrated by an extraordinarily long "train of examples"—fully a hundred quotations—whose tendency is generally moral, recommending self-denial and self-defense while condemning self-love, self-seeking, and self-murder. *Consciousness,* meanwhile, is "the perception of what passes in a man's own mind," a definition that fully endorses the empiricist notion that the self can somehow be inspected *by* the self.

A distinction between an epistemological and a moral self will help to clarify the characteristic emphases of Johnson and Hume. In the first book of the *Treatise of Human Nature*, Hume ties the paradox of the self-inspecting self into ever-tighter knots, and has sometimes been accused of ending up with no self at all. Johnson, very differently, relies on the dualistic religious assumption that the better self must stand watch over the worse, and that thought can control thought. "He therefore that would govern his actions by the laws of virtue, must regulate his thoughts by those of reason; he must keep guilt from the recesses of his heart, and remember that the pleasures of fancy and the emotions of desire are more dangerous as they are more hidden" (*Rambler* No. 8). But as the metaphor of "recesses" suggests, the self in Johnson's writings is not so much an identity as a murky scene of disturbance where order is fought for endlessly. "Vacuity" becomes an essential term in his psychological thinking, and as Arieh Sachs observes, "Johnson's basic metaphor for human experience is the empty receptacle which cannot tolerate its own emptiness" (3).

Closely related to the empty self is the passive self, bereft of adequate "objects" and victimized by forces that it will not or cannot resist.

> Where then shall hope and fear their objects find?
> Must dull suspense corrupt the stagnant mind?
> Must helpless man, in ignorance sedate,
> Roll darkling down the torrent of his fate?
> (*Vanity of Human Wishes*, ll. 343–46)

"Torrent" is a revision for "current," and Johnson often uses the two terms to suggest helplessness, particularly when initial efforts seem to have been in vain. "A man thus cut off from the prospect of that port to which his address and fortitude had been employed to steer him, often abandons himself to chance and to the wind, and glides careless and idle down the current of life, without resolution to make another effort, till he is swallowed up by the gulph of mortality" (*Rambler* No. 127). Many people never even struggle. "Most minds are the slaves of external circumstances, and conform to any hand that undertakes to mould them, roll down any torrent of custom in which they happen to be caught, or bend to any importunity that bears hard against them" (*Rambler* No. 70). One recalls that the passions, which play an essential role in Hume's psychology as in Johnson's, are in their original signification reactive rather than active, so that Locke can say, "When the ball obeys the motion of a billiard-stick, it is not any action of the ball, but bare passion" (*Essay* 2.21.4). The first two definitions of *passion* in Johnson's *Dictionary* are "1. Any effect caused by external agency. 2. Violent commotion of the mind."

Worst of all, bad habits may cooperate with indolence to produce melancholy—nowadays called neurosis—and ultimately despair. "They crawled on reluctant and gloomy, till they arrived at the depth of the recess, varied only with poppies and nightshade, where the dominion of Indolence terminates, and the hopeless wanderer is delivered up to Melancholy; the chains of Habit are riveted for ever; and Melancholy, having tortured her prisoner for a time, consigns him at last to the cruelty of Despair" (*Vision of Theodore* 174). In the face of this threat Johnson doggedly asserts the role of reason, demanding of it a perpetual vigilance that is exhausting if not impossible. Bate says, "The final, the most drastic compulsion of Johnson is that of reason itself—the compulsion to be fully and finally aware" (*Achievement* 162). Johnson's lifelong insomnia is undoubtedly symptomatic of the fear of losing consciousness. He is committed to an unceasing and relentless inspection of what goes on in his mind, with the goal of bringing his unruly mind under rigid control.

The empiricist theory of mind tends to assume that "madness" is a matter simply of misaligning and misinterpreting sense data; according to Lockean psychology you are either mad or else you are not. Johnson's psychological writings, often denounced in his own time as morose and misanthropic, take empiricism for granted but draw also on the very different assumptions of the Augustinian tradition. Like the Puritans of the previous century, Johnson regards "normal" life as an unrealizable abstraction and neurosis as a universal affliction, varying of course in degree.

Perhaps, if we speak with rigorous exactness, no human mind is in its right state. There is no man whose imagination does not sometimes predominate over his reason, who can regulate his attention wholly by his will, and whose ideas will come and go at his command. . . . All power of fancy over reason is a degree of insanity. . . . By degrees the reign of fancy is confirmed; she grows first imperious, and in time despotic. Then fictions begin to operate as realities, false opinions fasten upon the mind, and life passes in dreams of rapture or of anguish. (*Rasselas*, chap. 44)

To a striking degree this analysis is anticipated by Richard Sibbes in a treatise called—in language Freud would approve—*The Soul's Conflict* (1635). Even the metaphor of the dream is present:

Imagination, of itself, if ungoverned, is a wild and a ranging thing; it wrongs not only the frame of God's work in us, setting the baser part of a man above the higher, but it wrongs likewise the work of God in the creatures and everything else, for it shapes things as itself pleaseth. . . . By reason of the distemper of imagination, the life of many is little else but a dream. Many good men are in a long dream of misery, and many bad men in as long a dream of happiness, till the time of awakening come. (180)

Just so the deluded astronomer in Johnson's *Rasselas* is a good man tossing in a nightmare from which he is awakened at last to health.

"It is no vain speculation," Johnson declares in an essay on "moral discipline," "to consider how we may govern our thoughts, restrain them from irregular motions, or confine them from boundless dissipation" (*Rambler* No. 8). Here is a fundamental paradox of Augustinian as of empiricist psychology: what is the "we" that represents the true self, acting through "reason" but subject to chaotic collapse if it permits "imagination" to gain ascendancy? The imagination (or fancy) is somehow not oneself and needs constantly to be subdued or "repressed": "All power of fancy over reason is a degree of insanity; but while this power is such as we can control and repress, it is not visible to others, nor considered as any depravation of the mental faculties; it is not pronounced madness but when it comes ungovernable, and apparently [i.e., visibly] influences speech or action" (*Rasselas*, chap. 44). This mode of repression differs from Freud's in two crucial ways: it is consciously chosen, and it is regarded as wholly desirable.

Johnson's twin assumptions here—that the imagination is dangerous, but that it can be brought under control—reflect the widespread eighteenth-century attempt to hold back the psychological relativism that was soon to break through. Whereas Romantic thinkers would celebrate the boundless individuality of human imaginations, empiricists held that the imagination's basis in sensory experience guaranteed its uniformity. Burke puts it very clearly in the *Philosophical Enquiry*: "Since the imagination is only the representative of the senses, it can only be pleased or displeased with the images from the same principles on which the sense is pleased or displeased with the realities; and consequently there must be just as close an agreement in the imaginations as in the senses of men" (17). For Johnson, no one is in his right mind, but all people deviate from the same right mind that they *would* be in if they could.

Accordingly, Johnson proposes a double response to the precariousness of the self: introspection that produces stern control of imagination by reason, and a counterbalancing return from the depths to an outer world that can replace imaginary objects with real ones. On the empiricist model the mind will always be busy reshuffling images, but instead of inventing "delights which nature and fortune . . . cannot bestow" (*Rasselas*, chap. 44), it can learn to ground itself upon "truth."

When a number of distinct images are collected by these erratic and hasty surveys, the fancy is busied in arranging them; and combines them into pleasing pictures with more resemblance to the realities of life as experience advances, and new observations rectify the former. . . . We first discard absurdity and impossibility, then exact greater and greater degrees of probability, but at last become cold and insensible to the charms of falsehood, however specious, and from the imitations of truth, which are never perfect, transfer our affection to truth itself. (*Rambler* No. 151)

The move through probability to truth is a matter of resisting specious charms and redirecting affection. Johnson's passionate commitment to knowledge thus has a deeply emotional basis; but it seeks to rise above emotion, rejecting fantasy and exercising reason upon "the realities of life" that experience yields.

The plural noun is potentially significant: rather than being a unitary order such as idealist philosophers might conceive, the world is a mosaic of intersecting "realities" (though Johnson may only have in mind the Latin *realia,* specific real things). Any text, whether fictional or non-fictional, can only gesture toward particular versions of these realities, and the reader must assess and confirm them by comparison with his or her own experience. "Imitations produce pain or pleasure not because they are mistaken for realities, but because they bring realities to mind" (*Preface to Shakespeare* 78). Only rarely does Johnson admit that society itself may be nothing more than a conjunction of separate fantasies: "In solitude we have our dreams to ourselves, and in company we agree to dream in concert" (*Idler* No. 32). Out of his personal experience and out of shrewd observation of other people, Johnson has created a richly complex fiction of the self, unsparing in its pessimism but committed to a conception of truth based upon shared "realities" that can rescue the self *from* itself.

Hume's contribution to the theory of the self is particularly challenging and complex, and has often been represented as a thoroughgoing demolition of the notion of personal identity. It is certainly true that Hume, like other empiricists, distinguishes between any possible "real" world and the interior images that are one's only clues to it: "The mind is a kind of theatre, where several perceptions successively make their appearance; pass, re-pass, glide away, and mingle in an infinite variety of postures and situations" (*Treatise* 253). Hume goes far beyond Locke in denying that there *is* a self, except insofar as these fleeting perceptions add up to an uneasy sense of identity, and he points out that a metaphor is not an explanation. "The comparison of the theatre must not mislead us. They are the successive perceptions only, that constitute the mind; nor have we the most distant notion of the place where these scenes are represented, or of the materials of which it is composed" (253). It follows that "what we call a *mind*, is nothing but a heap or collection of different perceptions" to which we falsely ascribe "a perfect simplicity and identity" (207), and that other people "are nothing but a bundle or collection of different perceptions, which succeed each other with an inconceivable rapidity, and are in a perpetual flux and movement" (252).

But it is important to recognize that Hume considers it impossible to *believe* in a totally decentered self. His account of it is a stage in a polemical campaign against the exaggerated claims of reason and the Cartesian cogito, and Hume freely acknowledges that the self exists even while he denies that we can understand its mode of existence. As a modern commentator says, "It is not the case that men are bundles of perceptions but only that when each man examines his 'mind' all that he finds is a bundle of perceptions" (Capaldi, "Hume's Theory" 181). Perhaps more interesting than the theoretical deconstruction of the self, therefore, is the process of sign interpretation by which it reconstructs the world around it as well as the world within. Even though our mental system is subjectively concocted from impressions which "we are pleased to call a *reality*" (*Treatise* 108), that does not mean that provisional realities are inadequate for living. On the contrary, Hume insists on the priority of "nature" over thinking, of instincts that wed us to the world even while our minds confess their inability to define it. "Most fortunately it happens, that since reason is incapable of dispelling these clouds [of doubt], nature herself suffices to that purpose, and cures me of this philosophical melancholy and delirium, either by relaxing this bent of mind, or by some avocation, and lively impression of my senses, which obliterate all these chimeras" (269). Even though immediate sensory "impressions" are the only reality we know, that is more than enough reality to be getting on with, and as Johnson says, "The motions of sense are instantaneous; its objects strike unsought" (*Rambler* No. 7).

In its context, Hume's account of the mind as a heap of perceptions provides an object lesson in the need to attend to the complexity of philosophical argument, and not to generalize too quickly from it to a full-scale account of human experience, let alone to alleged existential tendencies in the age. Literary scholars often quote this passage as if it described a chaotically incoherent self, and fail to notice that in context its purport is diametrically opposed to such a claim. Hume makes his point in answer to a question by which empiricism had long been troubled, "how we can satisfy ourselves in supposing a perception to be absent from the mind without being annihilated"; and his answer is, "Now as every perception is distinguishable from another, and may be considered as separately existent, it evidently follows that there is no absurdity in separating any particular perception from the mind; that is, in breaking off all its relations with that connected mass of perceptions which constitute a thinking being" (*Treatise* 207). A human being is a *connected* mass of perceptions, and the point of Hume's maneuver is to provide evidence for the existence of the external world, not to expose the incoherence of the internal world. As John Yolton summarizes his argument here, "The mind is nothing but a heap of different perceptions, united by certain relations; every perception is distinguishable and hence can be separated from this collection; hence any perception can exist apart from mind" (153). At bottom this passage in Hume is an answer to Berkeleyan idealism, not an attack on the existence of the self.

By pressing epistemology to its conclusion Hume intends to redirect attention to a more useful question: not "What is the logic by which we know what we know?" but rather "What is the process by which we believe what we believe?" The imagination "produces the fiction of a continued existence" (*Treatise* 209), and this is a fiction that works. Each person continuously reconstructs reality, as Hume says in a meditation on the unprovable regularities that are assumed all the time:

I am here seated in my chamber with my face to the fire; and all the objects that strike my senses are contained in a few yards around me. My memory, indeed, informs me of the existence of many objects; but then this information extends not beyond their past existence, nor do either my senses or memory give any testimony to the continuance of their being. When therefore I am thus seated, and revolve over these thoughts, I hear on a sudden a noise as of a door turning upon its hinges; and a little after see a porter, who advances towards me. This gives occasion to many new reflections and reasonings. First, I never have observed, that this noise could proceed from any thing but the motion of a door; and therefore conclude, that the present phenomenon is a contradiction to all past experience, unless the door, which I remember on t'other side the chamber, be still in being. Again, I have always found, that a human body was possessed of a quality, which I call gravity, and which hinders it from mounting in the air, as this porter must have done to arrive at my chamber, unless the stairs I remember be not annihilated by my absence. (196)

By anatomizing every unexamined assumption in a casual experience, Hume defamiliarizes it and compels us to recognize how much we normally take for granted. But to do so *is* normal. Experience cannot bestow certainty but it can establish probability, and a world without certainty, even of one's own identity, can still be a comfortable one. As John Richetti comments, "Our reconstruction of the world from our impressions of it is designed to give us ease, comfort, and even pleasure, to make life as agreeable as possible" (211). Hume's contemporary Thomas Reid said sarcastically that we learn from Hume that "a succession of ideas and impressions may eat, and drink, and be merry" (Grave 98n). But that is precisely Hume's point.

Hume, with a secure sense of self, can afford to explode the self in theory; Johnson's situation is the very reverse. Yet indignant though he may sometimes be at Hume's insinuating paradoxes, Johnson gives a not dissimilar account of the reciprocal relation between imagination and world. Remarking on the barren uniformity of the Highland landscape in *A Journey to the Western Islands*, he comments that it might seem to offer nothing whatever to the mind:

It will very readily occur, that this uniformity of barrenness can afford very little amusement to the traveller; that it is easy to sit at home and conceive rocks and heath and waterfalls; and that these journeys are useless labours, which neither impregnate the imagination, nor enlarge the understanding. It is true that of far the greater part of things, we must content ourselves with such knowledge as description may exhibit or analogy supply; but it is true likewise, that these ideas are always incomplete, and that at least, till we have compared them with realities, we do not know them to be just. As we see more, we become possessed of more certainties, and consequently gain more principles of reasoning, and found a wider basis of analogy. (40)

Even a bare and unchanging landscape cannot really be *known* until one has seen it for oneself. No one can see and know everything, but an understanding of the world is achieved by working from as many direct perceptions of "realities" as possible (once again, Johnson uses the plural form).

The Highland scene, then, is valued for its actuality. Such a response is remote from conventional literary artifice. Surprisingly, however, Johnson moves immediately to an interior mediation that acknowledges, however ironically, the imaginative relevance of romance:

I sat down on a bank, such as a writer of romance might have delighted to feign. I had indeed no trees to whisper over my head, but a clear rivulet streamed at my feet. The day was calm, the air soft, and all was rudeness, silence, and solitude. Before me, and on either side, were high hills, which by hindering the eye from ranging, forced the mind to find entertainment for itself. Whether I spent the hour well I know not; for here I first conceived the thought of this narration. (40)

The mind turns inward almost as in Marvell's *Garden*, though encouraged here by an encircling emptiness that forces reflexivity. What it creates, however, is not Marvell's alternative universe, but a version of the surrounding outer world, "this narration" of the journey in Scotland. And although the scene irresistibly arouses romance associations in a person of literary tastes, Johnson's narration is no romance.

So there is a triple movement. First, it is always best to see a real scene instead of merely imagining it. Second, the scene throws one inward upon the imagination, which is not tied to the present but loves to range freely. But finally, since it *is* the real scene that has stimulated the imagination, what results is not fanciful invention, but a "narration" that recovers the scene and makes sense of it in a larger context of analogy and analysis. "The use of travelling," Johnson wrote from Scotland to Hester Thrale, "is to regulate imagination by reality, and instead of thinking how things may be, to see them as they are" (*Letters* 1:359).

It needs to be emphasized once again that the differences between Johnson and Hume flow not from epistemological premises but from assumptions that are guaranteed as much by temperament as by theory. There are moments in Hume that veer close to Johnson's preoccupations, but whenever that happens Hume slides quickly away. His procedure deserves to be examined closely:

Such is the unsteadiness and activity of thought, that the images of every thing, especially of goods and evils, are always wandering in the mind; and were it moved by every idle conception of this kind, it would never enjoy a moment's peace and tranquillity. Nature has, therefore, chosen a medium, and has neither bestowed on every idea of good and evil the power of actuating the will, nor yet has entirely excluded them from this influence. Though an idle fiction has no efficacy, yet we find by experience that the ideas of those objects, which we believe either are or will be existent, produce in a lesser degree the same effect with those impressions, which are immediately present to the senses and perception. . . . This effect it can only have by making an idea approach an impression in force and vivacity. (*Treatise* 119)

These wandering images, which Hume so easily dismisses as idle fictions without efficacy, are the bane of Johnson's existence, and he is more concerned with soul than with mind—"that part of any man where his reason and conscience join to fight, not so much against others as against his own sense-bombarded, windblown, and fallible impulses" (Van Tassel 466).

Two crucial assumptions underlie Hume's equanimity here: first, that "nature" has benevolently "chosen" a middle way that admirably suits the human condition; and second, that belief is reliably supported by the "force and vivacity" of the images that pass through the mind. *Nature* is a fundamental term in Johnson's criticism—"In this poem there is no nature, for there is no truth" (*Lives* 1:163)—but Hume's usage might strike him as smuggling in the anthropomorphic myth of his first *Dictionary* definition: "An imaginary being supposed to preside over the material and animal world." Johnson's illustration is, very tellingly, Edmund's speech in *King Lear*: "Thou, *nature*, art my goddess; to thy law / My services are bound." In so far as nature simply means the sum total of things that really exist, Johnson holds to it firmly, since it affords his chief defense against destructive imaginings. But in so far as nature implies a force that works through material phenomena, Johnson regards it with extreme suspicion, for he shares the Augustinian view that nature is fallen. Hume's usage ("nature has chosen") reveals, incidentally, that mythic thinking can continue to invest the language of someone who supposes that he has debunked all myths.

The different connotations of *belief* in Hume and Johnson are closely related to those of *nature*. In Hume we believe what nature impresses strongly upon us; in Johnson we look beyond or behind it because we know that nature—our own nature above all—cannot be trusted. For Hume the superior "vivacity" of certain impressions is sufficient reason to believe in them: "An opinion or belief is nothing but an idea, that is different from a fiction, not in the nature, or the order of its parts, but in the *manner* of its being conceived. . . . An idea assented to *feels* different from a fictitious idea that the fancy alone presents to us: and this different feeling I endeavour to explain by calling it a superior *force*, or *vivacity*, or *solidity*, or *firmness*, or *steadiness*" (*Treatise* 628–29). Johnson testifies repeatedly that the mere force of an image cannot guarantee belief in its reality, for the imagination continually projects images that the mind prefers to "the insipidity of truth" (*Preface to Shakespeare* 82).

For Johnson, therefore, belief must be justified by a higher power. "Persuasion; opinion" is only the fourth definition of *belief* in the *Dictionary*; the first two, along with their illustrations, establish the basis for true belief in "the authority by which it is delivered" and in "the theological virtue of faith, or firm confidence of the truths of religion." Johnson quotes Hooker as saying that "no man can attain *belief* by the bare contemplation of heaven and earth; for that they neither are sufficient to give us as much as the least spark of light concerning the very principal mysteries of our faith." Johnson accepts religion as the type and foundation of true belief, an authority that lies beyond the bare contemplation of heaven and earth. For Hume, who rejects all authority, religion is the type and often the foundation of false belief, a credulous acceptance (under social pressure) of notions that could never have been suggested by the bare contemplation of heaven and earth. (We will return to these themes in Chapter 4).

Hume holds that imagination, which for Johnson is so prompt to create unreal alternative worlds, cannot stray for long from the present moment: " 'Tis obvious, that the imagination can never totally forget the points of space and time, in which we are existent; but receives such frequent advertisements of them from the passions and senses, that however it may turn its attention to foreign and remote objects, it is necessitated every moment to reflect on the present" (*Treatise* 427–28). However fictive our experience of the present may be, past and future are still greater fictions, the former founded on sense impressions stored up in the memory, the latter a conjectural anticipation of impressions that may someday occur. Johnson seizes on this point to emphasize the importance of memory not just for a sense of identity, but for moral integrity as well. "The future is pliant and ductile, and will be easily moulded by a strong fancy into any form. But the images which memory presents are of a stubborn and untractable nature, the objects of remembrance have already existed, and left their signature behind them impressed upon the mind, so as to defy all attempts of rasure, or of change" (*Rambler* No. 41). Impressions are literally im-pressed on the tablet of the mind, and one's grasp of reality is dependent on the facility and accuracy with which one can retrieve them.

It is because he feels the pressure of the past so strongly that Johnson, whose extraordinary memory astonished all who knew him, often speaks of its unreliability. Emotionally, impressions take root and are ineradicable, yet their outlines tend to grow blurry: "He who has not made the experiment, or who is not accustomed to require rigorous accuracy from himself, will scarcely believe how much a few hours take from certainty of knowledge, and distinctness of imagery; how the succession of objects will be broken, how separate parts will be confused, and how many particular features and discriminations will be compressed and conglobated into one gross and general idea" (*Journey* 146–47). For all his skepticism, Hume needs to rely on the past and present stability of mental impressions, since he is committed to an epistemology that can never get beyond them. Johnson, committed to a psychology that aspires beyond the world of impressions even if they remain all that our minds can now know, has good reason to throw doubt on their ultimate reliability. But to permit the past to grow hazy is to condemn it to imaginative distortion, which is all the more reason to demand that the fading traces of memory be stabilized by the permanent traces of written language. Johnson's reflections on memory occur in a context of urging travelers to write down what they see, and it is easy to understand how the act of writing becomes essential to the perpetuation of a reality that begins to dissolve as soon as its constituent impressions grow vague. We shall consider later how Boswell's journals are the basis of a memory that constitutes the ongoing self, and how Gibbon, conceding his inability to recover the details of personal experience, displaces this preoccupation into the cultural memory of the *Decline and Fall*.

SKEPTICISM AND PROBABILISM

"Ourself," Hume declares, "independent of the perception of every other object, is in reality nothing: for which reason we must turn our view to external objects" (*Treatise* 340). Richard Rorty has trenchantly criticized the Cartesian tradition, with its focus on the inner arena of the mind, as "the triumph of the quest for certainty over the quest for wisdom" (*Philosophy and the Mirror* 61), and he condemns the assumption of some modern philosophers "that we can split ourselves up into knowers of true sentences on the one hand and choosers of lives or actions or works of art on the other" (364). This is a modern rediscovery of the position to which Johnson and Hume, in their opposing ways, committed their lives as thinkers and writers: that certainty is unattainable, that wisdom must be founded in experience, and that living takes priority over knowing. As Hume very clearly states, "All knowledge resolves itself into probability, and becomes at last of the same nature with that evidence, which we employ in common life" (*Treatise* 181).

Ian Hacking has demonstrated that the concept of probability is an index to the development of modern ideas about evidence, as contrasted with an older notion of truth which did not admit of degrees of likelihood. The concept can be divided into two aspects, "aleatory" and "epistemic." The former concerns the statistical regularities that emerge from chance processes; the latter, the procedure of assessing reasonable degrees of belief in a situation where decisive proof is impossible. The notion that chance might be quantified and predicted, rather than being merely "blind," was not easily grasped and seems to have been essentially unknown until about 1660. The other kind of probability goes back, as its etymology suggests, to the notion of "provability" (including the sense of "worthy of approval"), but during the Renaissance it gradually took on the sense of likelihood which was *not* strictly provable.

To estimate probability, one had to consider the implication of ambiguous signs, rather than supposing like Paracelsus or Boehme that "natural signs" encoded occult meanings, heart-shaped leaves for instance de-
noting aptness for curing heart disease (Hacking 42). Hobbes, writing on
Humane Nature a hundred years before Hume, discusses their interpretation in the modern empirical way: "The signs are but *conjectural;* and
according as they have often or seldom failed, so their *assurance* is more
or less; but *never full* and *evident:* for though a man have always seen
the day and night to follow one another hitherto, yet can he not hence
conclude they shall do so, or that they have done so eternally: *experience concludeth nothing universally*" (Hacking 48). Hume argues very
similarly that although we cannot be certain the sun will rise, experience
permits us to rely on the likelihood of its doing so. Whatever rigorous
theory might hold, "one would appear ridiculous, who would say, that
'tis only probable the sun will rise tomorrow, or that all men must die;
though 'tis plain we have no further assurance of these facts, than what
experience affords us" (*Treatise* 124).

According to Hume, then, nature gives us beliefs that enable us to live
successfully in the world, even though those beliefs are unprovable and
might conceivably be wrong. To Johnson this distinction is a paradox and
therefore frivolous. To Hume it is a paradox all right, but one that defines
the difference between living and knowing, or as more recent philosophers
would say, between "knowing how" and "knowing that." We know how
to live, and part of this knowledge is a baggage of assumptions—varying
a good deal from one culture to another—that shore up our confidence
without actually being "true" in a metaphysical sense. As John Passmore
puts it, "Our irrationality preserves our reason" (137). Experience is a
trustworthy teacher.

For modern minds, discussions of probabilism tend to make it sound
too much like "probability," which is one aspect of what is involved but
far from the whole story. The point is not so much that probabilism enables us to guess specific outcomes, as in rolling dice or making atomic
particles collide, as that it allows us to assert regularities of experience to
which we give shorthand names that have pragmatic rather than absolute
value. As William James observes, " 'Winter' is only the name for a certain
number of days which we find generally characterized by cold weather,
but it guarantees nothing in that line, for our thermometer tomorrow may
soar into the 70s. Nevertheless the word is a useful one to plunge forward
with into the stream of our experience. It cuts off certain probabilities and
sets up others" (*Pragmatism* 171–72). Johnson's *Dictionary* defines *winter*

simply as "the cold season of the year," and after some poetic quotations gives this one from Isaac Watts's *Logick*:

To define *Winter*, I consider first wherein it agrees with Summer, Spring, Autumn, and I find they are all seasons of the year; therefore a season of the year is a genus: then I observe wherein it differs from these, and that is in the shortness of the days; therefore this may be called its special nature, or difference: then, by joining these together, I make a definition. *Winter* is that season of the year wherein the days are shortest.

In some parts of the world winter may not be cold, but at least the days are short; at the equator, on the other hand, there can be no winter. Far from being a real entity, *winter* is simply a name for aspects of experience for which a shorthand sign is convenient. "Words are the daughters of earth."

We are now in a position to see why Hume and Johnson, for all their radical disagreement that seemed so real to them and their contemporaries, share at a deep level a commitment to "common life" that is the enabling premise of their writings. The disagreement occurs because Johnson takes common experience as a starting point that is simply given, while Hume reaches it by an elaborate dialectic that leaves a good many traditional assumptions badly damaged along the way. Johnson's position, in fact, has close affinities (as Chester Chapin has shown) with the Scottish "common sense" critique that was developed by Thomas Reid and popularized by James Beattie. Reid argues that since nature compels us to act *as if* certain assumptions are true, as Hume consistently declares, then very little is gained by insisting that they are false. Any philosophy which looks absurd to common sense is violating principles that are too fundamental to be called into question. They cannot be proved because they just *are*. Accordingly, it must be the basic assumptions of empiricism that are mistaken, rather than those of common sense which empiricism claims to explode.

As Reid sees clearly, empiricism rests upon the belief that knowledge is confined to "ideas" which are located in a place called "the mind" and are linked together by a process called "association."

By this system, three laws of association, joined to a few original feelings, explain the whole mechanism of sense, imagination, memory, belief, and of all the actions and passions of the mind. Is this the man that nature made? I suspect it is not so easy to look behind the scenes in nature's work. This is a puppet surely, contrived by too bold an apprentice of nature, to mimic her work. It shows tolerably by candle light, but brought into clear day, and taken to pieces, it will appear to be a man made with mortar and a trowel. (17)

Reid has a double aim here, to expose the flaws in Hume's reasoning and to show that Hume's system, even while it undertakes to expose the common fictions of the mind, is itself a specialized fictional creation that rests on nothing more substantial than "a rope of sand" (80).

For Johnson, common sense has to be more substantial than it is for Hume. Indeed, it must literally confirm the existence of substance.

> After we came out of the church, we stood talking for some time together of Bishop Berkeley's ingenious sophistry to prove the non-existence of matter, and that every thing in the universe is merely ideal. I observed, that though we are satisfied his doctrine is not true, it is impossible to refute it. I never shall forget the alacrity with which Johnson answered, striking his foot with mighty force against a large stone, till he rebounded from it, "I refute it *thus.*" This was a stout exemplification of the *first truths* of Père Bouffier, or the *original principles* of Reid and of Beattie. (*Life* 1:471)

H. F. Hallett has argued that the stone's independent reality is confirmed when it causes Johnson's foot to rebound, and Douglas Patey ("Johnson's Refutation") that Johnson is thinking of Hartley's claim that the sense of touch is our fundamental authority for knowledge of the world. But surely there is something tricky in refuting an argument by means of a physical gesture, especially when that gesture is enshrined in a text. Johnson felt the kick, Boswell only saw it, and a reader does neither. A pragmatist, Rorty says in an essay called "Texts and Lumps," "agrees that there is such a thing as brute physical resistance—the pressure of light waves on Galileo's eyeball, or of the stone on Dr. Johnson's boot. But he sees no way of transferring this nonlinguistic brutality to *facts,* to the truth of sentences" (4).

Johnson insists on a prelinguistic world of experience and takes it for granted that language (and literature) cannot prove anything in the way that physical activity can. But many people today would argue that Johnson's kick, let alone Boswell's account of it, relies on a context of socially conditioned linguistic expectations. Kicking a stone would prove nothing about physical reality to a Buddhist saint. To decide to kick the stone, and even to *perceive* it as a stone, already imply a complex chain of learned responses. William James asks, "What shall we call a *thing* anyhow? It seems quite arbitrary, for we carve out everything, just as we carve our constellations, to suit our human purposes" (*Pragmatism* 165). Even the initial "impression" of the stone, to use the empiricist term, is not naive and immediate, for "we can hardly take in an impression at all, in the absence of a preconception of what impressions there may possibly be" (162).

Hume's own account of the world, including the principle of causality which everyone believes but no one can prove, meets this line of response as Johnson's does not. " 'Tis certain," he concedes, "that all mankind, and even philosophers themselves, for the greatest part of their lives, take their perceptions to be their only objects, and suppose that the very being, which is intimately present to the mind, is the real body or material existence" (*Treatise* 206). But this is finally a psychological fact, not a metaphysical truth. "We may well ask, *What causes induce us to believe in the existence of body?* but 'tis in vain to ask, *Whether there be body or not?* That is a point which we must take for granted in all our reasonings" (187).

What really threatened to lead to solipsism was the absolute separation of mind and body postulated by Descartes, whereas post-Berkeleyan empiricism sought to reestablish a unified phenomenology of experience. An intellectual ideal of perfect objectivity, whose ghost continues to survive in the academic world today, is a legacy from Descartes. As Dale Porter says in *The Emergence of the Past*, "Cartesian dualism separated mind from matter, ensuring that our subjective experience of time and events would never interfere with the abstract, objective orderliness of physical entities. Causation took the place of perception as the fundamental activity" (64). Hume is profoundly modern in exposing the unacknowledged assumptions that underlie notions of causation, and in reinstating individual perception as the central feature of the world that each individual inhabits.

Once again, difficulties arise only when an ideal of certainty is first postulated and then denied. If it can be recognized that such an ideal is both impossible and irrelevant, then Humean skepticism can be seen as a direct ancestor of the various forms of pragmatism that are increasingly invoked today. When one seeks to *prove* what one believes, whether by logic or by stone kicking, one can never get closer to certainty than a set of varyingly reliable probabilities. But when one *believes* what one believes, one simply believes it. The context is then phenomenological rather than epistemological, and as Stanley Fish puts it, "No one can *be* a relativist, because no one can achieve the distance from his own beliefs and assumptions which would result in their being no more authoritative *for him* than the beliefs and assumptions held by others" (319). This is exactly what Hume means about returning to the world of backgammon and conversation from his temporary episodes of philosophical speculation. In Fish's words, "As soon as you descend from theoretical reasoning about your assumptions, you will once again inhabit them and you will inhabit them without any reservations whatsoever" (370).

Steven Knapp and Walter Benn Michaels are prepared to draw the conclusion that "the world of practice must be founded not on theoretical truth but on the repression of theoretical truth" (29). It would be less paradoxical to say that "theoretical truth," if opposed or irrelevant to practice, has no obvious right to be called "truth" at all. What we are left with, in Fish's terms, is a "standard story" that currently seems the true one (239). Johnson and Hume agree to a surprising extent on the general outlines of that story; the difference between them is that Hume wants his readers to admit that the story rests on social consensus rather than on metaphysical conviction. But that does not make the standard story any less compelling, and Hume's forthright rejection of Pyrrhonist skepticism needs to be emphasized: "Should it here be asked me . . . whether I be really one of those skeptics, who hold that all is uncertain, and that our judgment is not in *any* thing possessed of *any* measures of truth and falsehood, I should reply that this question is entirely superfluous, and that neither I nor any other person was ever sincerely and constantly of that opinion" (*Treatise* 183). Nature, Hume says, makes a wholesale skepticism impossible, and after all is said and done "we retain a degree of belief, which is sufficient for our purpose, either in philosophy or common life" (185).

Moreover, Johnson's practice—once his metaphysical premises are set aside—tends to be much more like Hume's than one might suppose, and beyond that it has many affinities with twentieth-century pragmatism. Johnson's well-known assertion that successful works of art must combine the natural with the new (*Lives* 1:163) embodies a principle whose application is much wider than literary criticism. It expresses an intellectual conservatism that denies the possibility of wholly new "truths," not because everything is already known but because the human mind simply cannot leap into a void. As James says in *Pragmatism*, "A new opinion counts as 'true' just in proportion as it gratifies the individual's desire to assimilate the novel in his experience to his beliefs in stock" (52). But the yearning for novelty is as significant as the need to assimilate it to what is already believed, and as Johnson says, "every new genius produces some innovation which, when invented and approved, subverts the rules which the practice of foregoing authors had established" (*Rambler* No. 125). To quote James again, "Experience has ways of *boiling over*, and making us correct our present formulas" (*Pragmatism* 145). Still, the process is and must be cumulative: "Truth grafts itself on previous truth, modifying it

47

in the process, just as idiom grafts itself on previous idiom, and law on previous law" (158). Johnson's *Dictionary* is an extended revelation of the way language evolves through social usage, and the common law of Great Britain, in Johnson's usage as in Burke's, reflects a similar process of change.

ETHICS, POLITICS, SOCIETY

The life of the individual is merged in that of society, which works constantly to shape experience and indeed to define it. Solipsism is averted because experience is socially conditioned; indeed, the radically individual self is a Romantic invention that neither Hume nor Johnson foresaw. As one commentator puts it, for Hume "the self is revealed in its social roles. Hence, there is no self apart from the social roles, or, put another way, the roles are real, not the self, but the self is an ultimate explanatory constituent of the roles" (Capaldi, "Hume as Social Scientist" 113). Quite similarly, even though much of Johnson's writing broods on the precariousness of the interior self, his solution is always a social interchange that banishes solipsism. "In order to regain liberty, he must find the means of flying from himself; he must, in opposition to the Stoic precept, teach his desires to fix upon external things; he must adopt the joys and the pains of others, and excite in his mind the want of social pleasures and amicable communication" (*Rambler* No. 89).

Hume goes still further: adopting the joys and pains of others is not just a good idea, it is instinctual and inevitable. His essay *Of the Origin of Government* begins not from a hypothetical social contract but from the practical facts of human experience: "Man, born in a family, is compelled to maintain society, from necessity, from natural inclination, and from habit" (*Essays* 37). "The minds of men are mirrors to one another" (*Treatise* 365), and such regularities as national characteristics are explained by the "contagion" with which human beings absorb the behavior of their fellows: "The propensity to company and society is strong in all rational creatures; and the same disposition, which gives us this propensity, makes us enter deeply into each other's sentiments, and causes like passions and inclinations to run, as it were, by contagion, through the whole club or knot of companions" (*Of National Characters, Essays* 202).

Beneath this harmonious social vision no doubt rests the disposition of *le bon David* himself: "A good-natured man finds himself in an instant of the same humour with his company" (*Treatise* 317). If Johnson sees society as a means of escaping the self, Hume prefers to see it as a stimulus to mutual enjoyment, and he is prepared—quite surprisingly in view of his own epistemology—to declare that we enter completely into each other's feelings: "Company is naturally so rejoicing, as presenting the liveliest of all objects, *viz.* a rational and thinking being like ourselves, who communicates to us all the actions of his mind; makes us privy to his inmost sentiments and affections; and lets us see, in the very instant of their production, all the emotions which are caused by any object" (*Treatise* 353).

Once again, Johnson and Hume tend to agree on the conditions of practical existence, while interpreting those conditions through different assumptions that reflect different temperaments. Just as nature for Hume is a benevolent guide, so sympathy is a unifying instinct that is apparent if we "take a general survey of the universe, and observe the force of sympathy through the whole animal creation, and the easy communication of sentiments from one thinking being to another." Man is distinguished as "the creature of the universe, who has the most ardent desire of society, and is fitted for it by the most advantages" (*Treatise* 363).

At the bottom of Hume's attitude is an ethics based on feeling, derived from such thinkers as Shaftesbury, Butler, and Hutcheson. At the bottom of Johnson's is a moral rationalism in the older Christian humanist tradition. "Sir, natural affection is nothing: but affection from principle and established duty is sometimes wonderfully strong" (*Life* 4:210). In Johnson's disillusioned analysis, society may be natural but cooperation is not: "We are formed for society, not for combination; we are equally unqualified to live in a close connection with our fellow beings, and in total separation from them: we are attracted towards each other by general sympathy, but kept back from contact by private interests" (*Adventurer* No. 45). Hume's notion of the binding force of sympathy is much closer to Sterne's. Nothing could be more Shandean than the declaration that "the tear naturally starts in our eye on the apprehension of a warm sentiment of [benevolence]; our breast heaves, our heart is agitated, and every humane, tender principle of our frame is set in motion and gives us the purest and most satisfactory enjoyment." But these words are in fact Hume's in the *Inquiry concerning the Principles of Morals* (80).

Hutcheson asserted, on empiricist principles, that the moral sense was literally a sense, apprehending impressions that correspond to moral ideas. Hume held that moral sentiments are complex ideas that derive from the simpler emotions, but he agreed with Hutcheson that they do not depend upon reason, and that ethics resembles aesthetics more than logic or metaphysics. And Hume followed Hutcheson in the view that what is ethically "good" is determined by what people in general believe to be so, just as a "good" novel, or for that matter a "red" object, is so determined. "The hypothesis which we embrace is plain. It maintains that morality is determined by sentiment. It defines virtue to be *whatever mental action or quality gives to a spectator the pleasing sentiment of approbation;* and vice the contrary" (*Inquiry . . . Morals* 107). Insofar as one believes that all persons feel the same emotions in the same way, this view can still support a standard of morality. But as soon as that notion begins to break down, it leads directly to relativism and utilitarianism; it was Hutcheson who coined the influential phrase "the greatest happiness for the greatest numbers."

If belief in virtue continues to prevail, that is because nature encourages the belief, just as "she" encourages us to believe in the integrity of the self and the dependability of causality.

MACHIAVEL himself discovers a true sentiment of virtue in his history of FLORENCE. When he talks as a *Politician,* in his general reasonings, he considers poisoning, assassination, and perjury as lawful arts of power; but when he speaks as an *Historian,* in his particular narrations, he shows so keen an indignation against vice, and so warm an approbation of virtue, in many passages, that I could not forbear applying to him that remark of HORACE, That if you chase away nature, though with ever so great indignity, she will always return upon you. (*Of the Study of History, Essays* 567)

The rules of society, including the language by which it understands itself, are merely conventional, but familiarity makes them seem so normal that people no longer perceive their artificiality. "Thus two men pull the oars of a boat by common convention, for common interest, without any promise or contract; thus gold and silver are made the measures of exchange; thus speech, and words, and language are fixed by human convention and agreement" (*Inquiry . . . Morals* 123).

If morality, like aesthetics, is based on taste and feeling, then everything depends on postulating the uniformity of human experience. The use of history, Hume declares, "is only to discover the constant and universal principles of human nature" (*Inquiry . . . Understanding* 93), and he believes just as fully as Johnson does that whatever its local variations may be, "human nature is always the same" (*Adventurer* No. 99). Such a view easily conduces to a conservative ethic, as Reynolds makes clear in his seventh *Discourse,* where a Lockean account of mind leads directly to submission to "the public voice":

The internal fabric of our minds, as well as the external form of our bodies, being nearly uniform, it seems then to follow of course that as the imagination is incapable of producing any thing originally of itself, and can only vary and combine those ideas with which it is furnished by means of the senses, there will be necessarily an agreement in the imaginations as in the senses of men. There being this agreement, it follows that in all cases, in our lightest amusements as well as in our most serious actions and engagements of life, we must regulate our affections of every kind by that of others. The well-disciplined mind acknowledges this authority, and submits its own opinion to the public voice. (107)

At the beginning of this passage Reynolds seems to say that all minds necessarily respond to the world in the same way; by the end, he tacitly acknowledges that they do not, since regulation and discipline must be imposed in order for an individual to submit to authority. But people are entirely willing to submit to this regulation, because exclusion from the group would be too painful to bear. "In fact," Reynolds continues, "we are never satisfied with our opinions, whatever we may pretend, till they are ratified and confirmed by the suffrages of the rest of mankind" (108).

Individuality is thus both selfish and painful, and ethical precepts merge easily with psychosocial analysis. The solidarity of the group is possible because all human beings have similar faculties and responses, and taste in art—as in Hume's essay *Of the Standard of Taste*—is developed in exactly the same way as socialization in its broadest sense. So Reynolds arrives at a triumphant (and very Johnsonian) affirmation of neoclassical permanence: "What has pleased, and continues to please, is likely to please again: hence are derived the rules of art, and on this immovable foundation they must ever stand" (108). A recurring theme throughout the *Discourses* is the individual's need to learn to share the values of the group, at once acquiring and confirming a "taste" whose universality depends on a communal willingness to perceive it so.

Versions of this attitude have persisted into our own day; Lionel Trilling could still declare in 1976, even while ruefully admitting that his students no longer saw what he did in Austen's novels, that "humanism takes for granted that any culture of the past out of which has come a work of art that commands our interest must be the product, and also, of course, the shaping condition, of minds which are essentially the same as our own" (251). But for many people the perspective of the twentieth century, with its experience of cultural and individual diversity, makes such an assumption look provincial. Louis Mink remarks that "the common sense of an age, we recognize when we compare that age with others, may well be for different times or places beyond the limits of comprehension or even of fantasy" (129). That process of comparison was just beginning in the eighteenth century, when even the most radical of the *philosophes* expected to deduce unchanging constants of human behavior from the variations they studied. "Would you know the sentiments, inclinations, and course of life of the Greeks and Romans?" Hume asks. "Study well the temper and actions of the French and English" (*Inquiry . . . Understanding* 93).

If the uniformity of experience explains and justifies the norms of society, then it also tends to justify the current status quo. Whether or not Hume thought of himself as a Pyrrhonist, the tendency of skepticism had always been conservative, resting the justification of institutions on tradition rather than on rational evaluation in order "to live tranquilly in accordance with instinct, custom, and tradition" (Hiley 186–87). Hume's rejection of ultimate knowledge claims and his emphasis on harmony with "nature" are very much in this tradition, as in the statement by Sextus Empiricus that skeptics "follow a line of reasoning which, in accordance with appearances, points us to a life conformable to customs of our country and its laws and institutions, and to our own instinctive feelings" (13). This kind of epistemological and political skepticism was easily shared by persons who differed as to theological "truth"; thus Burke, whose social views rest on a religious foundation very different from Hume's, speaks like Hume of "the happy effect of following nature, which is wisdom without reflection, and above it" (*Reflections* 119).

A common investment in perpetuating the social order explains the remarkable similarity between Hume's and Johnson's political views, once one looks beyond the superficial quarrels of "Whig" and "Tory." In fact Hume's skeptical Whiggism has a lot in common with Johnson's Toryism, and Johnson himself was compelled to admit it, though he grudgingly called Hume "a Tory by chance" (*Life* 4:194). They differ chiefly on the religious establishment and on the problem of dynastic succession (Johnson seems to have been a Jacobite sympathizer while Hume, as a Scot, was careful to dissociate himself from Jacobitism). But their politics rests on two shared assumptions: that subordination is essential to society, and that the current expressions of subordination in Great Britain have been legitimated by custom and ought not to be changed. The far-reaching extent of this conservatism deserves discussion, since modern readers are understandably reluctant to recognize it, and since the foundation of most eighteenth-century British writing is a commitment to the then-current social system.

Subordination is much more than simple obedience, though that is certainly its basis. Hume says decisively in *Of the Original Contract*, "If the reason be asked of that obedience which we are bound to pay to government, I readily answer, *because society could not otherwise subsist*" (*Essays* 481). So also Johnson in *Taxation No Tyranny*: "If the subject refuses to obey, it is the duty of authority to use compulsion. Society cannot subsist but by the power, first of making laws, and then of enforcing them" (*Political Writings* 448). But subordination—defined in Johnson's *Dictionary* as "The state of being inferior to another" and "A series regularly descending"—is not just the rule of force; it reflects a deeply held ideological belief in the value of hierarchy. The index entries for *subordination* in G. B. Hill's edition of the *Life of Johnson* indicate Johnson's (and Boswell's) deep emotional commitment: "Conducive to the happiness of society [five entries] . . . essential for order . . . French happy in it . . . grand scheme of it . . . high people the best . . . S. J. a friend to it . . . his favourite subject . . . his great merit in being zealous for it . . . mean marriages to be punished . . . men not naturally equal" (6:375). Such assumptions were encouraged by a society that did indeed emphasize continuity rather than separation; in a modern historian's account, "All these nice distinctions, and the supercharged snobbery they provoked and which sustained them, shaped a social order whose gross inequalities were landscaped in a gentle slope rather than in steps" (R. Porter 64). Politics might easily be seen as ratifying these stabilized gradations, though Johnson complained bitterly that this was changing: "Politics are now nothing more than means of rising in the world" (*Life* 2:369).

Meanwhile, people continued to believe in subordination because ideology perpetuated the fiction that the peculiarities of any given social system were natural and inevitable. Hume is very clear about this in *Of the Original Contract*: "Obedience or subjection becomes so familiar that most men never make any enquiry about its origin or cause, more than about the principle of gravity, resistance, or the most universal laws of nature" (*Essays* 470). In post-Marxian political thought, to recognize that the political order rests on a fiction is to expose its duplicities and to justify change. But if the fiction is itself natural, then to recognize it is simply to recognize it. John Barrell comments that in Johnson's political writings, "an account of the *status quo* is assumed to be, at the same time and without further justification, a defence of it" (147).

"The true rule of government," Hume states flatly, "is the present established practice of the age" (*Of the Coalition of Parties*, *Essays* 498). Johnson similarly derides social contract theories, and in *Taxation No Tyranny* he locates consent not in choices made but in a condition that precedes all choice: "As all are born the subjects of some state or other, we may be said to have been all born consenting to some system of government. Other consent than this, the condition of civil life does not allow. It is the unmeaning clamour of the pedants of policy, the delirious dream of republican fanaticism" (*Political Writings* 428). Just as in Burke's theory of prescription, it is irrelevant, though it would be easy enough, to show that existing states had their origins in force rather than in choice. "Time and custom," Hume says, "give authority to all forms of government, and all successions of princes; and that power, which at first was founded only on injustice and violence, becomes in time legal and obligatory" (*Treatise* 566).

If the present order is good, then to change it (as opposed to merely "reforming" it) must be bad, and by a kind of paradoxical extension, even those changes that produced the present order cannot have been altogether good; Johnson and Hume express very similar views of Charles I, Cromwell, and the Civil War (Vance 243–45). The American colonies must not repeal their charters, Johnson says, because "by such repeal the whole fabric of subordination is immediately destroyed, and the constitution sunk at once into a chaos; the society is dissolved into a tumult of individuals, without authority to command, or obligation to obey" (*Taxation No Tyranny* 425). So also Hume: "In reality, there is not a more terrible event than a total dissolution of government, which gives liberty to the multitude, and makes the determination or choice of a new establishment depend upon a number which nearly approaches to that of the body of the people" (*Of the Original Contract* 472). To be sure, Johnson said more than once that the people have a right to rebel against tyranny, but this was a truism that was universally shared; as Burke puts it in the course of denouncing the French Revolution, "The punishment of real tyrants is a noble and awful act of justice; and it has with truth been said to be consolatory to the human mind" (*Reflections* 178). Burke's position is that this kind of resistance is both inevitable and just, but only when actual experience has made it so: "The speculative line of demarcation, where obedience ought to end and resistance must begin, is faint, obscure, and not easily definable. . . . Governments must be abused and deranged indeed before it can be thought of, and the prospect of the future must be as bad as the experience of the past" (116). Hume held similarly that "since resistance was an extreme remedy that put everything in jeopardy, it could be justified only in cases of 'egregious' tyranny, like that of Nero" (Forbes 92).

Given the strength of this conservatism, one must be cautious of modern attempts to project contemporary preoccupations onto the past. Donald Greene has had remarkable success in recreating Johnson as a

North American liberal of the 1950s: "Johnson does not *like* the use of power by one individual over another; rather, he hopes that if men recognize that the ultimate sanction of government *is* power, they will be able to minimize its use" (247). It would be more accurate to say that Johnson distinguishes between moral principles, which no government has the right to abridge, and political ones, which may drastically curtail liberty whenever circumstances call for it. Greene makes much of Johnson's opposition to slavery, but Johnson clearly opposes it on moral grounds (see Voitle 84–93) that have little to do with political liberties. The famous question in *Taxation No Tyranny*, "How is it that we hear the loudest yelps for liberty among the drivers of negroes" (*Political Writings* 454), is mainly a sarcasm at the expense of the merchants who were claiming to seek "liberty" in England, and Johnson has no use at all for idealistic theories of the rights of man:

The argument of the irregular troops of controversy, stripped of its colours and turned out naked to the view, is no more than this. Liberty is the birthright of man, and where obedience is compelled, there is no liberty. The answer is equally simple. Government is necessary to man, and where obedience is not compelled, there is no government. If the subject refuses to obey, it is the duty of authority to use compulsion. (*Taxation No Tyranny* 448)

At bottom Johnson's defense of hierarchy is not a matter of obsequiousness to privilege, much less an assertion of it; Boswell "heard him once say, 'I have great merit in being zealous for subordination and the honours of birth, for I can hardly tell who was my grandfather'" (*Life* 2:261). Johnson's position, like Burke's, reflects rather a fear of the individualism that expresses itself in the dog-eat-dog survival of the cleverest—"these lords of themselves, these kings of *Me*, these demigods of independence," as Johnson contemptuously calls them in *Taxation No Tyranny* (*Political Writings* 429). Such a fear is felt with particular force by a clever person who resists (or perhaps suspects that he does *not* resist) the temptation to imitate people who are unscrupulously getting ahead.

This is the principle explicitly stated by Burke in the *Reflections*, that the property of individuals and families is the very basis of society, and that its preservation requires an institutional shoring-up by walls of privilege that can withstand the attacks of "ability":

As ability is a vigorous and active principle, and as property is sluggish, inert, and timid, it never can be safe from the invasions of ability, unless it be, out of all proportion, predominant in the representation. . . . The characteristic essence of property, formed out of the combined principles of its acquisition and conservation, is to be *unequal*. The great masses therefore which excite envy, and tempt

55

rapacity, must be put out of the possibility of danger. Then they form a natural rampart about the lesser properties in all their gradations. (140)

This is a vision of a threatened world, in which property is protected by being piled up in enormous "masses," even though their very size attracts envy and tempts the "rapacity" of persons with ability. The value of hierarchy is to distribute the threat by imposing an extended series of gradations, each step hemmed in and defined by the one just above it, and the whole series building up the "masses" of property in a carefully interlocked sequence. The conservative case against individualism is that there is no such thing as an autonomous individual, and that the alternative to the established hierarchy is not independent persons but new and more dangerous combinations of persons. As Burke aphoristically puts it in the *Reflections*, "Liberty, when men act in bodies, is *power*" (91).

Hume was just as appalled by the "Wilkes and Liberty" campaign of the 1760s as Johnson was, writing to Turgot in France, "They roar Liberty, though they have apparently ["evidently, openly"—*Dictionary*] more liberty than any people in the world; a great deal more than they deserve; and perhaps more than any men ought to have" (*Letters* 2:180). It is worth following closely the movement of Hume's thought as he entertains and then rejects the implications of human equality:

To be sure, an anatomist finds no more in the greatest monarch than in the lowest peasant or day-labourer; and a moralist may, perhaps, frequently find less. But what do all these reflections tend to? We, all of us, still retain these prejudices in favour of birth and family; and neither in our serious occupations, nor most careless amusements, can we ever get entirely rid of them. A tragedy that should represent the adventures of sailors, or porters, or even of private gentlemen, would presently disgust us; but one that introduces kings and princes acquires in our eyes an air of importance and dignity. Or should a man be able, by his superior wisdom, to get entirely above such prepossessions, he would soon, by means of the same wisdom, again bring himself down to them, for the sake of society, whose welfare he would perceive to be intimately connected with them. Far from endeavouring to undeceive the people in this particular, he would cherish such sentiments of reverence to their princes; as requisite to preserve a due subordination in society. (*Of the Protestant Succession, Essays* 504)

From this point of view society is literally sustained by a fiction, one whose roots are so deep that merely literary fictions violate it at their peril, and "prejudices"—as Burke often reiterates—are the means of internalizing the social fiction as a dependable way of life.

The conservatism of Johnson and Hume expresses the unease of a culture that venerates its past but is increasingly immersed in rapid and irreversible change—social, financial, and ultimately (though as yet only on the horizon) political. The notion that change might actually be beneficial was extremely difficult to entertain, and both Johnson and Hume relied on the venerable opposition between civic virtue and "corruption" that J. G. A. Pocock describes in *The Machiavellian Moment*. "Every government, say the politicians, is perpetually degenerating towards corruption, from which it must be rescued at certain periods by the resuscitation of its first principles, and the re-establishment of its original constitution" (*Rambler* No. 156). "By the middle of the eighteenth century," Pocock writes elsewhere, "the historically problematic individual, who could neither return to ancient virtue nor find means of completely replacing it, had made his appearance" (*Virtue* 71). Johnson and Hume speak for that problematic individual, and their reactionary outbursts— particularly in Hume's letters and in Johnson's conversation—are symptoms of a real dread of the new. "Tyburn itself is not safe from the fury of innovation."

What is at stake, very clearly, is an incipient breakdown of consensus. The authors of the American Declaration of Independence, aristocrats who were themselves deeply concerned with "corruption" in the Renaissance humanist sense, declared that "We hold these truths to be self-evident": they are self-evident because "we," the group whose views are being represented, perceive them so. But "these truths" were tinged with the Rights of Man rhetoric of the Continental Enlightenment, and did not seem in the least self-evident to Hume and Johnson. New and (to them) repellent values were increasingly dominant, and the whole basis of their social philosophy was thereby put at risk. What is the use of norms based on consensus if the new consensus has no room in it for Hume and Johnson?

For the time being, the accession of the popularly "British" George III, to whom Johnson paid solemn compliments, seemed to have dispelled the dynastic problem and ratified the social order:

After 1760, the whole disposition in favour of order, rank and subordination, which Johnson classically represents, found a single and undivided object of loyalty. And the impact upon the intelligentsia was profound. Many of the leading figures of the mid-eighteenth century, in a wide range of disciplines, pose problems for modern interpreters for the same reason. Born and educated in one political universe, they survived into another, labouring to adapt their now-anachronistic ideas, or to re-express them in a new form. (Clark 189)

In the 1790s it would become clear that new fictions accompanied and expressed new realities, and later on we shall consider the searching examination of this theme in Burke and Godwin. But by 1790 Hume had been dead for fourteen years and Johnson for six.

FICTION

If human beings live by unexamined fictions, they also make and enjoy representations of experience that are overtly fictional, and both Hume and Johnson have an active interest in these. I am not concerned here with their detailed views on literary criticism or aesthetic theory, but with their reflections on the ambiguous relationship between the fictional and the real.

In the *Dictionary* Johnson defines *fiction* as:

> 1. The act of feigning or inventing.
> 2. The thing feigned or invented.
> 3. A falsehood; a lie.

In Johnson's usage *fiction* is often synonymous with escapist "semi-slumbers" in which a person forgets "that misery is the lot of man" by indulging in "a voluntary dream, a temporary recession from the realities of life to airy fictions; and habitual subjection of reason to fancy" (*Idler* No. 32). Works of art are of course different from private daydreams, but when they do their work effectively they intoxicate readers into analogous bondage.

If the writer is sufficiently compelling, this bondage may be welcome. "Such is the power of his poetry," Johnson says of Milton, "that his call is obeyed without resistance, the reader feels himself in captivity to a higher and a nobler mind" (*Lives* 1:190). But captivity always threatens to be dangerously coercive, as Johnson states plainly in *Rambler* No. 4 when he warns that modern fiction may overwhelm rational control, "take possession of the memory by a kind of violence, and produce effects almost without the intervention of the will." Hume, brooding about the force of irrational convictions in his celebrated chapter "Of Miracles," makes a similar point: "Eloquence, when at its highest pitch, leaves little room for reason or reflection, but addressing itself entirely to the fancy or the affections, captivates the willing hearers, and subdues their understanding." Hume adds, rather complacently no doubt from Johnson's point of view, "Happily, this pitch it seldom attains" (*Inquiry . . . Understanding* 125–26).

Seen in this way, the mere existence of metaphor, let alone of elaborated fictions, is a threat to the integrity of language and thought. Johnson warns in the *Preface* to the *Dictionary* that although one might wish that language would cease changing, "the tropes of poetry will make hourly encroachments, and the metaphorical will become the current sense" (325). The art of poets, Johnson says in *Rambler* No. 202, "is imagined to consist in distorting words from their original meaning." Hume, though less alarmed than Johnson by the power of imagination, shows a similar inclination to identify metaphor with untruth: "Many of the beauties of poetry, and even of eloquence, are founded on falsehood and fiction, on hyperboles, metaphors, and an abuse or perversion of terms from their natural meaning" (*Of the Standard of Taste*, *Essays* 231). No wonder Johnson defends Addison's *Campaign*, stigmatized by Joseph Warton as "a gazette in rhyme," with the solemn pronouncement that "the rejection and contempt of fiction is rational and manly" (*Lives* 2:129).

This attitude reflects an uneasiness that had pervaded thinking about language, not to mention art, ever since the end of the seventeenth century. Thomas Sprat lamented in the *History of the Royal Society* that "the ornaments of speaking" had fallen into abuse: "They make the fancy disgust the best things, if they come sound and unadorned; they are in open defiance against reason, professing not to hold much correspondence with that, but with its slaves, the passions; they give the mind a motion too changeable and bewitching to consist with right practice. Who can behold, without indignation, how many mists and uncertainties these specious tropes and figures have brought on our knowledge?" (2.20). Johnson and Hume share Sprat's suspicion of the mists of metaphor, but they recognize as well its affinity with the fancy and confess an attraction to its bewitching energy. In addition, Hume explicitly reverses Sprat's formulation, holding that reason is and ought to be the passions' slave.

So metaphor is at once unavoidable, necessary, and dangerous. George Herbert had asked in *Jordan (I)*,

> Who says that fictions only and false hair
> Become a verse? Is there in truth no beauty?
> Is all good structure in a winding stair?
> May no lines pass, except they do their duty
> Not to a true, but painted chair?

By the time of Hume and Johnson it was becoming increasingly apparent that tropes are inseparable from truth, that viable structures are winding rather than straight, and that any "true" chair is already—by virtue of linguistic and conceptual mediation—a painted one.

If language were indeed able to refer reliably to a prior truth, what would that truth be? As we have seen, it must itself be fictive, but mental fictions that are tied to real experience differ from fictions that invent experience which no one has ever had. "The value of every story," Johnson told Boswell, "depends on its being true. A story is a picture either of an individual or of human nature in general: if it be false, it is a picture of nothing" (*Life* 2:433). Two notions of truth are invoked here: neoclassical generality, which summarizes the common features of a series of examples; and empiricist mimesis, which presents specific characteristics of actual individuals. As Johnson understands them, these apparently different modes of truth are not fundamentally different. They represent the poles of a continuum, in which generalizations must be checked constantly against the particulars that give them life. While Johnson often celebrates "the grandeur of generality," it is always with the understanding that a generality not founded on particularity is both empty and uninteresting. He once remarked, admittedly with polemical exaggeration, "I had rather see the portrait of a dog that I know, than all the allegorical paintings they can show me in the world" (Hill 2:15).

Such assumptions only partly coincide with older Renaissance attitudes, essentially Platonic in inspiration, that may sometimes seem to be echoed in the rhetoric of eighteenth-century aesthetics. For both Johnson and Hume, neoclassicism is an inherited system in which they only partly believe. Writing on the eclogues of Virgil, whose genre-bound character had interested most previous critics, Johnson characteristically declares of his two favorites, "It may be observed that these two poems were produced by events that really happened; and may, therefore, be of use to prove that we can always feel more than we can imagine, and that the most artful fiction must give way to truth" (*Adventurer* No. 92). This formulation is strikingly close to Hume's thought experiment in which a text is read with more interest if one believes it to be literally true:

If one person sits down to read a book as a romance, and another as a true history, they plainly receive the same ideas, and in the same order; nor does the incredulity of the one, and the belief of the other hinder them from putting the very same sense upon their author. His words produce the same ideas in both; though his testimony has not the same influence on them. The latter has a more lively conception of all the incidents. He enters deeper into the concerns of the persons; represents to himself their actions, and characters, and friendships, and enmities; he even goes so far as to form a notion of their features, and air, and person. While the former, who gives no credit to the testimony of the author, has a more faint and languid conception of all these particulars; and except on account of the style and ingenuity of the composition, can receive little entertainment from it. (*Treatise* 97–98)

In this account an identical sequence of words produces different results, and reader response is tied to the reader's assumptions about reality. Hume takes precisely the opposite position from a Romantic critic or a twentieth-century New Critic, who would say that the fiction is *more* vivid, because it creates an internally guaranteed world of imagination. Literary works are autotelic, the New Critics used to say. According to Hume, the telos of every text lies outside it, and it becomes more vivid for the reader who receives it as true—as a reliable report of a world beyond itself. Later on Hume developed a subtler literary theory, in which aesthetic experience differs significantly from real-life experience. But he never abandoned the essential assumption that we are most deeply struck by what we believe to be real. In Hume's philosophy, we live by fictions that add up to at least a *kind* of reality: our experience of millions of "impressions" generates a reasonably stable picture of the world, even if it must remain ultimately hypothetical. It is no accident that Hume became a historian.

The crucial issue is what the reader does with the text, not what it somehow "is" in some absolute sense. Hume certainly did not need to be told, by poststructuralist theorists or anyone else, that human notions of the world are imaginative and psychological, and that they bear no necessary relation to an ontologically stable "reality" outside of human consciousness. It was Hume himself who brought these issues into the central area of philosophical discourse. But it does not follow that all texts are equally fictive. Texts embody conventions that readers have learned to interpret, and the very different expectations of fiction and nonfiction are among the most fundamental of those conventions. In the case of Hume's thought experiment, the status of the text is established by the conventions the reader supposes are being invoked, which are allied either with straightforward references to the actual state of affairs, or with fictive language that elaborates an invented world (which may well contain references to the "actual" world). Of course, any interpreter may choose to ignore or defy the conventions implied in a text. Much poststructuralist criticism has been committed to precisely this procedure. But from Hume's point of view, that simply reflects an unwillingness to play the game by its own rules, a tactic that is bound to be counterproductive since the rules of language are socially determined, and therefore not open to arbitrary redefinition by individuals.

Moreover, it is not just a matter of recognizing that individual readers interpret texts differently. Beyond that, the words on the page have literally no meaning—are not *words* at all—until they are apprehended and interpreted by a living mind. As Barbara Herrnstein Smith says, "Texts are altogether mute objects" (6), awaiting performance just as musical scores do. And when a text is performed, much will depend on the assumptions the reader brings to it. In his essay *Of the Study of History* Hume recounts, rather condescendingly, how he once got "a young beauty" to read Plutarch's *Lives* on the pretense that they were fictional, and how she reproached him indignantly when "she came to the lives of ALEXANDER and CAESAR, whose names she had heard of by accident" (*Essays* 564). One might suppose that she rejected Plutarch because fiction is exciting and history dry, and that her behavior refutes Hume's thought experiment, since she finds the lives interesting only if fictional. But it is equally plausible to conclude that what she wants from fiction is an escapism that depends upon an explicit awareness of its unreality. Christensen comments that the names of Alexander and Caesar "summon a historical reality (a world where actions have consequences) which is not the domain of novels and romances, and which cannot help but disturb an attention based on the pleasant illusion that at least one action, reading novels and romances, has no consequences" (109).

Johnson has a similar stake in discounting the power of literary fiction. More than once (*Rambler* No. 151, *Idler* No. 84) he claims that as we gain experience of life, judgment predominates over fancy and we abandon fiction for truth. "We endeavor, or wish, to find entertainment in the review of life, and to repose upon real facts, and certain experience" (*Rambler* No. 203). Hume says that "a painter, who intended to represent a passion or emotion of any kind, would endeavor to get a sight of a person actuated by a like emotion, in order to enliven his ideas, and give them a force and vivacity superior to what is found in those which are mere fictions of the imagination" (*Treatise* 85). So also Shakespeare, according to Johnson, "caught his ideas from the living world, and exhibited only what he saw before him" (*Preface* 63–64), with the result that his dialogue, for instance, "seems scarcely to claim the merit of fiction, but to have been gleaned by diligent selection out of common conversation and common occurrences" (63). In Johnson as in Hume, *common* is rescued from its pejorative meanings ("Vulgar; mean") and is made to speak for the shared experience of the race ("Frequent; usual; ordinary"). Art is not life, but it succeeds in proportion as it invokes life: "Imitations produce pain or pleasure not because they are mistaken for realities, but because they bring realities to mind" (*Preface* 78).

Fearing the power of art less than Johnson does, Hume develops a psychological aesthetics in which art arouses the same passions as life and then gives them artistic form. This provides his answer to the puzzle with which *Of Tragedy* begins, the "unaccountable pleasure, which the spectators of a well-written tragedy receive from sorrow, terror, anxiety, and other passions, that are in themselves disagreeable and uneasy" (*Essays* 216). Like Johnson, Hume stresses fictionality, but unlike Johnson, he holds that emotions are transformed rather than dispelled. "It is thus the fiction of tragedy softens the passion, by an infusion of a new feeling, not merely by weakening or diminishing the sorrow" (221). Johnson takes a homeopathic view of catharsis, in which art arouses the same passions that real life does, but in a controlled way that works to moderate them (*Life* 3:39). In Hume's theory, as Ralph Cohen has shown, they are not the same passions as those of real life, but specifically aesthetic ones. Yet, once again, the affinity between the two positions is closer than may appear. Johnson says that art intoxicates, but also that no one ever mistakes it for reality; Hume says that art transforms passion, but also that it becomes unacceptably painful if the reality it represents is too intensely felt.

"The truth is," Johnson declares, "that the spectators are always in their senses" (*Preface* 77); yet he writes of a speech in *Macbeth*, "He that peruses Shakespeare looks round alarmed, and starts [i.e., gives a start] to find himself alone" (*Johnson on Shakespeare* 8:770). Seated in the social environment of a theater and watching actors impersonate dramatic characters, the spectator is unlikely to forget the artificiality of the occasion. Reading Shakespeare in solitude, one may well lose oneself in the imaginary world, and Johnson regards this immersion as a threat rather than an advantage. "Whilst we are absorbed in the novel," William James says in *The Principles of Psychology*, "we turn our backs on all other worlds, and, for the time, the Ivanhoe-world remains our absolute reality. When we wake from the spell, however, we find a still more real world, which reduces Ivanhoe, and all things connected with him, to the fictive status, and relegates them to one of the sub-universes" (2:922n). For Johnson there is only one universe, and one must never turn one's back on it. Fictions of reality therefore generate a special kind of uneasiness in Johnson, since he wants to assert simultaneously that they are grounded in fact and that they work by exciting the imagination. The cruelty of Lear's daughters is justifiable as being "an historical fact" attested by the chronicles Shakespeare followed, but the death of Cordelia is simply intolerable: "I was many years ago so shocked by Cordelia's death, that I know not whether I ever endured to read again the last scenes of the play till I undertook to revise them as an editor" (*Johnson on Shakespeare* 8:703–704).

Hume too holds that a tragic action may be so "atrocious" as to excite "such movements of horror as will not soften into pleasure" (*Of Tragedy*, *Essays* 224), and also that an actual event, for those who have lived through it, may remain too emotionally fraught to be capable of artistic transformation.

Lord CLARENDON, when he approaches towards the catastrophe of the royal party [in the Civil War], supposes that his narration must then become infinitely disagreeable; and he hurries over the king's death without giving us one circumstance of it. He considers it as too horrid a scene to be contemplated with any satisfaction, or even without the utmost pain and aversion. He himself, as well as the readers of that age, were too deeply concerned in the events, and felt a pain from subjects which an historian and a reader of another age would regard as the most pathetic [i.e., moving] and most interesting, and, by consequence, the most agreeable. (223–24)

Literary experiences are more powerful if the reader believes them to be true, but if they press too closely on the reader's (or the writer's) own experience they can seem *too* true.

Johnson says sternly in *Rambler* No. 4, where the immorality of recent novels is under review, "If the world be promiscuously described, I cannot see of what use it can be to read the account, or why it may not be as safe to turn the eye immediately upon mankind, as upon a mirror which shows all that presents itself without discrimination." The principle of selection (Johnson) or aesthetic rearrangement (Hume) implies a way of looking more clearly at the world, but it is not otherwise different from looking at it "immediately," without mediation. The two kinds of looking provide a mutual check: you evaluate the work of art by comparing it with your own experience of the world, and you look at the world with closer attention because works of art have helped you to know what to look for. In other words, art is a model of reality. Just as a well-made model of a ship helps you to understand ships, so *Othello* helps you to understand jealousy. But Johnson also says in the *Preface to Shakespeare*, "Upon every other stage the universal agent is love. . . . But love is only one of many passions, and as it has no great influence upon the sum of life, it has little operation in the dramas of a poet who caught his ideas from the living world, and exhibited only what he saw before him" (63–64). It is thus not enough to say that love is a convention of the drama, or that people are fascinated by love and enjoy seeing it in art even if it can't always have a central place in their lives. Art has to *be* life.

In a subtle passage in *Rasselas* Imlac declares, "Example is always more efficacious than precept. A soldier is formed in war, and a painter must copy pictures. In this, contemplative life has the advantage: great actions are seldom seen, but the labours of art are always at hand for those who desire to know what art has been able to perform" (chap. 30). This might conceivably mean, "Art can perform a lot; contemplative people have an advantage because they are always free to learn from art." But it is more likely to mean, "Whatever art can perform is permanently available, but it's different from life and there is a lot that it can't perform. Contemplative people may always have art at hand, but don't forget that they are dropouts from life." Imlac's theme in this discourse, after all, is that "while you are making the choice of life, you neglect to live." In the end it is life to whose temporal flow one must submit, whether waiting like Johnson for "the choice of eternity" (chap. 48) or accepting like Hume the finality of present existence. "I may, nay I must yield to the current of nature" (*Treatise* 269). "Do not suffer life to stagnate; it will grow muddy for want of motion: commit yourself again to the current of the world" (*Rasselas*, chap. 35). Both Hume and Johnson speak for an age that replaces fiction with nonfiction, even while it recognizes the fictive status of the experience that nonfiction seeks to represent. And the ultimate point of their fictions of reality is that these, unlike the fictions of traditional art, are *felt to be true,* both by the community that has internalized them and by writers like Hume and Johnson who are dedicated to clarifying and confirming them.

2

Boswell
Life as Art

DIARY AND SELF

ON THE sixteenth of May, 1763, four years after the publication of Johnson's *Rasselas*, a twenty-two-year-old Scot named James Boswell was introduced to Johnson in a London bookseller's shop. Not until 1950 did the public see the volume edited by Frederick Pottle as *Boswell's London Journal, 1762–1763*, the richest and most fully integrated of the journals Boswell kept throughout his life, in which that meeting is reported not as the crucial event of a lifetime but merely as one incident among many. *Rasselas* is a fable about young people pondering the choice of life; the *London Journal* dramatizes the same theme in richly circumstantial detail, and demonstrates (more or less naively) that life is inevitably lived as art.

The essayistic mode of Johnson and Hume is built upon personal experience, but often idealized, and always generalized to such an extent that biographical references are likely to be apparent only to readers who recognize them from other contexts:

Poor Sober! I have often teased him with reproof, and he has often promised reformation; for no man is so much open to conviction as the idler, but there is none on whom it operates so little. What will be the effect of this paper I know not; perhaps he will read it and laugh, and light the fire in his furnace; but my hope is that he will quit his trifles, and betake himself to rational and useful diligence. (*Idler* No. 31)

In this disguised self-portrait, Johnson has set up an ironic dialogue between his best and worst selves, the former hoping against hope for reformation, the latter preparing to laugh at advice and to burn the paper which his best self has just written. But the effect is almost of a private joke; only because of Boswell's biographical labors are we able to penetrate the disguise and smile (or wince) at the self-reference. Boswell himself, by contrast, is completely *there,* a man in his book.

Boswell was passionately eager to win fame as a writer, and in 1762 had already begun the output of doggerel verse and other ephemera that would continue throughout his life. What he could not know, as Pottle observes in his masterly biography, was that his journal was developing into an "unrecognized, nameless work of art" (94). Nonetheless, the *London Journal* is a book and is meant to be. Boswell wrote it out on neat quarto sheets that make a volume of more than seven hundred manuscript pages, and these were mailed regularly to his friend John Johnston in Scotland, with hints that posterity might someday be interested.

On the one hand, the *London Journal* is filled with literary assumptions; more than most diaries it forces one to recognize that experience is perceived in artificial and conventional ways. On the other hand, its grounding in actuality has to be recognized, and much of its literary force derives from its openness to preliterary or extraliterary experience. Boswell has the very rare gift of transforming circumstantial experience into art, giving imaginative form to the quotidian. Leslie Stephen, reflecting on the feeble unconnectedness of most of the materials reprinted by G. B. Hill as *Johnsonian Miscellanies*, observes that "Boswell seems to be alone in the art of presenting us in a few lines with a conversation which is obviously as real as it is dramatic" ("Johnsoniana" 126). Such a judgment refers not just to literal accuracy, to which most of the writers in the *Miscellanies* aspired, but to the psychological and imaginative accuracy that gives body and meaning to the "real." Stephen could not have seen the journals, which were as yet unpublished and unknown, but he had read Boswell's letters to William Temple and was able to call him, very aptly, "one who lives in a dream world, and yet one whose dreams are always a version of realities" (133). As in the thinking of Johnson and Hume, reality in Boswell's letters and journals exists as the multiple "realities" of individuals, each one idiosyncratic but overlapping with the rest in so many ways that a world of shared experience is confirmed.

"Truth shall ever be observed," Boswell declares at the outset, saying that he will omit sensitive matters when necessary but never misrepresent them (*London Journal* 40). He then proposes an interesting series of reasons for maintaining the journal, each of which addresses some aspect of the relation between writing and life:

In this way I shall preserve many things that would otherwise be lost in oblivion. I shall find daily employment for myself, which will save me from indolence and help to keep off the spleen, and I shall lay up a store of entertainment for my after life. Very often we have more pleasure in reflecting on agreeable scenes that we have been in than we had from the scenes themselves. I shall regularly record the business or rather the pleasure of every day. I shall not study much correctness, lest the labour of it should make me lay it aside altogether. I hope it will be of use to my worthy friend Johnston, and that while he laments my personal absence, this journal may in some measure supply that defect and make him happy. (40)

A wide range of motives for diary keeping is here implied. First of all, regular writing will rescue experience from "oblivion." Boswell prides himself on a fertile imagination, but memory is the presiding muse of this incipient epic of the self, which will accumulate into a book that will afford "entertainment" just as a work of fiction might, but with the added charm of giving a literary shape ("scenes") to one's own life. Second, the journal is a means of keeping busy, a defense against the "spleen" (an emotional disturbance made worse by "indolence" and perhaps even caused by it). It is not just the record of a life, but an essential therapy in that life. And finally, the journal's basis in personal friendship is deeply important. Its liveliness and frankness are made possible by addressing an ideal reader who is also a real reader, Boswell's close friend Johnston. The writer can examine himself intimately because his friend shares his concern, but he must not be so self-absorbed as to bore or disgust his friend. (Similarly, Wordsworth's *Prelude* represents itself as a letter to Coleridge, and other readers are in effect invited into the friendship, encouraged to care about the writer as his intimates do.)

Nothing is more characteristic of Boswell than a scrupulous attention to accuracy. He distinguishes strictly between fiction and fact, as a much later journal entry notes: "Carelessness as to the exactness of circumstances is very dangerous, for one may gradually recede from the fact till all is fiction" (Brady 7). Hobbes said that memory was decaying sense; Boswell seems almost to be saying that fiction is decaying fact. But while factual truth must be faithfully observed, not everything should be revealed, let alone explained. At the very end of the journal we discover that before coming to London Boswell fathered, and has continued to support, an illegitimate child. In a novel the concealment of this information would be a piece of design; in the journal it is simply a reticence which the writer permits himself.

More significantly, Boswell's tormented relation with his stern father, who was literally a judge, is consistently elided. It is shocking to read the wounding paternal letter that Pottle prints as an appendix to the *London Journal*, threatening disinheritance and "selling all off, from the principle that it is better to snuff a candle out than leave it to stink in a socket"

(341). This is the great suppressed subject of a journal that is carried on in defiance of Lord Auchinleck's wishes and (as Felicity Nussbaum notes) is filled with imagery of conflict between fathers and sons. Boswell's canon of veracity is itself a legacy from his implacable father, as he indicates in an autobiographical sketch written for Rousseau (translated by Pottle from Boswell's French):

> I preferred being weak and ill to being strong and healthy. . . . It is surprising that I did not often say that I was ill when I was actually well. But my worthy father had impressed upon me a respect for the truth which has always remained firm in my mind. Accordingly I never lied, but I hung my head down towards the floor until I got a headache, and then I complained that I was ill. (Pottle 1–2)

Boswell may not fully notice the implication that although he will not falsify reality, he can try to influence reality in the direction of his wishes. But at bottom the function of writing is to fix the traces of memory, which are linked to experience in the empiricist sense that Johnson expounds in *Rambler* No. 41. Without the journal, fact would indeed recede into fiction, and for Boswell that would be an unbearable loss.

His increasing mastery of language gives Boswell keen satisfaction. Friends keep urging him to develop a formal style, but he is drawn instinctively to an expressive plain style, exhibiting glee at his developing ability to recreate experience in language:

> How easily and cleverly do I write just now! I am really pleased with myself; words come skipping to me like lambs upon Moffat Hill; and I turn my periods smoothly and imperceptibly like a skilful wheelwright turning tops in a turning-loom. There's fancy! There's simile! In short, I am at present a genius. (*London Journal* 187)

Boswell's sentences are still periodic, but they are produced with the confident ease of a master craftsman whose art is so familiar that he hardly needs to think about it. This is a style in which Boswell can tell a story, but like Sterne's flashier style it can also take the place of story. "I am not at all unsatisfied with this [housebound] kind of existence. It is passing my portion of time very comfortably. Most philosophically do I reason upon this subject, being certainly the most important one to me at present" (184). Boswell is indeed his own true subject at all times, even when eliciting the opinions of the majestic Johnson: "We then talked of Me" (326). And because he is his own subject, nothing is irrelevant that relates to himself, as Johnson observes with specific reference to Boswell's journal: "I told Mr. Johnson that I put down all sorts of little incidents in it. 'Sir,' said he, 'there is nothing too little for so little a creature as man'" (305).

At times the obligation to write may seem Sisyphean, "bringing up my lagging journal, which, like a stone to be rolled up a hill, must be kept constantly going" (324). But it also represents the sustaining framework of existence. "I lately had a thought that appeared new to me," Boswell writes many years afterward, "that by burning all my journal and all my written traces of former life, I should be like a new being" (Brady 147). Or perhaps he would then be nobody at all. His journals closely resemble *Tristram Shandy* in their dedication to the ever-unfolding moment: if the writing were to stop, it would mean that the author had stopped. And even more than *Tristram Shandy* they are committed to recording the ongoing present. "We do not *live* stories," Hayden White says, "even if we give our lives meaning by retrospectively casting them in the form of stories" (*Tropics* 90). But Boswell does live stories, and his periods of depression are marked by an inability to feel that satisfying stories are happening.

In this sense the journal is Boswell's formalized version of what goes on in everyone's head, "that story of our own lives that we narrate to ourselves in an episodic, sometimes semi-conscious, but virtually uninterrupted monologue" (Brooks 3). Rather than winning something new from the void as fictions do, Boswell's journals strive to rescue what has already existed from disappearing into the void. Milan Kundera says of one of his characters who hopes to recover her lost diaries,

She is aware, of course, that there are many unpleasant things in the notebooks—days of dissatisfaction, quarrels, even boredom. But that is not what counts. She has no desire to turn the past into poetry, she wants to give the past back its lost body. She is not compelled by a desire for beauty, she is compelled by a desire for life. (86)

But this character is herself a fictional invention, seeking the body of a past that never was—and even in the fiction she never gets the diaries back. She is an invented person recovering reality; Boswell is a real person whose reality is mediated through fictions, striving to embody the ongoing present before it can turn into the irrevocable past.

Even if Boswell had sat down to write every evening—in fact he sometimes postponed doing so for several days—the material of the journal would already have receded into that past. His theme is as much presentness as pastness, and more than once he recognizes that his mission is to recreate a lost presence. "I have all along been speaking in the perfect tense, as if I was writing the history of some distant period. I shall after this use the present often, as most proper. Indeed, I will not confine myself, but take whichever is most agreeable at the time" (*London Journal* 65). Like Richardson in *Pamela* and *Clarissa*, Boswell combines still-happening thoughts with just-happened events, and of course he is committed literally to what Richardson presents fictionally, an anticipation of the not-yet-happened future. In Robert Fothergill's helpful phrase, the journal is a "serial autobiography" (2) that embodies provisional structures but resists definitive ones.

Boswell understands clearly that what gives significance to facts is the sensibility that perceives and orders them. To the passion for veracity he joins "my genius for poetry, which ascribes many fanciful properties to everything" (42), whether he is bowing farewell to the "lofty romantic mountain" that overlooks Edinburgh (41) or admiring the wintry Thames in the language of the sublime: "We . . . went upon the top of London Bridge, from whence we viewed with a pleasing horror the rude and terrible appearance of the river, partly froze up, partly covered with enormous shoals of floating ice which often crashed against each other" (153). Cultural categories determine what is there to be seen, much as Gombrich's medieval artist sat in front of a living lion and drew a heraldic emblem (79).

Beyond the conventional terms, though inarticulate without them, is "the true language of my heart" (205)—which, as it happens, is a tag from the artful Pope (*Epistle to Arbuthnot*, l. 399). In Johnson's writings sensibility or "feeling" is a dangerous if not vicious guide; Boswell, very differently, "thought myself right from feeling, which is the great test to every man" (228). Johnsonian ethics are prescriptive and authoritative, which is why Boswell is drawn to Johnson as a mentor. The ethics of feeling, as Hume's moral philosophy makes clear, are based in the end on the conventions of the group, even when these are said to reflect the instinctive responses of universal human nature. But Boswell has strongly contradictory feelings and can easily imagine himself adopting the standards of very different groups.

However much he may agonize over the conflict between ethical codes, Boswell is most himself when reveling in the sensations of the moment, in a world of phenomenology rather than of epistemology or moral doctrine: "I had my feet washed with milk-warm water, I had my bed warmed, and went to sleep soft and contented" (81). Deeper and fuller than the world of official literature is the recreated world of the senses, into which even the most formidable figures are drawn by the force of Boswell's imagination. "As Smith used to observe, a time of indisposition is not altogether a time of misery. There is a softness of disposition and an absence of care which attend upon its indolent confinement" (164). In the luxury of sensory relaxation, "indisposition" and "disposition" grow indistinct and merge. And who would guess that "Smith" here is Adam Smith, Boswell's former teacher and founder of the science of economics?

But if everything that Boswell sees is assimilated to what he feels, one should not suppose that he fully anticipates the modern preoccupation with consciousness. On the contrary, he usually finds himself defeated by the gaze within and projects his feelings outward. When he does look within, his aim is to take his emotional temperature rather than to anatomize his psychological life in a novelistic way. In any case he does not and cannot have the comprehensive perspective that writers of fiction enjoy, and he is under no obligation to describe thematic or structural patterns if he does not see them. John Updike comments in an essay on one of Boswell's later journals, "The writer of a novel or a history holds over his reader the tyranny of a plan, of withheld secrets and staged revelations. The writer of a journal is at sea in his tides of detail, and after enough immersion with him we develop a kind of infantile, pre-conscious sensibility, which knows at least where the warm spots and the cold spots are" (336).

In contrast to the vividness of sensation, Boswell's inner life remains murky, above all with respect to the "melancholy" that deeply tormented him. He has "dismal dreams almost every night" (195) but does not describe them; he feels "too great a hurry of spirits" (211), is "very bad" for days on end (246), finds himself "quite unhinged" (248), and endures "gloomy terrors" so disturbing that he has to sleep at a friend's lodgings (253). The descriptions seem deliberately vague. Boswell is a man in pain, fleeing anxieties which he does not care to record, and meanwhile recording a stream of sensations that confirm at least that he is alive. But even as it evades interiority, the *London Journal* conveys a powerful impression of consciousness in Updike's sense if not in Wordsworth's.

Boswell's way of living, in his own opinion, exhibits a paradoxically inactive mode of activity: "I am rather passive than active in life. It is difficult to make my feeling clearly understood. I may say, I act passively. That is, not with my whole heart, and thinking this or that of real consequence, but because so and so things are established and I must submit" (77). In later life this reluctance to submit would contribute to intense melancholia; Boswell agonized endlessly about determinism and free will because —in the terms of the Calvinism in which he was raised—he felt both guilty and unfree. In a 1780 essay his self-portrait of a "hypochondriac" transposes the active passiveness of the *London Journal* into a darker key, unwillingly embracing the standards of the external world through shame rather than desire:

He is distracted between indolence and shame. Every kind of labour is irksome to him. Yet he has not resolution to cease from his accustomed tasks. Though he reasons within himself that contempt is nothing, the habitual current of his feelings obliges him to shun being despised. He acts therefore like a slave, not animated by inclination but goaded by fear. (*The Hypochondriack* 2:41)

Boswell's conversational merriment looks compensatory, and that is how he describes it in what appears to be another self-portrait in the *Life of Johnson*: "There is no doubt that a man may appear very gay in company who is sad at heart. His merriment is like the sound of drums and trumpets in a battle, to drown the groans of the wounded and dying" (4:304n).

Even in the *London Journal*, moments of intensely gratified vanity, for instance when Lady Northumberland shows particular favor, open out into detached curiosity and then into intimations of an existential abyss.

I could observe people looking at me with envy, as a man of some distinction and a favourite of my Lady's. Bravo! thought I. I am sure I deserve to be a favourite. It was curious to find of how little consequence each individual was in such a crowd. I could imagine how an officer in a great army may be killed without being observed. I came home quiet, laid by my clothes, and went coolly to bed. There's conduct for you. (71)

Boswell's pleasure in being noticed gives way to thoughts of being lost in the crowd, and then to thoughts of anonymous death; but he ends with a reaffirmation of controlled "conduct," even when there is no one at all to see it.

ACTING AND MIRRORING

This doubleness of experience is central to Boswell's achievement as a writer. Re-presenting his life of feeling, he surveys his behavior as a spectator might, viewing himself affectionately but also critically in the mirror of social relationships. In a conversation recorded in the *Life of Johnson* he seizes on the analogy between his journal and a mirror:

JOHNSON. "A man loves to review his own mind. That is the use of a diary, or journal." LORD TRIMLESTOWN. "True, Sir. As the ladies love to see themselves in a glass, so a man likes to see himself in his journal." BOSWELL. "A very pretty allusion." JOHNSON. "Yes, indeed." BOSWELL. "And as a lady adjusts her dress before a mirror, a man adjusts his character by looking at his journal." (3:228)

In this conception, which comes perilously close to Swift's satire on clothes as souls in *A Tale of a Tub*, character is essentially external and can be adjusted like clothing. One thinks of Boswell's lifelong predilection for eye-catching costumes. The mirror metaphor is not very suggestive of

introspection, and Frank Brady, calling Boswell "shrewd rather than penetrating," says that he is limited by "his unwillingness to go deeper than
the mirror image" (145). But to look unflinchingly even at one's external image requires a good deal of self-knowledge, and Boswell's journals
testify richly to his recognition of his follies as well as his charms.

Playing roles so self-consciously, Boswell was bound to be interested
in acting and actors; one of his models when he arrived in London was
West Digges, who had been a great success as Macheath in *The Beggar's Opera*. Thomas Sheridan, actor and teacher of elocution, maintained
"that an actor ought to forget himself and the audience entirely, and be
quite the real character; and that for his part, he was so much so that he
remembered nothing at all but the character." Boswell, recording this pronouncement, finds himself agreeing with another person who urges that
"an actor in that case would not play so well, as he would not be enough
master of himself" (*London Journal* 109). A few years later Boswell wrote
an essay—at about the same time as Diderot's celebrated *Paradoxe sur le
comédien*—that specified "a kind of double feeling" in the actor's consciousness: the role "must take full possession, as it were, of the ante-
chamber of his mind, while his own character remains in the innermost
recess" (Brady 16–17). The essay goes on to detect the same doubleness
in a lawyer pleading a case, as Boswell himself did professionally many
times a year.

Just as the actor must be conscious of artifice in order to seem the person he feigns, so in actual life one cannot avoid playing a role or roles, and
nothing is gained by pretending that they do not exist. The *London Journal* is sustained by Boswell's personality, but personality is not a concept
that he entertains or wants. From his own point of view he is committed
to a continual search for character: he needs to *have* a character and to *be*
one. So he tries on a long series of roles and plays each one with as much
conviction as he can manage, having learned "that we may be in some
degree whatever character we choose" (47). When the journal begins he is
a son with "warm filial regard" just leaving home, and he enjoys thinking
about the "scene" that that calls up: "The scene of being a son setting
out from home for the wide world, and the idea of being my own master,
pleased me much" (41). At the same time he indulges pleasant fantasies
about a remote period when "I shall certainly be a religious old man"
(46).

What Boswell wants above all is to overcome the "style" in which
his London friends knew him three years before, "raw, curious, volatile,
credulous" (52), a mode of behavior in which "I was, in short, a charac-

ter very different from what God intended me and I myself chose" (62). The equation is significant: does Boswell choose (like a good Calvinist) to concur with the life plan that God has already determined as inevitable, or is he free to stray from it? And if he strays, is he disobeying, or merely fulfilling God's wishes in a different way?

In episodes of pleasure seeking Boswell likes to imagine himself "one of the wits in King Charles the Second's time" (140), but he needs to be reassured that he has "no love for riot, no ambition to be a buck" (129), and Digges strikes him as an appropriate role model on such occasions:

I attempted to be like Digges, and considered the similarity of our genius and pleasures. I acquired confidence by considering my present character in this light: a young fellow of spirit and fashion, heir to a good fortune, enjoying the pleasures of London, and now making his addresses in order to have an intrigue with that delicious subject of gallantry, an actress. (94)

Here "my present character" clearly implies a role that has been newly assumed and may someday be supplanted by others. Digges is not so much a role model, perhaps, as a "type" that one can play at being. When spending the night at an inn with his subject of gallantry, Boswell goes so far as to "assume the name of Mr. Digges" (137).

But on the whole Digges is too frivolous, and Boswell prefers to merge his example with those of graver masters.

I felt my mind regain its native dignity. I felt strong dispositions to be a Mr. Addison. Indeed, I had accustomed myself so much to laugh at everything that it required time to render my imagination solid and give me just notions of real life and of religion. But I hoped by degrees to attain to some degree of propriety. Mr. Addison's character in sentiment, mixed with a little of the gaiety of Sir Richard Steele and the manners of Mr. Digges, were the ideas which I aimed to realize. (62)

At the theater "I wrought myself up to the imagination that it was the age of Sir Richard Steele, and that I was like him sitting in judgment on a new comedy" (177). Neither Steele nor Addison is literally emulated, but rather their mutual persona: "I imagined myself the Spectator taking one of his rural excursions" (244).

In these experiments in imagination, Boswell's object is to acquire, but also to verify that he intrinsically is, a character of mature judiciousness.

I . . . pride myself in thinking that my natural character is that of dignity. My friend Temple is very good in consoling me by saying that I may be such a man, and that people will say, "Mr. Boswell is quite altered from the dissipated, inconstant fellow that he was. He is now a reserved, grave sort of a man. But indeed that was his real character; and he only deviated into these eccentric paths for a while." Well, then, let me see if I have resolution enough to bring that about. (258)

Meanwhile Boswell indulges himself with less sober literary analogues, as if he were "the hero of a romance or novel" (206). On a single excursion he impersonates in rapid succession a scruffily dressed "blackguard," a half-pay officer, and a highwayman, but is flattered to discover that "I was always taken for a gentleman in disguise" (273).

In the finest of all these vignettes, Boswell poses as a Scottish High-lander—he was very much a Lowlander—and enjoys a pair of young prostitutes in the character of Macheath:

I then sallied forth to the Piazzas in rich flow of animal spirits and burning with fierce desire. I met two very pretty little girls who asked me to take them with me. "My dear girls," said I, "I am a poor fellow. I can give you no money. But if you choose to have a glass of wine and my company and let us be gay and obliging to each other without money, I am your man." They agreed with great good humour. So back to the Shakespeare [Tavern] I went. "Waiter," said I, "I have got here a couple of human beings; I don't know how they'll do." "I'll look, your Honour," cried he, and with inimitable effrontery stared them in the face and then cried, "They'll do very well." "What," said I, "are they good fellow-creatures? Bring them up, then." We were shown into a good room and had a bottle of sherry before us in a minute. I surveyed my seraglio and found them both good subjects for amorous play. I toyed with them and drank about and sung *Youth's the Season* and thought myself Captain Macheath; and then I solaced my existence with them, one after the other, according to their seniority. (263–64)

It is active passivity again, the self-abnegation of the actor who facilitates the acting of a whole ensemble; many of the most memorable episodes in the *Life of Johnson* are products of this gift.

It is important to recognize that Boswell's impersonations, however much they reflect his psychological needs, are also an expression of a tendency in his culture. A central preoccupation of eighteenth-century literature is the liberation afforded by role playing, and indeed by imposture and faking. Clearly it gave theater audiences pleasure to see people manipulate the network of social roles by plausible feats of impersonation. It is a question not just of pretending to be someone you're not, but of realizing that you might be all sorts of persons besides the one you currently are. Benjamin Franklin's *Autobiography* has given offense to many post-Romantic readers because of its apparent insincerity, but from Franklin's own point of view he was simply choosing to be a person of a particular kind, or kinds. Hume and Gibbon seem to have fashioned themselves (or their selves) in similar ways.

A world of role playing, Berger and Luckmann observe, is characterized by "a network of reciprocal manipulations" (172). Boswell's fervent social and political conservatism is in part a reaction against the instability of this world of manipulations, as is the sentimentality with which he and many of his contemporaries extol the language of the heart. One notices that eighteenth-century plays about imposture always end with a rush of sentiment when the masks are taken off: "Such goodness who could injure! I find myself unequal to the task of villain; she has gained my soul, and made it honest like her own" (Aimwell in the final scene of Farquhar's *Beaux' Stratagem*).

Boswell's street roles in the *London Journal* are reflections both of personal preoccupations and of social schemas. In every one of them he plays at being an outsider and at exercising power. They obviously flow from his anomalous status as a young Scot in London, hoping to become an insider with socially sanctioned power, and they occur in the intervals of his decorous visits to patrons like Lady Northumberland. The escapism is itself socially conditioned, since the romantic highwayman is just as much a projection of eighteenth-century society as Squire Allworthy or the Man of Feeling. "Sincerity," Peter Berger says dryly, "is the consciousness of the man who is taken in by his own act" (109). Boswell's problem perhaps is that he has too many acts and can't be secure in any one of them. The episode in the tavern comes just two weeks after "a very deep melancholy" excited by seeing the execution of a "genteel, spirited" young highwayman who was known as "Captain" and who appeared "just a Macheath" (251–52).

The theatrical metaphor, as recent scholarship has made clear, opens out into the deepest concerns of eighteenth-century thinking about the self, gaining its power from the twin facts that the stage imitates life and that people play roles. Adam Smith's *Theory of Moral Sentiments* (published four years before Boswell began the *London Journal*) has recently attracted interest for its extended account of sympathy as a reciprocal mirroring between persons that is duplicated by a self-reflexive interior process. As David Marshall summarizes Smith's view, "One becomes a spectator to oneself in order to determine if one can enter into one's own feelings; one knows if one sympathizes with oneself because one sympathizes with the sentiments of the spectator-judge one has become" (598). It may seem reasonable to conclude, as Marshall does, that "identity itself is undermined by the theatrical model which pictures the self as an actor who stands beside himself and represents the characters of both spectator and spectacle" (599). But Smith's point in fact is that sympathy, rather than deconstructing identity, works to confirm it.

To be sure, the self is defined and indeed constituted by its social context, which is to say that it is as much sociological as psychological. John

Bender comments that Smith's position looks forward to such theorists of behavior as George Herbert Mead, for whom "self-identity comes to being only when the sensations of a particular individual pass through the medium of social norms and expectations as personified in the 'generalized other,' or, in Dr. Johnson's terminology, 'the public eye' " (222). This position will seem a daring challenge to personal identity only for persons who assume a Romantic definition of the self. What Smith and Hume and Johnson have in mind is that we can understand our world only through constant reference to the worlds of others. The social construction of experience is what makes life possible, and as Hume very concisely puts it, "the minds of men are mirrors to one another" (*Treatise* 365).

The cult of sincerity finds its apogee in Rousseau, and as Hannah Arendt says, "The search for motives, the demand that everybody display in public his innermost motivation, since it actually demands the impossible, transforms all actors into hypocrites; the moment the display of motives begins, hypocrisy begins to poison all human relations" (98). Rousseau was notoriously accused of hypocrisy. Boswell, very differently, tends to *become* whatever role he assumes; rather than concealing a "real" self behind a mask, he tries on a series of selves that all succeed in expressing aspects of his nature.

Such a procedure, moreover, is fully in accord with the empiricist theory of the self, in which man is simultaneously a natural object and a cultural product. As Nicholas Capaldi puts it in "Hume as Social Scientist," man is by definition "a role-playing or rule-following agent" (99). Moreover, human roles are enacted in a temporal process. As Capaldi says, once Hume has exploded causal explanation he is driven upon historical explanation as the only means of making sense of life, and his exposition of Hume's position is deeply relevant to Boswell's practice:

Within [the] temporal order is revealed our past self, our past choices. In this sense we can truly say that the self is not the thing which chooses, rather we as selves emerge from our choices. This situation also reveals why we cannot escape our history. . . . Since we ourselves are not something other than our social roles, we need the participation of others to maintain our self-image. This means we require some sort of predictable pattern. This means we cannot choose in a manner inconsistent with the past. . . . The only frame of reference Hume will allow for determining relevance is the historical past, not any independent ontological order. (122)

Measured against a Rousseauvian or Romantic notion of the self, the Boswell of the *London Journal* may seem unstable and inconsistent. Measured against a Humean notion of the self, he is engaged in a continuous process of deducing himself from his own ongoing history. He keeps making choices to become something different from what he has been, but the choices are themselves temporally conditioned; unlike the "second birth" of spiritual autobiography, Boswell never claims to acquire a totally new self unconnected with the old one. Tracing the chain of resemblances, both as he himself perceives them and as others do, is the fundamental theme of the journals.

Boswell views Johnson, of course, as a massively stable identity, a memorable image of which is the central achievement of the *Life of Johnson*. But this is very much a compensatory idealization, and as W. H. Auden once remarked, Boswell's devotion to Johnson is "as remarkable in its way as Dante's to Beatrice" (148). The Johnsonian self of the *Life of Johnson* is an expression of Boswell's emotional need; the socially triangulated identity of the journals is an expression of his emotional experience.

What is most problematic about this complex of mirroring and role playing is not so much its ethical status as its truth status, whether the narratives that embody it are entirely mental or are written down. Bender says persuasively that even in Adam Smith's theoretical account of self-mirroring, the operative analogy is not really with the drama but with third-person narration, so that Smith's account of imaginative sympathy resembles "a play staged fictionally within a novel" (228). Insofar as Boswell can successfully be an actor on a public stage, encouraging those around him to play roles in the same drama, he is able to recover the Renaissance improvisatory freedom of Lanham's *homo rhetoricus*. Insofar as he tells stories in his head, both while they are happening and later on when he records them in his journal, he is imprisoned in the infinite regress of *homo seriosus'* search for sincerity.

Boswell's experiences of sex, or rather his interpretations of those experiences, epitomize the difficulty of resting secure in the conventional roles he is forever trying to cast himself in. His is a temperament in which, to quote Mary Wollstonecraft's strictures on romantic sensibility, "sentiments become events" (183). In the *London Journal* Boswell enjoys decorous conversations with women of good family, but (like Rousseau) he seems a perfect instance of the type Freud describes in "The Most Prevalent Form of Degradation in Erotic Life," who is inhibited from sexual pleasure with women of his own class and enjoys it with women whom he perceives as degraded. The day after the episode in which Boswell roisters as a blackguard—having picked up a whore, "I dipped my machine in the Canal and performed most manfully" (272)—he attempts the elegant Miss Temple and is chagrined to find himself impotent: she "used every endearing amorous blandishment," but his exhaustion from the previous day, "joined with my being really in love with her, had quite enervated me, and I had no tender inclinations" (273).

Just what all of this means is a constant puzzle to Boswell, and often a source of anxiety as well. In his day, when poverty was desperate and the streets of London unlit, it was easy to procure what he wanted for a shilling or even for sixpence. At times he is more than a little uneasy about the implications in human terms: "She who submitted to my lusty embraces was a young Shropshire girl, only seventeen, very well-looked, her name Elizabeth Parker. Poor being, she has a sad time of it!" (227). Clearly there has been some conversation, though Boswell does not report it, and it has left disquieting thoughts.

The next entry in the *Journal* is devoted to a conceit about a reinvented world in which religion might bestow sexual pleasure instead of repressing it:

Erskine and I sauntered up and down some hours. I should have mentioned some time ago that I said to him that if venereal delight and the power of propagating the species were permitted only to the virtuous, it would make the world very good. . . . Preachers would incite the audience to goodness by warmly and lusciously setting before their imaginations the transports of amorous joy. This would render the pleasures of love more refined and more valuable, when they were participated only by the good. Whereas at present it is the common solace of the virtuous and the wicked, the man of taste and the man of brutality. (227)

Boswell is at once the man of taste and the man of brutality, and he is profoundly confused by the tension between the two, not to mention by the fantasy that virtue would be more appealing if its reward could be what is normally stigmatized as vice. A generation later, subtler thinkers like Wollstonecraft and Blake would subject this dilemma to trenchant analysis: the worm of secrecy destroying the sick rose, the priests in black gowns "binding with briars my joys and desires" (Blake's *Garden of Love*), and above all the parasitical relationship of prostitution to cultural inhibition. From a Blakean point of view, forbidding sexual pleasure is precisely the institutional role of preachers, and it is no wonder that they do not recommend "the transports of amorous joy."

Boswell cannot quite get the matter into focus, but his language betrays discomfort that sometimes rises to disgust:

At night I strolled into the Park and took the first whore I met, whom I without many words copulated with free from danger, being safely sheathed. She was ugly and lean and her breath smelt of spirits. I never asked her name. When it was done, she slunk off. I had a low opinion of this gross practice and resolved to do it no more. (230–31)

Elizabeth Parker (six days earlier) was young and pretty, so Boswell asked her name, but the more he knew about her the more her plight seemed distressing. The ugly whore, selected at random and used without conversation, remains an anonymous appurtenance in "this gross practice" of which Boswell admits to having a low opinion. What he wants to avoid, of course, is having a low opinion of *himself*, no Captain Macheath now but a man of brutality indeed.

At times Boswell euphemizes his behavior as "promiscuous concubinage" (304), as if he were some sort of oriental potentate, but usually the gulf between actual and ideal is clearly marked by levels of language.

At night I took a streetwalker into Privy Garden and indulged sensuality. The wretch picked my pocket of my handkerchief, and then swore that she had not. When I got home, I was shocked to think that I had been intimately united with a low, abandoned, perjured, pilfering creature. I determined to do so no more; but if the Cyprian fury should seize me, to participate my amorous flame with a genteel girl. (280)

The gap between the "low creature" and the "genteel girl" remains unbridgeable, as does the gap between everyday "sensuality" and the "amorous flame" of romance. Boswell's good resolutions have predictably temporary results: "This afternoon I had some low debauchery with girls who patrol the courts in the Temple" (300).

Sympathetic though Boswell may be toward prostitutes, he imagines their lives in essentially sentimental terms, as a comparison with Johnson's much grimmer picture makes evident: "If those who pass their days in plenty and security could visit for an hour the dismal receptacles to which the prostitute retires from her nocturnal excursions, and see the wretches that lie crowded together, mad with intemperance, ghastly with famine, nauseous with filth, and noisome with disease; it would not be easy for any degree of abhorrence to harden them against compassion, or to repress the desire which they must immediately feel to rescue such numbers of human beings from a state so dreadful" (*Rambler* No. 171). There is much more here than Boswell wants to know. Wide open though his diary ostensibly is, its margins are in fact tightly controlled.

If the *London Journal* were a novel, one would have to ask what the author intends by this kind of uneasiness, and to speculate perhaps that Boswell is an unreliable narrator whom the real author holds up to Johnsonian or Blakean censure. But the inconsistencies that might produce a confused novel make a fascinating journal. It is enough that Boswell gives life on the page to experience that was lived on the streets and in his head. His dilemmas are those of his culture (the widower Johnson avoided them, painfully, by total abstention from sex), and if he does not understand them very clearly, neither do most of his contemporaries. Moreover, to say that the *London Journal* is no novel is to make a formalist judgment that could easily be turned around: if Boswell had tried to write a novel he would almost certainly have been constrained to smooth over contradictions, damping down the revelations of conflicted behavior and of unconscious motivation. The truth-telling naiveté of the diary reveals much that would have been concealed by the *vraisemblance* of eighteenth-century aesthetics.

What Boswell does understand is the ironic collapse of the one extended amour in the *London Journal*, his campaign to conquer the actress Anne Lewis, whose name he disguises as "Louisa." (Curiously, the name of the executed highwayman was Paul Lewis.) An actress, Boswell had already noted, was a "delicious subject of gallantry" (94), combining elegant manners with easy morals, and allowing him to pretend he was making love to a lady while knowing that she was no such thing (a neat solution to "the most prevalent form of degradation"). "Louisa had an exquisite mixture of delicacy and wantonness that made me enjoy her with more relish. Indeed I could not help roving in fancy to the embraces of some other ladies which my lively imagination strongly pictured" (139). And again, "I . . . had vast pleasure as I enjoyed her as an actress who had played many a fine lady's part" (149). The much-postponed seduction, in which both parties know exactly what is going on, is described with relish; they collaborate both as actors and as playwriting team. When Boswell finally gets Louisa to bed he celebrates the moment in a joyous stream of clichés: "Sweet delirium . . . snowy arms . . . milk-white bosom . . . amorous dalliance . . . luscious feast . . . godlike vigour . . . noble game . . . supreme rapture" (139).

Boswell is profoundly self-regarding here, playing out a particularly choice role: "Surely I may be styled a Man of Pleasure" (140). When he goes to Lady Northumberland's house a couple of days later, he is still much inflated by his triumph. "I strutted up and down, considering myself as a valiant man who could gratify a lady's loving desires five times in a night; and I satisfied my pride by considering that if this and all my other great qualities were known, all the women almost in the room would be making love to me" (142). But all too soon manifestations appear which a sustained flight of euphemism only partly veils, "a little heat in the members of my body sacred to Cupid, very like a symptom of that distemper with which Venus, when cross, takes it into her head to plague her votaries" (149). More bluntly, it is "Signor Gonorrhoea" (155), and the consequences—"these damned twinges, that scalding heat, and that deep-tinged loathsome matter" (156)—cannot really be disguised as jolly trophies from the sports of Venus.

Boswell has been rightly admired for his skill in recreating the whole tragicomic sequence; apparently he wrote it down after he knew he was sick, but without betraying that fact in the earlier stages. From a literary point of view, he was making the story dramatic; from a personal point of view, he was recreating it as it actually felt. But of course what he "actually felt" was a life already fictionalized, perceived and conducted through imaginative categories even as he lived it. The story he tells the reader is the story he has been telling himself. The ending is bitter enough, certainly: "She is in all probability a most consummate dissembling whore" (160). It is possible, incidentally, that Louisa was not actually the source of the infection, and quite likely that even if she was infected she did not know it (Ober 6–8). And one should not forget that Boswell's chagrin derives, above all, from the way in which the outcome mocks his coolly prudential foresight: "Thus ended my intrigue with the fair Louisa, which I flattered myself so much with, and from which I expected at least a winter's safe copulation" (161). As so often, he discovers that he has been unsuccessful in the attempt to be author of his own story. Life is lived as art, but that does not mean that art can control life.

As is indicated by the strong eighteenth-century interest in the "signs" of passion, both in everyday life and as codified on the stage, there was a deep wish to read human motives accurately and a corresponding fear that they might remain unreadable. Hume says in the *Treatise*,

'Tis evident, that when we praise any actions, we regard only the motives that produced them, and consider the actions as signs or indications of certain principles in the mind and temper. The external performance has no merit. We must look within to find the moral quality. This we cannot do directly; and therefore fix our attention on actions, as on external signs. (477)

A similar dilemma haunts the pages of *Tom Jones*: we ought to be judged for what we are, but our actions, which furnish the only available evidence, are often unworthy of us or are liable to misconstruction. Hume goes so far as to say that what we see "has no merit," and is therefore obliged to hope that in studying "signs" we can somehow peer beneath them. Given the fluctuating and disconnected experience of the self, those signs represent an individual's best hope of piecing together the story of his or her continued existence. We understand our selves by seeing ourselves as others see us.

In the *Philosophical Enquiry* Burke says that when the seventeenth-century physiognomist Campanella "had a mind to penetrate into the inclinations of those he had to deal with, he composed his face, his gesture, and his whole body, as nearly as he could into the exact similitude of the person he intended to examine; and then carefully observed what turn of mind he seemed to acquire by this change. So that, says my author, he was able to enter into the dispositions and thoughts of people, as effectually as if he had been changed into the very men" (133). By "composing" one's own outside, one is enabled to "penetrate" the inside of other people. Once again, of course, it is the uniformity of human nature that makes the maneuver possible.

Knowing what the signs signify is made still more difficult by the fact that civilized behavior is a systematic disguise of natural impulses. In *The Rise and Progress of the Arts and Sciences* Hume describes "gallantry" in terms that are very appropriate to Boswell: "As nature has given *man* the superiority above *woman,* by endowing him with greater strength both of mind and body, it is his part to alleviate that superiority, as much as possible, by the generosity of his behaviour, and by a studied deference and complaisance for all her inclinations and opinions" (*Essays* 133). In the *London Journal* Boswell reflects that no felicity exceeds "the participation of genuine reciprocal amorous affection with an amiable woman" because the male partner "exults with a consciousness that he is the superior person" (84). Johnson, characteristically, is more acid than either Boswell or Hume on this theme: "The whole endeavour of both parties, during the time of courtship, is to hinder themselves from being known, and to disguise their natural temper, and real desires, in hypocritical imitation, studied compliance, and continued affectation. From the time that their love is avowed, neither sees the other but in a mask" (*Rambler* No. 45).

Sparring playfully with Louisa, Boswell the gallant thinks he knows what lies under her mask (and under his own), but after discovering the infection he refuses to believe her protestations of ignorance. What he fears most is a world in which one can't know what is really happening. No wonder Sheridan's *School for Scandal*, with its climactic exposure of hypocrisy when a screen overturns, was one of the most popular comedies of the age. But the theatrical convention that allows the audience to see behind screens is regularly used to expose, as Jerome Christensen says of Goldsmith's *She Stoops to Conquer*, "an incomplete synthesis of personality with role" (36). Boswell's journals display a subtler complication than the stage comedies do. Sheridan's Joseph Surface *is* one thing (his character) but *appears to be* another (his role), whereas Boswell's character is itself an uneasy anthology of contradictory roles.

Even if the truth could be known—even if in life, as on stage, the reality behind the screen could always be revealed—the fact that consciousness is mediated through language poses an insuperable obstacle to what Jean Starobinski calls "transparency" of self-understanding. In the later eighteenth century, theoretically inclined writers often pondered the dilemma that verbal representation is incapable of immediacy, contaminated as it is with pastness and with what modern theory would call absence. The classic aesthetic exposition is Lessing's *Laocoon*; here is Diderot on the same theme:

> The state of our soul is one thing, the account we give of it, to ourselves and others, is another. The total and instantaneous sensation of that state is one thing, the successive and detailed attention that we are forced to give it in order to analyze it, to manifest it, and to make ourselves understood, is another. Our soul is a moving *tableau* which we depict unceasingly; we spend much time trying to render it faithfully, but it exists as a whole and all at once. The mind does not proceed one step at a time as does expression. (*Lettre sur . . . les muets*, Fried 91)

That moving *tableau* is Boswell's subject too, and the journal represents his ever-renewed attempt to stop it in its tracks and make it intelligible.

If mental experience is ephemeral, then the act of writing is all the more crucial: an artificial coherence is better than no coherence at all. Pondering the mind's operations in *The Hypochondriack*, Boswell elaborates strikingly on the familiar empiricist metaphor of an internal theater:

> How then can we represent, by a sensible image, the mind as a theatre to its own actings? Let us conceive a spacious saloon, in which our thoughts and passions exert themselves, and let its walls be encrusted with mirror, for the purpose of reflection, in the same manner that rooms in voluptuous oriental countries are said to be finished for the purpose of increasing sensual delight. (1:152–53)

Not only is character adjusted in the mirror, but consciousness itself is a system of internal mirroring, with a self-regard so autoerotic that Boswell finds his analogy in pornography. As we have noticed, however, it is just when he gets Louisa to bed that Boswell's language collapses into conventionality. Nabokov once said that pornography is the copulation of clichés. Narrated sex is bound to be reduced to clichés because a fundamentally private mode of experience is being described in a public language that seeks to escape embarrassment—as is obvious even in the once-notorious *Fanny Hill*—by flights of elegant periphrasis.

Boswell writes most convincingly when he stands outside himself, Adam Smith's spectator indeed, in a moment of calculated anticipation rather than in the "supreme rapture" itself.

> She declined to undress before me, and begged I would retire and send her one of the maids. I did so, gravely desiring the girl to go up to Mrs. Digges. I then took a candle in my hand and walked out to the yard. The night was very dark and very

cold. I experienced for some minutes the rigours of the season, and called into my mind many terrible ideas of hardships, that I might make a transition from such dreary thoughts to the most gay and delicious feelings. (138–39)

Boswell cannot describe the gratification itself, but he can describe the humorously earnest little scene that precedes it, and the sensory contrast that helps him to savor it.

DIARY AND PUBLICATION

At bottom, the world of social and internal mirroring has uncomfortable affinities with the prison house of language, and it is no wonder that Boswell seeks to escape it for a more substantial and "objective" world. The counterplot of the *London Journal* is Boswell's imaginative submission to the massive authority of Johnson, whose philosophical fable he welcomes as the personal voice of a wise counselor: "*Rasselas*, where we find a humane preceptor delighting the fancy and mending the heart" (291). Mr. Spectator might be an impossible model, but the *Rambler* is suddenly transformed into human relationship: "Will you really take a charge of me? It is very good in you, Mr. Johnson, to allow me to sit with you thus. Had I but thought some years ago that I should pass an evening with the Author of *The Rambler*!" (285). Soon Boswell is recording that most Johnsonian of dicta, "that human experience, which was constantly contradicting theory, was the great test of truth" (326). And even while he continues to record the moving tableau of his experience in a long series of journals, he seeks ways to fix experience in sustained narratives of a more public kind.

An alternative to recreating one's own ongoing life, with all the instability and problematic self-exposure that that entails, is to reconstruct a past that can never change. Boswell's public monument was not the journals, which remained unknown until the 1930s, but the *Life of Johnson*, in which his own conversations (along with much else) were stabilized as historical artifacts. And the trial run for the *Life* was a journal that began like the others but was shown to Johnson during its composition, and a year after Johnson's death was revised for the public as *A Journal of a Tour to the Hebrides, with Samuel Johnson, LL.D.* (1785), published twelve years after Boswell's trip with Johnson and ten years after Johnson's own account of it in *A Journey to the Western Islands of Scotland*.

In *The Hypochondriack* Boswell remarks, "There is a certain strange mysteriousness propagated as to *appearing in print,* as the phrase is; as if there were some charm in a printing press, and a man's character were to be sealed by an irrevocable sentence as soon as any work of his hath passed through that engine" (1:313). But this is said in an essay about revision, and Boswell goes on to talk about the ways in which a piece of writing can be continually revised right up to the moment of publication, and afterward too in later editions. His own impulse is incurably essayistic, preferring open-endedness to closure. In another paper he suggests that writing is a compulsive gratification not unlike his well-known weakness for alcohol: "Writing upon drinking is in one respect, I think, like drinking itself: one goes on imperceptibly, without knowing where to stop; and as one calls for the other bottle to his friends, I press the other paper upon my readers" (1:341). Neither the *Tour* nor the *Life of Johnson* would ever have been completed if Edmond Malone had not supervised them relentlessly, rescuing the essayist from his bottle and his revising.

Johnson's *Journey to the Western Islands* belongs to a tradition of objective travel writing that focuses on the places seen rather than on the traveler who does the seeing. "The learned English Rambler," Ralph Griffiths wrote in the *Scots Magazine*, "seems . . . to confine his views to the naked truth,—to moralize on the occurrences of his journey, and to illustrate the characters and situation of the people whom he visited, by the sagacity of remark, and the profundity of reflection" (Curley 192). In this not very searching conception, there can be such a thing as "the naked truth" about Scotland, which can be clearly segregated from reflections upon it (*illustrate* carries its root meaning of throwing light).

The problem of truth is indeed a presiding theme in Johnson's book, though he is more skeptical than Griffiths about the possibility of stripping it naked. Johnson as traveler is constantly measuring and questioning, debunking marvels and dangers as he goes. "No man," he solemnly declares, "should travel unprovided with instruments for taking heights and distances," and he deplores the readiness of memory to blur recollection so that "many particular features and discriminations will be compressed and conglobated into one gross and general idea" (*Journey* 146–47). If even Johnson admits to experiencing this dispersal of knowledge, the Highlanders, who depend entirely on oral tradition, are bound to suffer it far more drastically.

He that goes into the Highlands with a mind naturally acquiescent, and a credulity eager for wonders, may come back with an opinion very different from mine; for the inhabitants, knowing the ignorance of all strangers in their language and antiquities, perhaps are not very scrupulous adherents to truth; yet I do not say that they deliberately speak studied falsehood, or have a settled purpose to deceive. They have inquired and considered little, and do not always feel their own ignorance. They are not much accustomed to be interrogated by others, and seem never to have thought upon interrogating themselves; so that if they do not know what they tell to be true, they likewise do not distinctly perceive it to be false. (117)

These strictures, though stern, are not entirely a condemnation of Scottish credulity. Johnson's point is that a self-enclosed culture cannot apply canons of veracity that depend upon a detached and essentially literary perspective. He himself, of course, embodies that perspective, moving through Scotland (he says) "like some being of another world" (103), much as Rasselas moves through the nations of the East.

Boswell's book is just as concerned with veracity as Johnson's, but presents its mission in different terms. Johnson looks at Scotland; Boswell looks at Johnson looking at Scotland, at his own role in bringing the two great subjects together, and at the sparks that are sometimes struck by their collision. In the *London Journal* Johnson appears episodically; in the *Tour* he is not only the central figure but is made privy to the narrative even as it gets written down. "He came to my room this morning before breakfast, to read my Journal, which he has done all along. . . . 'Sir,' said he, 'it is not written in a slovenly manner. It might be printed, were the subject fit for printing'" (*Tour* 226–27; I cite Boswell's unpublished version as *Journal* and his published version as *Tour*).

In the same conversation, Boswell acknowledges that the labor of recording actually encroaches upon the experience that is being recorded. In order to put Johnson into the journal, he must see less of Johnson.

He asked me today how it happened that we were so little together: I told him, my Journal took up much time. Yet, on reflection, it appeared strange to me, that although I will run from one end of London to another to pass an hour with him, I should omit to seize any spare time to be in his company, when I am settled in the same house with him. But my Journal is really a task of much time and labour, and he forbids me to contract it. (227)

The inadmissible suspicion is that Boswell could ever have enough of Johnson, let alone more than enough; so he is glad to let the act of writing be the explanation for not being with Johnson, and to record Johnson's command to keep on writing. Only once does he confess, with touching ingenuousness, "I did not exert myself to get Dr. Johnson to talk, that I might not have the labour of writing down his conversation" (159).

From this point of view the journal exists to present, as Johnson himself tells Boswell, "a very exact picture of a portion of his life" (*Tour* 279). But it is still Boswell's journal after all, not a formal biography like the *Life*, and much of its interest derives from the tension between Boswell as Johnson's chronicler and Boswell as independent human being. In fact the Highland jaunt, which while it was happening was a single experience (or two experiences, Johnson's and Boswell's) has distributed itself into a series of texts that overlap and complement each other. Knowing that Johnson is reading the journal, Boswell has to censor himself to some extent, though he also hopes that Johnson will comment on what he reads and thereby add to it; he is disappointed, for instance, when Johnson ignores the speculations about his compulsive gestures (*Tour* 307n). The journal is not just about the relationship between the two men, it is part of it. Johnson, in turn, writes long letters to Mrs. Thrale, sometimes exciting Boswell's jealousy because he is so anxious to get them posted, and these later form the basis for his own *Journey to the Western Islands*. Then, a decade afterward, when Johnson has died and Boswell feels free to make his version public, he revises his journal with Malone's help, adopting a more "correct" style and deleting material that seems irrelevant or that would give offense to living persons.

Most of the original diary survives intact, allowing us to compare the two versions, but Boswell worked up the final fifty pages from scrappy notes—"portable soup" (*Journal* 165) that had never been rehydrated—and ruefully admits the loss: "My Journal cannot have the same freshness and fullness when written now as when written recently after the scenes recorded" (346). Moreover, for this final section the manuscript itself is now missing, so that the published version is all that survives. And other potentially valuable documents are absent too, particularly "a pretty full and curious Diary of his Life" which Johnson left in a drawer in Boswell's house, and which, to Boswell's lasting grief, his wife never thought to transcribe (*Tour* 53). Whatever text we read is filled with embedded texts—letters, inscriptions, material from other versions—and irreparable holes are left by the texts that aren't there.

In the published *Tour*, Boswell gives the impression that the only changes are trivial expansions and that "*the very Journal which Dr. Johnson read,* shall be presented to the public" (78n). In fact, however, the changes are extensive and significant. In part it is a simple matter of euphemizing, with the loss that always occurs when Boswell strives for elegance. The sentence "He called Hanbury Williams a wretched scribbler" (*Journal* 233) becomes "He spoke contemptuously of our lively and elegant, though too licentious, lyric bard, Hanbury Williams" (*Tour* 268). But Boswell is right to say that in spirit the published version is faithful to the original. A canceled passage declares, "I once thought of writing it anew, but Sir Joseph Banks, Sir Joshua Reynolds, and other friends thought it would be better to give the genuine transcript of what passed at the time and add notes to explain or enlarge. A great part of its value is its authenticity and its having passed the ordeal of Dr. Johnson himself" (*Journal* 411–12). It must have been an ordeal indeed, since Johnson was so implacable a spokesman for factual veracity, and since he often deplored the excesses of Boswell's lively imagination.

A consequence of the focus on Johnson is that Boswell himself tends to drop out of sight except as tour guide and social facilitator. In the unpublished *Journal* we read, "I exerted myself in an extraordinary degree in dancing tonight, drinking porter heartily at intervals, and thinking that I was fit to lead on Highlanders" (140). This is very much the Boswell of the *London Journal*, who vanishes however in the elliptical version in the published *Tour*: "We . . . piqued ourselves at not being outdone at the nightly ball" (168). And the rich Boswellian world of phenomenology largely fades from view. The published *Tour* is filled with unmemorable remarks like this one: "We here enjoyed the comfort of a table plentifully furnished, the satisfaction of which was heightened by a numerous and cheerful company" (157). How different is the original!

We had for supper a large dish of minced beef collops, a large dish of fricassee of fowl, I believe a dish called fried chicken or something like it, a dish of ham or tongue, some excellent haddocks, some herrings, a large bowl of rich milk, frothed, as good a bread-pudding as I ever tasted, full of raisins and lemon or orange peel, and sillabubs made with port wine and in sillabub glasses. There was a good table-cloth with napkins; china, silver spoons, porter if we chose it, and a large bowl of very good punch. It was really an agreeable meeting. (*Journal* 120)

The tone is affectionate and the detail circumstantial, with Boswell's usual careful accuracy ("lemon *or* orange peel"). No one in 1785 would have expected him to present such a paragraph to book-buying readers, who might well have derided it as a pointless indulgence. But that in itself is a measure of what Boswell can do in a private mode that the public mode rejects or ignores.

Venerating Johnson as he does, Boswell is bound to idealize him in the *Tour*. But even so, one often grasps that Johnson is an alien in these surroundings and that all of Boswell's social energy is necessary to integrate him even temporarily.

We for the first time had a specimen of the joyous social manners of the inhabitants of the Highlands. They talked in their own ancient language, with fluent vivacity, and sung many Erse songs with such spirit, that, though Dr. Johnson was treated with the greatest respect and attention, there were moments in which he seemed to be forgotten. For myself, though but a *Lowlander*, having picked up a few words of the language, I presumed to mingle in their mirth, and joined in the choruses with as much glee as any of the company. Dr. Johnson, being fatigued with his journey, retired early to his chamber, where he composed the following Ode, addressed to Mrs. Thrale. . . . (*Tour* 157)

Johnson is lionized by those who know his literary reputation, but he disappears when the Gaelic-speaking Highlanders, for whom the *Rambler* is not even a name, turn to merriment. Boswell exuberantly joins in while Johnson retires to write a poem—in Latin!—to Boswell's rival for his affections, the absent Hester Thrale.

Surprisingly often, Johnson seems to be what Coleridge said Wordsworth was, a *spectator ab extra*. As Hugo Reichard has shown, passivity is characteristic of Johnson throughout the *Life of Johnson*, though Boswell often disguises the fact that other people "generate most of his conversation, extract most of his writing, elicit most of his charities, launch most of his frisks and frolics, conduct most of his tours, and preside over his meals, introductions, and encounters" (225). So also in the *Tour* Johnson retreats regularly to a book or to the conversation of an individual admirer. "It entertained me to observe him sitting by while we danced, sometimes in deep meditation,—sometimes smiling complacently,—sometimes looking upon Hooke's Roman History,—and sometimes talking a little, amidst the noise of the ball, to Mr. Donald M'Queen, who anxiously gathered knowledge from him" (*Tour* 166). What Johnson requires is listeners able to appreciate his powers. "Professor Shaw said to me, as we walked, 'This is a wonderful man: he is master of every subject he handles' " (*Tour* 70).

Boswell's special genius is at once a matter of life and of art: his ability to get Johnson talking and then to give memorable literary form to what is said.

I . . . may be allowed to claim some merit in leading the conversation: I do not mean leading, as in an orchestra, by playing the first fiddle; but leading as one does in examining a witness—starting topics, and making him pursue them. He appears to me like a great mill, into which a subject is thrown to be ground. It requires, indeed, fertile minds to furnish materials for this mill. I regret whenever I see it unemployed; but sometimes I feel myself quite barren, and have nothing to throw in. (*Tour* 264–65)

Of course to lead a witness is to guide his responses in some desired direction, and Johnson did not always care to be led: "I will not be baited with *what*, and *why*; what is this? what is that? why is a cow's tail long? why is a fox's tail bushy?" (*Life* 3:268). More seriously still, "Sir, you have but two topics, yourself and me. I am sick of both" (3:57). But it was his obsession with Johnson, and with his own relationship to Johnson, that enabled Boswell's recovery of otherwise ephemeral experience in the *Life*.

In the happiest moments in the *Tour*, life and art merge in vignettes in which Johnson gaily responds to Boswell's dramatizing imagination.

Dr. Johnson was curious to know where [the old woman] slept. I asked one of the guides, who questioned her in Erse. She answered with a tone of emotion, saying, (as he told us,) she was afraid we wanted to go to bed to her. This *coquetry*, or whatever it may be called, of so wretched a being, was truly ludicrous. Dr. Johnson and I afterwards were merry upon it. I said, it was he who alarmed the poor woman's virtue.—"No, sir, (said he,) she'll say, 'There came a wicked young fellow, a wild dog, who I believe would have ravished me, had there not been with him a grave old gentleman, who repressed him: but when he gets out of the sight of his tutor, I'll warrant you he'll spare no woman he meets, young or old.' "—"No, sir, (I replied,) she'll say, 'There was a terrible ruffian who would have forced me, had it not been for a civil decent young man, who, I take it, was an angel sent from heaven to protect me.' " (132–33)

At one point in the *Tour* Boswell ruefully admits, "I find a great difficulty in describing visible objects" (173). In the unpublished *Journal* the expression is stronger—"a wretched deficiency" (148)—and he speculates further about it: "I find I can do nothing in the way of description of any visible object whatever. Whether it is owing to my not seeing with accuracy, or to my not having the use of words fitted to such sort of description, I cannot say" (220). One might conjecture that Boswell is not really *interested* in visible objects, but rather in the invisible emotional currents that sustain human intercourse. What is central to the *Tour* is not Scotland, or even Johnson in Scotland, but the experience of watching the two as they get to know each other.

A passage that is much abridged in the published *Tour* meditates on the relationship of language to memory and to the temporality of consciousness.

Mr. Johnson said, as we were going up the narrow sound between Mull and Nun's Island, with solemn-like rocks on each side of us, and the waves rising and falling, and our boat proceeding with a dancing motion, "This is roving among the Hebrides, or nothing is." A man has a pleasure in applying things to words, and comparing the reality with the picture of fancy. We had long talked of "roving among the Hebrides." It was curious to repeat the words previously used, and which had impressed our imaginations by frequent use; and then to feel how the immediate impression from actually roving differed from the one in fancy, or agreed with it. It will be curious too, to perceive how the impression made by reading this my Journal some years after our roving will affect the mind, when compared with the recollection of what was felt at the time. Mr. Johnson said I should read my Journal about every three years. (*Journal* 328–29)

The first part of this formulation agrees closely with Johnson's own reflections in the *Journey* (40) on comparing one's notions of a thing with the thing itself. But the second part goes on to imagine a continually changing self for which the journey in turn will continue to alter, as the past self is held up for comparison by a series of future selves. Words preceded the experience of roving among the Hebrides, and words will survive it.

Boswell then meditates on the inevitable alteration of remembered events: the journal may preserve them in some sense, but not as they originally were.

> I have often experienced, that scenes through which a man has passed improve by lying in the memory; they grow mellow. *Acti labores sunt jucundi* [Cicero: "Past labors are sweet"]. This may be owing to comparing them with present listless ease. Even harsh scenes acquire a softness by length of time; and some are like very loud sounds, which do not please, or at least do not please so much, till you are removed to a certain distance. They may be compared to strong coarse pictures, which will not bear to be viewed near. Even pleasing scenes improve by time, and seem more exquisite in recollection than when they were present; if they have not faded to dimness in the memory. (*Tour* 333)

Lived experience turns into "scenes," imagined on the analogy of pictures that cannot appear beautiful when the brush strokes are too closely seen. And memory itself turns out to be in part an enemy, for only when experiences are imperfectly remembered can they give full pleasure. At the end of this passage in the *Journal* Boswell notes, "I must hear Mr. Johnson upon this subject" (329). One doubts that Johnson would have endorsed the mood of nostalgia that Boswell evokes. For him the Hebridean journey is a rebuke to imagination, not an invitation to it; as he writes to Mrs. Thrale from Skye, "The use of travelling is to regulate imagination by reality, and instead of thinking how things may be, to see them as they are" (*Letters* 1:359). But nostalgia is very much an eighteenth-century invention, born perhaps of the twin interests in the subtleties of consciousness and the novelty of rapid cultural change, and Boswell is deeply moved by it.

The journey itself is long gone by now, two centuries into our own past, and what remains is a series of prismatic reflections of it. No text is perfectly self-contained, and Boswell's texts are less so than most, in their multiple forms as well as in their external referentiality. Moreover, these complementary texts are read today in scholarly editions that supplement and supersede each other, so that it is less possible than ever to return innocently to "what Boswell wrote." William Epstein aptly compares the productions of the Yale "Boswell factory" to those of the Mellon family that helped to underwrite them: "the discovering, extracting, cornering, denaturing, producing, packaging, promoting, and distributing of a natural resource like coal or oil" (250).

Still more to the point, even for its first readers—even for *the* first reader—no journal, however circumstantial and well written, can really preserve the past. In one of his early journals Boswell comments,

According to the humour which I am in when I read it, I judge of my past adventures, and not from what is really recorded. If I am in gay spirits, I read an account of so much existence, and I think, "Sure I have been very happy." If I am gloomy, I think, "Sure I have passed much uneasy time, or at best, much insipid time." Thus I think without regard to the real fact as written. (*Germany and Switzerland* 143–44)

There is such a thing as "real fact"—the verifiable data of events that have actually occurred, as events in a novel have not—but "the real fact as written" is something else, both because it imposes a retrospective structure on what happened, and because readers (including the author himself at different times) will inevitably transform it in varying ways. Experience is a matter of feeling rather than of data. Boswell can hope to get the facts right, but what really matters is the emotional climate that gives them their life and significance.

All of Boswell's writing shows an interesting tension between these two poles, the objective (though filtered through consciousness) and the subjective (though based in a world of fact). Planning the *Life of Johnson* in 1785, the year in which the *Tour* was published, Boswell imagined a rather macabre triumph over temporality: "I tell every body it will be an Egyptian pyramid in which there will be a complete mummy of Johnson, that literary monarch" (*Correspondence*, ed. Waingrow 96). But when the *Life* was finished it turned out to be more like a journey than a mausoleum, allowing its readers, as Boswell says at the outset, "to see [Johnson] live, and to 'live o'er each scene' with him, as he actually advanced through the several stages of his life" (1:30). Paul Alkon (246) notes that Boswell may expect the reader to recall the rest of Pope's line in the *Prologue to Cato*, "Live o'er each scene, and be what they behold." As always, Boswell wants to give narrative the immediacy of drama; but we have seen that drama in this sense is compromised by narrativity.

As for subjectivity, even in the *Life of Johnson*, whose subject is exclusively Johnson, the "subject" in the philosophical sense must be Boswell, through whose imagination Johnson is recreated. While representing others Boswell necessarily represents himself. Still more than the *Life*, the published *Tour* and unpublished *Journal* are filled with his voice and presence. Among the monastic ruins of Iona, Johnson was inspired as usual to think of elevation above the present moment: "Whatever withdraws us from the power of our senses; whatever makes the past, the distant, or the future predominate over the present, advances us in the dignity of thinking beings. Far from me and from my friends, be such frigid philosophy as may conduct us indifferent and unmoved over any ground which has been dignified by wisdom, bravery, or virtue. That man is little to be envied, whose patriotism would not gain force upon the plain of Marathon, or whose piety would not grow warmer among the ruins of Iona" (*Journey* 148). Boswell quotes this passage reverently "as conveying my own sensations much more forcibly than I am capable of doing" (*Tour* 334), but his own account centers on personal feelings of a kind that Johnson keeps firmly out of sight.

Even in the published version, Boswell is willing to share with his readers (as Johnson certainly is not) the immediate sensations of guilt, piety, and hope for repentance that the scene at Iona excites. The unpublished version goes further still: "I read with an audible voice the fifth chapter of St. James, and Dr. Ogden's tenth sermon. I suppose there has not been a sermon preached in this church since the Reformation. I had a serious joy in hearing my voice, while it was filled with Ogden's admirable eloquence, resounding in the ancient cathedral of Icolmkill" (*Journal* 336). Yielding very deliberately to emotion in a romantic setting, Boswell chooses to bring ordered speech to the ruinous walls, and it is not his own speech; rather than speaking for himself, he "fills" his voice with someone else's eloquence. The sound is Boswell's, the words Ogden's, with Boswell the mediator who juxtaposes modern piety with ancient. As so often, he is a ventriloquist, but a ventriloquist who is most himself when enacting a role and adopting, or absorbing, the language of others. Johnson in Iona abstracts his mind from the present. Boswell immerses himself in the present, appropriates the past by placing it in dialogue with the present, and then uses writing to create a structure in which he and other readers can repeatedly reimagine and understand what has happened.

3

Gibbon
Commanding the Past

FACT, ART, MEANING

WHAT BOSWELL does for himself and his friends, Gibbon hopes to do for an entire culture. In writing his kind of history there can be no question of personal experience, but rather of reinventing experience that happened long ago, in distant places, to people whose very languages are now dead. The author of such a work, far from responding to the fluctuations of daily life, aspires to perceive what has happened with a more than human clarity and comprehensiveness.

In his youth Gibbon cast about widely for possible subjects, and the eventual decision struck him afterward as a conversion experience. "In my Journal the place and moment of conception are recorded; the fifteenth of October 1764, in the close of evening, as I sat musing in the Church of the Zoccolanti or Franciscan friars, while they were singing Vespers in the Temple of Jupiter on the ruins of the Capitol" (*Memoirs* 143). Increasingly Gibbon came to perceive himself as "the historian of the Roman Empire," and he remembered—perhaps even invented—the scene in Rome from the perspective of the completed *Decline and Fall* (Jordan 18–23). It is a self-created myth of origins presented as literal fact. Rather than tracing the development of a forever-unfinished self like Boswell, Gibbon wanted to believe that an essential unity had lain in wait from the beginning. He is a statue, not a moving picture: "Such as I am in genius or learning or in manners, I owe my creation to Lausanne [where he lived in his teens]. It was in that school, that the statue was discovered in the block of marble" (*Memoirs* 105).

The picture is heavily idealized, of course, particularly when simplified in the composite versions of the *Memoirs* that editors have put together from the six overlapping and competing drafts that Gibbon left at his death. To study the separate drafts, as Barret Mandel and W. B. Carnochan have done, is to see how uneasy Gibbon was about representing himself as the hero of his own story and how hard he found it to tell the story in a definitive way. The solution was to imagine himself from outside. Boswell places himself at the center of his writing; Gibbon withdraws to its margins. His *Memoirs* are notoriously unconfessional, and it is clear that he values himself almost exclusively as the Historian of the Roman Empire. References to personal feeling are carefully distanced, ironized, and made subservient to the official story.

For example, the short, portly, bookish Gibbon enlisted with other gentlemen in the militia to repel a possible invasion by the French. His comment in the *Memoirs* is: "The discipline and evolutions of a modern battalion gave me a clearer notion of the phalanx and the legion, and the captain of the Hampshire Grenadiers (the reader may smile) has not been useless to the historian of the Roman Empire" (128). Instead of Boswellian ingenuousness, there is self-deprecation of an almost Popean subtlety, deflecting the reader's laughter by preempting it. And whereas Boswell strives to write from and about his whole self, Gibbon chooses to speak from a specialized and intellectualized part of his self. Moreover, Gibbon's military service probably stimulated in him a specific nostalgia, suggesting identification with the landowning citizen-soldiers of the Roman Republic as contrasted with the mercenaries of the Empire (Pocock, *Politics* 146).

When Gibbon's father forbade him to marry a brilliant young Swiss woman, "I sighed as a lover, I obeyed as a son" (*Memoirs* 208n). Whether or not feeling is compromised here by being stylized, there is no doubt that Gibbon prefers it cool rather than hot. Of his disappointment in love he goes on to say, "My wound was insensibly healed by time, absence, and the habits of a new life; and my cure was accelerated by a faithful report of the tranquility and cheerfulness of the lady herself" (*Autobiographies* 204). As Spacks observes (105), the passive constructions in the *Memoirs* are very telling. Presented with contradictory roles, Gibbon allows the more dutiful but also the more habitual to prevail. As is clear from his letters at the time, he has seized upon the time-honored topos of conflict between love and duty as a way of managing the situation; disturbing experience is made to assume formal shape.

Lacking authority and mastery in his life, Gibbon found in the Roman story the perfect alternative world, at once fascinatingly complex and comfortably distant. In contrast with an illiterate peasant, he remarks in the first volume, a man of learning "by reading and reflection multiplies his own experience, and lives in distant ages and remote countries" (*Decline and Fall* 1:236). But this is a matter of enlarged perspective rather than of imaginative identification, and some thousands of pages later it leads to a memorable expression of Olympian detachment:

A being of the nature of man, endowed with the same faculties but with a longer measure of existence, would cast down a smile of pity and contempt on the crimes and follies of human ambition, so eager, in a narrow span, to grasp at a precarious and short-lived enjoyment. It is thus that the experience of history exalts and enlarges the horizon of our intellectual view. In a composition of some days, in a perusal of some hours, six hundred years have rolled away, and the duration of a life or reign is contracted to a fleeting moment; the grave is ever beside the throne; the success of a criminal is almost instantly followed by the loss of his prize; and our immortal reason survives and disdains the sixty phantoms of kings, who have passed before our eyes and faintly dwell in our remembrance. (5:258–59)

As a historian Gibbon can rise above precarious enjoyments and speak with the voice of immortal reason, almost as if he had mutated into that ideal being with human faculties but extended life. His reiterated appeal to "our" view and reason is particularly seductive. "To enlarge a horizon," Carnochan comments, "is to give the reader peripheral vision" (68). Reading the *Decline and Fall* one gratefully accepts the illusion of omniscience.

If the remoteness of the subject is part of its charm, the object of writing is to recover the lost subject, to close the gap between dead events and living readers. The perspective may be Olympian but it is not uninvolved; to adopt Gibbon's own distinction, he aspires to impartiality but not to indifference (*Decline and Fall* 2:306). He speaks at the outset of "the ardent pursuit of truth and knowledge" (1:xlvii), and he seems to have been a person for whom books were more seductive, and in a sense more real, than life itself. At an early age "the dynasties of Assyria and Egypt were my top and cricket-ball" (*Memoirs* 72–73), and later on the metaphors become sexual: the publication of his first essay was "the loss of my literary maidenhead" (117), and he says (using a metaphor that Boswell also favored) that when he had assembled a library of seven thousand volumes "my seraglio was ample, my choice was free, my appetite was keen" (172).

The conversion experience in Rome, accordingly, was the direct fruit of a love of books. "I cannot forget the joy," Gibbon says, "with which I exchanged a bank-note of twenty pounds for the twenty volumes of the

Memoirs of the Academy of Inscriptions" (*Memoirs* 113). The details of his early trip to Italy have become indistinct, just as empiricist psychology would predict: "The pleasing vision cannot be fixed by the pen; the particular images are darkly seen through the medium of five and twenty years" (135). But the countless texts which Gibbon read before traveling can never become indistinct, since they may always be reread.

I . . . finished the *Italia Antiqua* of Cluverius, a learned native of Prussia, who had measured on foot every spot, and has compiled and digested every passage of the ancient writers. . . . I separately read the descriptions of Italy by Strabo, Pliny and Pomponius Mela, the catalogues of the epic poets, the itineraries of Wesseling's Antoninus, and the coasting voyage of Rutilius Numatianus. . . . After glancing my eye over Addison's agreeable Dialogues, I more seriously read the great work of Ezechiel Spanheim, *De praestantia et usu Numismatum*, and applied with him the medals of the kings and emperors, the families and colonies, to the illustration of ancient history—And thus was I armed for my Italian journey. Perhaps I might boast that few travellers more completely armed and instructed have ever followed the footsteps of Hannibal. (140)

Gibbon's seraglio is also his armory.

A temperament like Gibbon's, shy and bookish, might have been drawn to fiction like Richardson or to poetry like Gray, and his passionate attraction to history does reflect a vicariousness analogous to theirs. It entails a commitment to the truth of facts, but safely distant ones, and to the texture of human experience, but experience as reconstructed from ancient texts. To Gibbon, much of the appeal of Latin, so tedious when brutal schoolmasters inculcated it during his boyhood, was its recreation as a living language. When he arrived in Switzerland in his teens he experienced a powerful sense of alienation, and he describes himself almost as if he had suffered shipwreck: "When I was thus suddenly cast on a foreign land, I found myself deprived of the use of speech and of hearing; and during some weeks, incapable not only of enjoying the pleasures of conversation, but even of asking or answering a question in the common intercourse of life" (*Memoirs* 93). By the time he returned to England, however, "French, in which I spontaneously thought, was more familiar than English to my ear, my tongue, and my pen" (94). So sudden and complete a loss of English suggests a desire to repudiate the land of his willful and demanding father (Gossman, *Empire* 20–21).

Having conquered French, at any event, Gibbon used it as a weapon with which to conquer its ancestor, Latin, translating passages from one language into the other and later, when "the words and phrases were obliterated from my memory," seeing how closely he could retranslate into the original (97). The outsider had made himself an insider in two different foreign cultures, one contemporary and one long vanished. And this achievement, whatever its basis in vicariousness or escapism, was of crucial importance for the successful recreation of the past. As H. G. Gadamer has said, the deepest dilemmas of hermeneutics are implicit in translation, which stands as the model for "the linguisticality of all human behavior in the world" and for "the general problem of making what is alien our own" (19). And Dominick LaCapra observes, "The dialogue with the text may even be experienced as more immediate and engrossing than most conversations" (*Rethinking* 51).

The self-imposed task of composing the *Decline and Fall* was a reliable source of pleasure, as Gibbon comments (with a passing slap at the gloomy Emperor Seghed in Johnson's *Rambler*) in a footnote about a caliph who claimed to have had only fourteen happy days in a peaceful reign of fifty years: "If I may speak of myself (the only person of whom I can speak with certainty), *my* happy hours have far exceeded, and far exceed, the scanty numbers of the caliph of Spain; and I shall not scruple to add that many of them are due to the pleasing labour of the present composition" (6:27n). Trapped in life, Johnson laments its miseries, reads with desultory haste, and neglects writing so much that Boswell wonders at it; "Sir, you *may* wonder," is Johnson's bitter reply (*Life* 2:15). Ensconced in books, Gibbon finds life satisfactory, and gives more than twenty years to the prodigies of research that undergird the *Decline and Fall*.

As a boy, Gibbon devoured histories as if they were exotic fictions. "Many crude lumps of Speed, Rapin, Mézeray, Davila, Machiavel, Father Paul, Bower etc. passed through me like so many novels, and I swallowed with the same voracious appetite the descriptions of India and China, of Mexico and Peru" (*Memoirs* 71–72). Voracious swallowing indicates a hunger that needs to be satisfied, but the metaphor of "passing through" implies imperfect digestion; the past will not yield up its secrets to that kind of brutal consumption. Gibbon never lost his fascination with the exotic, and there is much in the *Decline and Fall* about the steppes of Asia and the sands of Arabia where "whole caravans, whole armies, have been lost and buried in the whirlwind" (5:334). But he learned to be deeply skeptical of histories that resembled fictions, such as the "holy romances" in which medieval monks told the history of the church (2:67). Similarly the early history of Britain must remain obscure, since upon a "slight foundation" of facts "a huge superstructure of fable was gradually reared by the bards and the monks: two orders of men who equally abused the privilege of fiction" (3:44).

Like Hume, Gibbon is willing to declare that fiction is not only untrue, but less interesting than truth. "The *Cyropaedia* is vague and languid, the *Anabasis* circumstantial and animated. Such is the eternal difference between fiction and truth" (2:551n). This was an age in which the Aristotelian equation of poetry and truth was rapidly breaking down, and no less a novelist than Fielding says in his last book, "I must confess I should have honoured and loved Homer more had he written a true history of his own times in humble prose, than those noble poems that have so justly collected the praise of all ages; for though I read these with more admiration and astonishment, I still read Herodotus, Thucydides and Xenophon with more amusement and more satisfaction" (*Voyage to Lisbon* 182).

But to tell the truth about the past is a daunting project, since as Hume constantly emphasizes, "actions are, by their very nature, temporary and perishing" (*Inquiry . . . Understanding* 107). Only those actions can be reconstructed for which evidence happens to survive. Gibbon's famous assertion that history is "little more than the register of the crimes, follies, and misfortunes of mankind" (*Decline and Fall* 1:84) is a direct echo of Voltaire: "En générale toute cette histoire est un ramas de crimes, de folies, et de malheurs" (Brownley 637). Johnson says very similarly, "If we view past ages in the reflection of history, what do they offer to our meditation but crimes and calamities?" (*Adventurer* No. 120). Gibbon's meaning, however, seems to be not that human experience is uniformly dreadful, but rather that only the dreadful things get recorded. Anticipating George Eliot's aphorism that the happiest nations have no history, Gibbon discusses Spain's "remote and sequestered" situation and adds, "We may observe, as a sure symptom of domestic happiness, that in a period of four hundred years Spain furnished very few materials to the history of the Roman empire" (3:364). Even for Rome itself, history has tended to dwell on sensational wickedness at the expense of positive achievement. "It is sincerely to be lamented, that whilst we are fatigued with the disgustful relation of Nero's crimes and follies, we are reduced to collect the actions of Trajan from the glimmerings of an abridgement, or the doubtful light of a panegyric" (1:82).

In his essay *Of the Study of History* Hume claimed that lapse of time could improve clarity of vision, and announced as a goal "to see all the human race, from the beginning of time, pass, as it were, in review before us, appearing in their true colours, without any of those disguises which, during their lifetime, so much perplexed the judgment of the beholders" (*Essays* 566). This is indeed to stand in imperial superiority over the pygmy figures of the past. Gibbon is far less sanguine than Hume, however, about the apparent clarity that distance confers. As he observes in a typical note, "The elder Victor, who wrote under the next reign, speaks with becoming caution. . . . If we consult the succeeding writers, Eutropius, the younger Victor, Orosius, Jerom[e], Zosimus, Philostorgius, and Gregory of Tours, their knowledge will appear gradually to increase, as their means of information must have diminished: a circumstance which frequently occurs in historical disquisition" (2:221n). It is not just that historians tend to romanticize or fictionalize the past, but also that an abundance of information, by forcing a recognition of complexity, makes it harder rather than easier to detect intelligible patterns. And narration entails a process of selection and arrangement that further distances what is represented. Virginia Woolf comments in her essay on Gibbon that "the innumerable figures are suffused in the equal blue of the far distance" (57).

It is fashionable among modern historians to say that Gibbon accepts his sources too much at face value, but this seems unjust. No doubt his criteria for evaluating them are sometimes intuitive rather than scientific, but he does interrogate them shrewdly, well aware that the recovery of truth is an arduous process of criticism and that even the least tendentious sources often resemble "honest Froissard . . . who read little, inquired much, and believed all" (*Decline and Fall* 7:37n). Facts are not facts until they are interpreted, as Gibbon indicates with a jab at Johnson: "In one of the *Ramblers*, Dr. Johnson praises Knolles (*A General History of the Turks to the Present Year*, London, 1603) as the first of historians, unhappy only in the choice of his subject. Yet I much doubt whether a partial and verbose compilation from Latin writers, thirteen hundred folio pages of speeches and battles, can either instruct or amuse an enlightened age, which requires from the historian some tincture of philosophy and criticism" (7:25–26n). Throughout the *Decline and Fall* "philosophical" is a regular term of praise, reflecting "the spirit of inquiry" which Gibbon finds in such works as Montesquieu's *De l'Esprit des lois* (7:332n). But inquiry must not soar too confidently: "The brilliant imagination of Montesquieu is corrected . . . by the dry cold reason of the Abbé de Mably" (1:245n). The available evidence must be pondered with a patience and caution that are not found, for example, in the most famous philosophical historian, Voltaire, "who casts a keen and lively glance over the surface of history" (5:446n). Gibbon's aim is to get below the surface, an aim which the theoretical bias of "philosophical" history may well counteract. The historian's task is to build up a probable sequence of narration and explanation, weighing each purported fact against the probabilities of human experience, and against the myriad of other purported facts with which it has to be reconciled. Since no single fact is ever indisputable, it is the interrelationship of many facts that adds up to a persuasive whole.

Gibbon calls Tacitus "the first of historians who applied the science of philosophy to the study of facts" (1:230). In this usage "facts" are not detached bits of data verifiable by theory or experiment, but organic constituents of the chains in which they occur. The modern *American Heritage Dictionary* defines *fact* as "Something known with certainty; something asserted as certain; something that has been objectively verified; something having real, demonstrable existence." In this sense there can be no such thing, strictly speaking, as historical facts, since no evidence can guarantee absolute certainty. But Johnson's *Dictionary* in 1755 defines *fact* very differently, echoing the Latin *facta* (something that has been done):

1. A thing done; an effect produced; something not barely supposed or suspected, but really done.
2. Reality; not supposition; not speculation.
3. Action; deed.

Evidence is often untrustworthy, but that does not mean that all evidence is worthless; things have certainly been done. And Hume's point about the historian's superior vantage point, according to Donald Livingston, is that "we understand things only after they have occurred and in the light of later occurrences" (104). Facts *become* facts through being understood.

Gibbon is well aware of the implications of the "universal Pyrrhonism" of Bayle, exhibited in "the wonderful power, which he so boldly exercised, of assembling doubts and objections" (*Memoirs* 89). The answer, in Gibbon's opinion, is to reverse the destructive process that had dissolved the past into bits of doubtful data. The purpose of philosophical history, as Frank Manuel well describes it, is "to single out those facts that dominated a whole system of interrelationships" (167).

Johnson remarked to Boswell, in a deliberate parody of Humean skepticism, that one could easily argue that Britain had not really taken Canada from France, since the government and soldiers had obvious motives for lying. "Yet, Sir, notwithstanding all these plausible objections, we have no doubt that Canada is really ours. Such is the weight of common testimony" (*Life* 1:428). The testimony is believed not just because many persons concur in it, but also because it fits into a whole structure of confirmatory evidence. Moreover, "truth" in this context is secured by social exchange rather than by any kind of absolute verification. As William James puts it in *Pragmatism*,

Truth lives for the most part on a credit system. Our thoughts and beliefs "pass," so long as nothing challenges them, just as bank-notes pass so long as nobody refuses them. But all this points to direct face-to-face verifications somewhere, without which the fabric of truth collapses like a financial system with no cash basis whatever. . . . Beliefs verified concretely by *somebody* are the posts of the whole superstructure. (137)

Johnson agrees with Hume that just this kind of interchange undergirds the belief that Canada has been taken, and elsewhere he claims (in direct opposition to Hume) that the same kind of interchange guarantees the biblical miracles.

In assessing the evidence for putative facts, Gibbon was strongly influenced by the method of probabilism, in which ancient testimonies are weighed against what seems most likely to have happened, a procedure made possible by the assumption that human motives and behavior remain constant (Trowbridge 224). But one would always prefer the certain to the probable if one could get it, confirming "probable suppositions" by "the evidence of authentic facts" (*Decline and Fall* 2:88). Sometimes Gibbon feels confident that he can extract the truth from his sources by applying "a gentle pressure and paraphrase of their words" (4:211n). Sometimes the truth can be approximated by a method of dismantling: "I shall endeavour to form a just estimate of the famous vision of Constantine . . . by separating the historical, the natural, and the marvelous parts of this extraordinary story, which, in the composition of a specious argument, have been artfully confounded in one splendid and brittle mass" (2:317–18). But there are other times when the only hope is to see through the sources rather than with them: "A faint light may be obtained from the smoke of George of Pisidia" (5:93n).

No wonder Gibbon is grateful above all for eyewitness accounts, even granting that allowance for bias always has to be made. "For the troubles of Africa, I neither have nor desire another guide than Procopius, whose eye contemplated the image, and whose ear collected the reports, of the memorable events of his own times" (4:415n). The eyewitness may be all the more compelling if he is not a professional historian. "A simple citizen describes with pity, or perhaps with pleasure, the humiliation of the barons of Rome" (7:282). Gibbon quotes the account, and adds in a footnote, "He saw them, and we see them." But reliable eyewitness accounts are all too rare, both because the documentary record is imperfect and because few eyewitnesses know how to make sense of what they see. "[Athanasius] preserved a distinct and unbroken view of a scene which was incessantly shifting; and never failed to improve those decisive moments which are irrecoverably past before they are perceived by a common eye" (2:384).

Introducing the inflammatory topic of Roman persecution of the Christians, Gibbon declares as his aim "to separate (if it be possible) a few authentic, as well as interesting, facts from an undigested mass of fiction and error, and to relate, in a clear and rational manner, the causes, the extent, the duration, and the most important circumstances of the persecutions" (2:77). Some facts are authentic but not interesting. Many alleged facts are interesting but fictional. So they have to be digested and sorted, and then as Gibbon says *related*—that is, presented in narrative form.

In an obvious sense, narrated truth will always take the form of art. "The past is [Gibbon's] material," Leo Braudy says, "but history is what he has created" (214). Unlike a painter's oils and turpentine, however, the material remains of primary value. As Gibbon says in his polemical *Vindication*, a brilliant defense of his scholarly integrity against religious critics, "If my readers are satisfied with the form, the colours, the new arrangement which I have given to the labours of my predecessors, they may perhaps consider me not as a contemptible thief, but as an honest and industrious manufacturer, who has fairly procured the raw materials, and worked them up with a laudable degree of skill and success" (*English Essays* 277). Historians tend to emphasize the evidentiary basis of the *Decline and Fall* and literary scholars its imaginative status, but the work's power flows from the interaction between the two—from what Gossman calls "its ability to function simultaneously as literature, stimulating the imagination, and as history, limiting and restraining it" (*Empire* xi).

Gibbon would certainly not concede that the facts are compromised or fictionalized by the act of narration, as Johnson once suggested in his presence:

JOHNSON. "We must consider how very little history there is; I mean real authentic history. That certain kings reigned, and certain battles were fought, we can depend upon as true; but all the colouring, all the philosophy, of history is conjecture." BOSWELL. "Then, Sir, you would reduce all history to no better than an almanac, a mere chronological series of remarkable events." Mr. Gibbon, who must at that time have been employed upon his *History*, of which he published the first volume in the following year, was present; but did not step forth in defence of that species of writing. He probably did not like to *trust* himself with JOHNSON! (Boswell, *Life* 2:365–55)

Had he wished to speak, Gibbon would certainly have conceded that every history is built upon conjecture and selection, but he might well have added that the process of historical narration is no different from that by which all human experience is understood. Events make sense when they are organized in a narrative, and any narrative is necessarily what LaCapra calls it, a feat of "retrospective reconstruction" (*Rethinking* 17).

Not only must "facts" be organized in narrative in order to make sense; in addition, there can never be enough facts to generate a continuous story. The historian's role is therefore to join up the facts, or to fill in the gaps between them, in the way that empiricist theory ascribes to all interpretations of the past, personal as well as historical. A positivist historiography might aspire to recover *all* the facts, and would regard any gaps between them as lamentable omissions. But eighteenth-century empiricism holds that even in a person's individual experience there will always be gaps, and that these are bridged by the imagination in its continuous work of constructing the world. As one Hume scholar puts it, we reconstruct episodes in our own lives by stringing "threads of reminiscence" between fragmentary "memory tokens," and in an analogous way "spanning the gaps between tokens, when composing a coherent historical narrative, is work which is left to the imagination" (Noxon 290). The historian performs, for cultural memory, an act of reconstruction identical to that which the individual performs for personal memory. Indeed, as we have seen, for Hume the printed "traces" that describe Caesar's death derive from, and have the same status as, the memory "traces" of the original eyewitnesses.

Eighteenth-century thinking about narrative, Louis Mink argues, presupposes a model of "universal history" from which the individual historian has selected certain details. In such a conception, which most people probably take for granted to this day, history is not a series of inventions by historians but a bedrock of actuality into which they have sunk exploratory shafts. As Mink puts it, "Narrative form in history, as in fiction, is an artifice, the product of individual imagination. Yet at the same time it is accepted as claiming truth—that is, as representing a real ensemble of interrelationships in past actuality" (145). Somewhere too deep for ordinary recognition lies the unconscious assumption that "the past has in its own right a narrative structure which is discovered rather than constructed" (148). No doubt Gibbon does believe this: his art shows more of the past than other historians have done, or it shows the past more clearly, but "the past" stands stable and intact as a story waiting to be told.

At all events, it is only when a human mind gives meaning to facts —when the story gets told as a story—that they become "facts" at all. In Hayden White's words, historical discourse "makes the real desirable

. . . and does so by its imposition, upon events that are represented as real, of the formal coherency that stories possess" ("Value of Narrativity" 20). Johnson says rather casually in one of his essays, "He that writes the history of past times undertakes only to decorate known facts by new beauties of method or style, or at most to illustrate them by his own reflections" (*Idler* No. 94). Gibbon's narrative goes far beyond decoration and illustration, elaborating a form whose function is to inculcate truth by clarifying what actually happened. But it is essential to recognize that aesthetics is subordinated to the real, insofar as human intelligence can deduce a version of the real from the available evidence. Gibbon's standard of truth, like Johnson's, is as much moral as factual, but the two categories are finally inseparable. So he declares in the *Vindication*, "If I am capable of wilfully perverting what I understand, I no longer deserve to live in the society of those men, who consider a strict and inviolable adherence to truth, as the foundation of every thing that is virtuous or honourable in human nature" (*English Essays* 234). Gibbon adds that readers have a right to know "whether they must content themselves with reading the History of the Decline and Fall of the Roman Empire as a *tale amusing enough,* or whether they may venture to receive it as a fair and authentic history" (235).

The truth-disclosing potentiality of form is so crucial that Gibbon is willing to exalt it over the primary sources themselves. Setting out to describe the history of the Arabs, he modestly concedes, "I must profess my total ignorance of the Oriental tongues, and my gratitude to the learned interpreters who have transfused their science into the Latin, French, and English languages" (*Decline and Fall* 5:332n). But before long he is soaring with the confidence of a philosophical historian who can make better sense of Arabian history than Arabs can:

The art and genius of history have ever been unknown to the Asiatics; they are ignorant of the laws of criticism; and our monkish chronicles of the same period may be compared to their most popular works, which are never vivified by the spirit of philosophy and freedom. The *Oriental Library* of a Frenchman would instruct the most learned mufti of the East; and perhaps the Arabs might not find in a single historian so clear and comprehensive a narrative of their own exploits, as that which will be deduced in the ensuing sheets [i.e., of the *Decline and Fall*]. (5:428–29)

Just as the young Gibbon had to discover his own statue in the block of marble, so the historian must find or create form in the confused materials of the past.

The *Decline and Fall* is often described as an epic. The analogy is helpful in many ways, not least of which is a recognition of amplitude: this work needs to be read at length rather than in excerpts, as its tireless narrative voice presents the cumulative story of thousands of individual lives. In praising *Paradise Lost*, which of course he regards as a true story, Johnson describes epic in terms that are entirely applicable to the *Decline and Fall*: "History must supply the writer with the rudiments of narration, which he must improve and exalt by a nobler art, must animate by dramatic energy, and diversify by retrospection and anticipation; morality must teach him the exact bounds and different shades of vice and virtue; from policy, and the practice of life, he has to learn the discriminations of character, and the tendency of the passions, either single or combined" (*Lives* 1:170). But *Paradise Lost* turned out to be an unrepeatable fiction that was uniquely guaranteed by doctrinal truth. In an age that grieved because epic had become unwritable, Gibbon achieved a *kind* of epic by resting his presiding themes on a foundation of rich detail, while rising above the chaotic welter of immediacy that fascinated Boswell or Sterne or Diderot.

In another sense, however, Gibbon's history may seem anti-epic in insisting that real events are more significant and moving than fictionalized ones. "A plain narrative of facts," he remarks in a footnote, "is much more pathetic than the most laboured descriptions of epic poetry" (3:327n). But actually Gibbon is concerned here with rhetorical effects (the "descriptions") rather than with the truth status of what is described. So long as the rhetoric is kept reasonably "plain," the two modes approach each other very closely. As Gossman shows, eighteenth-century theorists saw history and epic as closely allied, and not just in rhetorical technique: "Voltaire, in short, preferred his epics to be true and his histories to be epic" ("History and Literature" 13). Similarly Pope, in the notes to his translation of the *Iliad*, contrasts the foreknown events of epic with the fictional suspense that romance and tragedy excite:

It must be owned that a surprise artfully managed, which arises from unexpected revolutions of great actions, is extremely pleasing: in this consists the principal pleasure of a romance or well writ tragedy. But besides this, there is in the relation of great events a different kind of pleasure which arises from the artful unravelling [of] a knot of actions, which we knew before in the gross. This is a delight peculiar to history and epic poetry, which is founded on history. In these kinds of writing, a preceding summary knowledge of the events described does no way damp our curiosity, but rather makes it more eager for the detail. (Note to 15.67)

History and epic interpenetrate in this conception, and what is at stake is not the veridicality of the narrative but its means of interesting and persuading the reader.

Whether epic or not, the *Decline and Fall* is a story of failure. Rome's greatness was tragically inseparable from its weakness, and its collapse was not only bound to happen but might well have happened sooner.

> The decline of Rome was the natural and inevitable effect of immoderate greatness. Prosperity ripened the principle of decay; the causes of destruction multiplied with the extent of conquest; and, as soon as time or accident had removed the artificial supports, the stupendous fabric yielded to the pressure of its own weight. The story of its ruin is simple and obvious; and, instead of inquiring why the Roman empire was destroyed, we should rather be surprised that it had subsisted so long. (4:173–74)

An account like this tends to represent Rome as a living creature that grows, decays, and "falls." "History in the main," Edward Said remarks, "has acquired its intelligibility through a kind of anthropomorphism projected onto and into events and collectivities of various sorts" (293). Clarendon described a "venom" of corruption spreading through the body of England, and Robertson, whom Gibbon greatly admired, called the Roman Empire "a vast body, languid and almost unanimated" (P. Burke 88). Gibbon says similarly, "This long peace, and the uniform government of the Romans, introduced a slow and secret poison into the vitals of the empire" (*Decline and Fall* 1:62), and indeed an animist notion of cultural growth and decay is common to most eighteenth-century thinkers. Rousseau states as a truism, "The body politic, as well as the human body, begins to die from its birth, and bears in itself the causes of its own destruction. But both may have a constitution more or less robust, and fitted to preserve them a longer or shorter time" (*Social Contract* 93). Buried metaphors provide the conceptual logic underlying historical narrative, and the double meaning of *constitution* is felt to be a significant homology rather than a mere analogy.

A historian preoccupied with virtue and corruption could hardly avoid being a moralist. According to Hume, "The advantages found in history seem to be of three kinds, as it amuses the fancy, as it improves the understanding, and as it strengthens virtue" (*Essays* 565). But in contrast with older, providential historiography, the philosophical historian develops moral reflections from within himself, by meditating on the welter of historical experience, and does not claim to identify such themes within the historical process itself. It is possible, Gibbon says, that "even in this world, the natural order of events will sometimes afford the strong appearances of moral retribution" (*Decline and Fall* 6:500). But more often the tangle of events, even when arranged in coherent sequence, refuses to yield up a moral in any traditional sense. "Such is the empire of Fortune (if we may still disguise our ignorance under that popular name) that it is almost equally difficult to foresee the events of war or to explain their various consequences" (4:126).

For a Christian moralist like Johnson or Fielding, fortune is another name for providence, or at any rate for chance as a strictly controlled subset of providential occurrences. For Gibbon, fortune is chance pure and simple, but it is important not to exaggerate the threat to intelligibility that this poses. As we have seen in Chapter 1, Hume's skepticism about proving causality does not diminish its relevance in practical life, and in the *Inquiry concerning Human Understanding* Hume states,

The most usual species of connection among the different events which enter into any narrative composition is that of cause and effect; while the historian traces the series of actions according to their natural order, remounts to their secret springs and principles, and delineates their most remote consequences. . . . Sometimes unavoidable ignorance renders all his attempts fruitless; sometimes he supplies by conjecture what is wanting in knowledge; and always he is sensible that the more unbroken the chain is which he presents to his readers, the more perfect is his production. He sees that the knowledge of causes is not only the most satisfactory, this relation or connection being the strongest of all others, but also the most instructive; since it is by this knowledge alone we are enabled to control events and govern futurity. (34)

Chance plays its role in life without making life incomprehensible; causes can be identified, with probability if not with absolute certainty, and the historian can assemble them into an "unbroken chain" that not only affords insight into the past, but even gives some measure of control over the future.

Donald Livingston gives an example from Hume's *History of England*: Charles I might have chosen not to give an order that prevented his future enemy Cromwell from emigrating, so in a sense huge and unforeseeable consequences flowed from a small action; but that does not mean that Charles and Cromwell were themselves randomly motivated. Stated philosophically, "Hume does not grant any ontological status to chance. To talk of chance is always to talk about our ignorance of causes relative to some system of determination" (Livingston 228). In retrospect the causes are in principle discoverable, whereas one could never predict in advance the immense changes that flow from apparently trivial impulses. As Burke eloquently puts it in the *First Letter on a Regicide Peace*, "It is often impossible, in these political enquiries, to find any proportion between the apparent force of any moral causes we may assign and their known operation. . . . The death of a man at a critical juncture, his disgust, his retreat, his disgrace, have brought innumerable calamities on a whole nation. A common soldier, a child, a girl at the door of an inn, have changed the face of fortune, and almost of nature" (*Works* 8:79–89).

This is not to say that causality is unknowable, but rather that it is inseparable from narrative and unintelligible apart from it. Robin Winks remarks (rather condescendingly) that by abstaining from causal claims, Gibbon escapes the datedness of most historians: "Gibbon manages to live because he rarely explains anything, although he gives an appearance of explaining all" (501). But from the point of view of Humean empiricism, causality is a fiction of narrative that has no existence apart from the stories in which it is embedded (or, if one prefers, invented). "Historical-narrative accounts are superior to causal accounts, and . . . causal accounts are all ultimately narrative-historical in character" (Capaldi, "Hume as Social Scientist" 107). If the model of understanding for science is predictive, for history it is retrospective. As a modern theorist says, "A historian can show that the destruction of the English monasteries was an intelligible incident not because it followed necessarily from some set of initial conditions but because the whole temporal process of which it was a part exhibits an intelligible structure" (D. Porter 34). The historian's narrative is not just an artistic vehicle through which his or her conclusions are presented, it *is* the conclusions.

STYLE, STORY, IDEOLOGY

Gibbon's style is celebrated for its witty ironies, in which—just as in Swift's—the insertion of a single incongruity can explode the solemnity of narration. "[Alexius Comnenus] dissembled till the moment of revenge; invited the chiefs to a friendly conference; and punished the innocent and guilty by imprisonment, confiscation, and baptism" (*Decline and Fall* 6:127). Parallelism is much used, and the reader grows accustomed to sentences that turn inside out: "The sons of Constantine seemed impatient to convince mankind that they were incapable of contenting themselves with the dominions which they were unqualified to govern" (2:244). But the implications of the style go far beyond aphorism and epigram, and like any artificial style it embodies a message that human life, though unpredictable and sometimes frightening, is finally intelligible.

Carlyle, in his *French Revolution*, found present-tense narration essential to recreate accurately the emotional texture of experience.

Indeed it is a most lying thing that same Past Tense always: so beautiful, sad, almost Elysian-sacred, "in the moonlight of Memory," it seems; and *seems* only. For observe, always one most important element is surreptitiously withdrawn from the Past Time: the haggard element of Fear! Not *there* does Fear dwell, nor Uncertainty, nor Anxiety; but it dwells *here;* haunting us, tracking us; running like an accursed ground-discord through all the music tones of our Existence;—making the Tense a mere Present one! (4:81)

Richardson's *Clarissa* gains its power from this immediacy, living in the present tense of fear. Gibbon's *Decline and Fall*, like Fielding's *Tom Jones*, exorcises fear by placing it in the past and illuminating it in the cool moonlight of a lapidary style. To make the reader relive the event would probably strike Gibbon as an illicit aim. In his view, one understands best what one can stand apart from and categorize ("I sighed as a lover, I obeyed as a son").

In Gibbon's careful structuring, the unit is the paragraph rather than the sentence. He reports in his *Memoirs*, "It has always been my practice to cast a long paragraph in a single mould, to try it by my ear, to deposit it in my memory, but to suspend the action of the pen till I had given the last polish to my work" (161). Boswell developed an expressive plain style to embody the experience of the moment; Gibbon developed a complex, ornate rhetoric to recreate the experience of the ages. In analyses of this rhetoric, too much has probably been made of its famous irony, which is certainly brilliant but is not really the dominant note. More characteristic is the trick of analyzing actions into parts, which implies a narrator who can stand above them, grasp them, and reduce them to elegant clarity: "The weak and guilty Lupicinus, who had dared to provoke, who had neglected to destroy, and who still presumed to despise, his formidable enemy, marched against the Goths" (*Decline and Fall* 3:105). Frequently Gibbon employs an "*A or B*" construction to evoke in passing the various lights under which the same event may be seen: "After their conversion from idolatry, or heresy, the Franks and the Visigoths were disposed to embrace, with equal submission, the inherent evils, and the accidental benefits, of superstition" (4:152).

Character sketches work similarly to analyze behavior into constituent parts, often in paired phrases or clauses. "Cruelty and superstition were the ruling passions of the soul of Maximin. The former suggested the means, the latter pointed out the objects, of persecution" (2:142). In effect Gibbon assigns behavior to whatever aspect of character seems operative in a particular context, almost as if he were writing allegory. The artifices of style are particularly appropriate for a summary kind of portraiture: it may be impossible to unravel the deepest strands of behavior in persons long dead, but one can summarize the impression they made on those who saw them. "Jealous of his wives, liberal of his wealth, prodigal of his own blood and of that of others, [Abu Moslem] could boast with pleasure, and possibly with truth, that he had destroyed six hundred thousand of his enemies; and such was the intrepid gravity of his mind and countenance that he was never seen to smile except on a day of battle" (6:20). Gibbon cannot and does not psychologize Abu Moslem, reporting instead an external fact about a man who carefully concealed his inside, a fact that works both to illustrate Abu Moslem's rigid self-control and to disclose a disturbing element of his temperament.

It would be a mistake to see this kind of characterization merely as neoclassical abstraction. On the contrary, it reflects a characteristically eighteenth-century recognition that people are known only through the roles they play and that their roles alter over the course of time. Gibbon's final comment on Mohammed acknowledges not only the difficulty of understanding a person long dead, but also the changeableness of apparent character even within that person's lifetime:

At the conclusion of the life of Mahomet, it may perhaps be expected that I should balance his faults and virtues, that I should decide whether the title of enthusiast or impostor more properly belongs to that extraordinary man. Had I been intimately conversant with the son of Abdallah, the task would still be difficult and the success uncertain: at the distance of twelve centuries, I darkly contemplate his shade through a cloud of religious incense; and, could I truly delineate the portrait of an hour, the fleeting resemblance would not equally apply to the solitary of mount Hera, to the preacher of Mecca, and to the conqueror of Arabia. (5:400)

Even Mohammed's contemporaries, assuming that any of them were disinterested observers, would have found it difficult if not impossible to define the "real" Mohammed. The Humean "signs" of character, always ambiguous and unclear, would have remained puzzling even to them. Gibbon, with his philosophical detachment and historical hindsight, may hope to interpret the structure of events more persuasively than tendentious Moslem historians, but he has no illusions about his ability to probe the personality of the Prophet. His notebook "Hints" contain the pregnant remark: "Ignorance why *we* have acted—how *we* shall act—how *others* will act" (*English Essays* 89).

Powerful as Gibbon's style is as an instrument of control, it is vulnerable to Lytton Strachey's wicked parody, written when he was a schoolboy of seventeen:

At last, having traversed twice as quickly as Red Riding Hood a road twice as short as that which she had taken, [the wolf] arrived in triumph at the house of the redoubtable though comatose octogenarian. History does not reveal the details of the interview. It can only be gathered that it was a short and stormy one. It is known for certain, however, that the wolf obtained at the same moment a victory and a meal, and that when Little Red Riding Hood entered her grandmother's abode, the arch deceiver, occupying the bed and arrayed in the nightgown of his unfortunate victim, was prepared to receive the child with a smile of outward welcome and of inward derision. (Holroyd 1:72)

But Gibbon is not without a line of defense against this kind of critique. He could well retort that his rhetorical structures work to deploy the fragments of past experience in intelligible relationships, and that their very artificiality warns the reader not to mistake re-creation for the thing itself.

William Empson speaks of the Augustan style as a mode of control and adds, "The *Decline and Fall of the Roman Empire* is one enormous panorama of these little witticisms" (82). The metaphor of the panorama suggests exactly what Gibbon is aiming at: temporality is broken down into significant moments, which are then distributed into an extended picture, every part of which is available to view. This insistence on the significant moment, rather than on the continuous flow of experience, is suggestive of the immense prestige of "history painting," which many eighteenth-century theorists explicitly compared to historical writing, in which perspective is used to give the viewer a single all-embracing viewpoint so as to be able "truly to *read* the canvas before him" (Gossman, "History and Literature" 17). The aesthetic theorizing that accompanied these didactic tableaus, as Michael Fried describes it, focused on a series of "heroic or pathetic actions" that permit "the causal necessity of every element to be instantaneously apparent" (76). Gibbon's omniscient narration places the reader at the proper viewing point, just as a painter might. And if the *Decline and Fall* is built up in a series of scenes, that is entirely in keeping with the theory, as Fried's quotation from Du Bos suggests: "The painter who makes a painting of the sacrifice of Iphigenia represents for us on the canvas only one moment of the action. Racine's tragedy puts before our eyes several moments [*plusieurs instants*] of this action, and these various incidents enhance one another's pathos" (Fried 77). Gibbon mentions approvingly a Byzantine historian who "has the uncommon talent of placing each scene before the reader's eye" (*Decline and Fall* 7:110n).

By way of illustrating how Gibbon's method works in extended narrative, consider the death of the emperor Decius fighting the barbarians. The abstract nouns and the leisurely unwinding of dependent clauses impose a pattern of inevitability:

An obscure town of Maesia, called Forum Terebronii, was the scene of the battle. The Gothic army was drawn up in three lines, and, either from choice or accident, the front of the third line was covered by a morass. In the beginning of the action, the son of Decius, a youth of the fairest hopes, and already associated to the honours of the purple, was slain by an arrow, in the sight of his afflicted father; who, summoning all his fortitude, admonished the dismayed troops that the loss of a single soldier was of little importance to the republic. The conflict was terrible; it was the combat of despair against grief and rage. The first line of the Goths at length gave way in disorder; the second, advancing to sustain it, shared its fate; and the third only remained entire, prepared to dispute the passage of the morass, which was imprudently attempted by the presumption of the enemy. (1:269)

At this point Gibbon gives a passage in quotation marks, which only a footnote reveals to be a description by Tacitus of a similar engagement two centuries earlier:

"Here the fortune of the day turned, and all things became adverse to the Romans: the place deep with ooze, sinking under those who stood, slippery to such as advanced; their armour heavy, the waters deep; nor could they wield, in that uneasy situation, their weighty javelins. The barbarians, on the contrary, were enured to encounters in the bogs; their persons tall, their spears long, such as could wound at a distance."

The quotation ends here, and Gibbon concludes,

In this morass the Roman army, after an ineffectual struggle, was irrecoverably lost; nor could the body of the emperor ever be found. Such was the fate of Decius, in the fiftieth year of his age; an accomplished prince, active in war, and affable in peace; who, together with his son, has deserved to be compared, both in life and death, with the brightest examples of ancient virtue.

One can't help feeling that even in the brief excerpt, Tacitus' account is more vivid than Gibbon's stately harmonies. Gibbon's account of Decius rises to a commemorative image, like that of the medallions he often invoked for historical evidence.

Moreover, in the original context the difference between Gibbon and Tacitus is still greater. Tacitus describes the horror with which before the battle the Roman troops gathered the unburied bones of their comrades, massacred six years before, their skulls nailed to trees; and he relates a haunting vision of the dead general Varus (here, in Michael Grant's translation):

The night brought no rest. And there was a contrast between the echoes resounding in the low-lying valleys and the forests, as the natives feasted with their savage shouting and triumphant songs, and the occasional murmuring of the Romans round their smouldering fires, as they lay here and there by the breastwork or wandered around the tents, dazed but sleepless. The general had a horrible dream —Varus, covered with blood, seemed to rise out of the morass, and call him: but he would not obey; and when Varus held out his hand he pushed it back. (69)

The solemn scene, with its striking details, seems almost Shakespearean. Gibbon, by contrast, needs his distance. History is distinguished from fiction not just in being true, but also in being detached and generalized. Syntax and rhetoric are kept firmly in the foreground so that relics of long-ago life, rescued from a thousand books, may take their orderly place in Gibbon's supreme book. And yet Gibbon does, after all, let Tacitus speak; it is as if the ancient historian has forced his way in, though held at arm's length by Gibbon's very un-Tacitean style.

It is important to recognize that Gibbon knows what he is doing and expects the reader to accept it. It would have been easy enough to string together a mass of vivid anecdotes, as many of his sources do; what is harder is to maintain proportion among the parts, and sufficient detachment to weigh them all fairly. As Tacitus himself says in the *Annals*, "What interests and stimulates readers is a geographical description, the changing fortune of a battle, the glorious death of a commander. My themes on the other hand concern cruel orders, unremitting accusations, treacherous friendships, innocent men ruined—a conspicuously monotonous glut of downfalls and their monotonous causes" (173). Gibbon says similarly that his survey of Roman administrative methods "will suspend, for some time, the course of the narrative; but the interruption will be censured only by those readers who are insensible to the importance of laws and manners, while they peruse, with eager curiosity, the transient intrigues of a court, or the accidental event of a battle" (*Decline and Fall* 2:168–69).

Such incidents do not, in fact, *deserve* to be made interesting: "Events by which the fate of nations is not materially changed leave a faint impression on the page of history, and the patience of the reader would be exhausted by the repetition of the same hostilities, undertaken without cause, prosecuted without glory, and terminated without effect" (5:42). Historical distance provides the possibility of deciding which events are significant and which are not. "The tedious warfare and alternate successes of the Roman and Persian arms cannot detain the attention of posterity at the foot of mount Caucasus" (4:407). But if time has made many details irrelevant, that is all the more reason why the historian, who decides what constitutes relevance, must throw light on their meaning as a whole. "This narrative of obscure and remote events is not foreign to the decline and fall of the Roman empire. If a Christian power had been maintained in Arabia, Mahomet must have been crushed in his cradle, and Abyssinia would have prevented a revolution which has changed the civil and religious state of the world" (4:414).

Even in an individual's memory, Johnson says, "many particular features and discriminations will be compressed and conglobated into one gross and general idea" (*Journey* 147), and historical memory is of course hazier still. Fredric Bogel comments on Johnson's remark, "Like the sand raised so profusely by a tempest that 'an estate was overwhelmed and lost,' time buries the particulars of the past beneath its featureless uniformity" (*Literature and Insubstantiality* 83). But in the opinion of most eighteenth-century commentators on history, an important counterforce works to rescue objects from those shifting sands: the written records whose "traces," as even Hume holds, add up to a reliable cultural memory. If anything, we have at our disposal too many traces rather than too few. It is not enough simply to exhume buried facts, since the resulting sandstorm of data particles will overwhelm understanding. Gibbon's art represents a monumental attempt to reinvigorate cultural memory by selection and interpretation, bringing significant facts into the light and aligning them with other facts that permit an intelligible story to emerge.

The insertion of the anachronistic Tacitus passage has further implications for Gibbon's control of his subject. Auerbach has shown in *Mimesis* (33–40) how Tacitus can vividly describe an army revolt without the least interest in, or even awareness of, the social forces that drive the soldiers to act as they do. By remaining exclusively ethical, his perspective excludes the possibility of historical mutation (e.g., a development of proletarian consciousness) as contrasted with cyclical repetition (rebelliousness as a threat to every form of authority). Pocock makes a related point about Gibbon's treatment of nomad invasions: "It was a rhetorical advantage, as well as an intellectual relief, to be able to present these peoples as sociologically indistinguishable; the same tropes and *topoi* could be used to introduce each in its turn" ("Gibbon and the Shepherds" 199).

As opposed to the novelistic kind of historian who aspires to "recreate" the past, Gibbon uses hindsight to detect patterns that were invisible to those who blindly lived inside them. In Arthur Danto's words, "The whole point of history is *not* to know about actions as witnesses might, but as historians do, in connection with later events and as parts of temporal wholes" (183). This is the heart of what was meant by philosophical history. As Gossman says, the ideal reader postulated by eighteenth-century historians is a detached observer "who masters history by reducing it to order or theory," not an actor whose perspective is enclosed by the action itself ("History and Literature" 17).

It is very much on purpose, then, that Gibbon goes beyond Tacitus in elevation and generalization. Like Johnson at Iona, he wants to withdraw from merely personal experience in order to survey history from above, grasping in a comprehensive vision what had appeared local and specific to the participants. Tacitus describes a swamp battle two centuries earlier than the one Gibbon invokes it to illustrate; Gibbon implies that what really matters is the endless confrontation of Rome and barbarism. It was *always like that*. Moreover, this procedure turns out to have been closer to Tacitus' own methods than Gibbon himself may have realized. Tony Woodman has shown that Tacitus engages in "substantive self-imitation" in this very passage: he echoes his own account of a similar engagement in order to fill in details, otherwise unavailable, of an event that happened a full century before his own time. "Tacitus would not, I believe, have regarded it as in any way unusual that he should describe the latter [event] in terms of the former: this was an illustration of history repeating itself" (Woodman 153). As the analogy of epic suggests, eighteenth-century theorizing, far from fearing the contamination of the fictive, explicitly recognized the alliance between history and fiction. D'Alembert remarked that the writings of Tacitus "would not lose much if we were to consider them only as the first and truest of philosophical novels" (Gossman, "History and Literature" 22). He does not say that *nothing* would be lost, only that the central significance would remain pretty much intact.

But there remains an essential respect in which Gibbon does resist the appeal of the fictive: he avoids any trace of the novelistic, even as much of it as appears in Tacitus. If in Bakhtin's terms the novel interweaves layers of discourse in all their social vitality while poetry imposes a single voice upon its materials, then the *Decline and Fall* is poetic while a work like Boswell's *London Journal* is novelistic. Boswell's reality is the fullness of the moment. Gibbon's reality is an armature of connections between *significant* moments, extracted from masses of confused documents and clarified by a deliberately artificial style. And this rejection of novelizing, which Gibbon no doubt sees as a refusal to seduce the reader with merely titillating details, results in a minimizing of phenomenological experience. The interlocking abstractions reflect a neoclassical ethos that regards the uniqueness of personal and cultural experience as either irrelevant or unreal. Nineteenth-century historicism is, perhaps, an essentially novelistic invention. "Gibbon's incomprehension of Medieval Europe," G. M. Young comments, "is the measure of what history owes to Scott" (14).

Just as Pope's verse is pervaded by the heroic mode, even when parodied or inverted in antiheroism, so Gibbon's prose tends to soar above ugliness and misery even when alluding to them. While following his sources with the utmost veracity, he creates a special kind of tone that laminates past suffering beneath a smooth veneer. This procedure is best illustrated, once again, by an extended example. First, here is a modern historian's account of the moment when a Persian fortress fell to Julian's soldiers, who had tunneled into it from beneath:

By evening Dagalaifus, who was in charge of the mining operations, reported that one of the mines was nearly through. Julian decided not to wait until the next day. The wearied soldiers mounted yet another general attack on the walls to distract the defenders' attention and to drown out the noise of the tunnellers. As dusk was falling the miners broke through the surface and found themselves in a room where a woman was grinding corn. As she was opening her mouth to scream the first of them killed her with a single blow. They went on to dispatch the other occupants of the house without attracting attention and crept up on the guard at the nearby gate. The Persian soldiers, pleased with the day's events, were singing in the guard house and did not hear their approach. Within a minute they were all killed, the gates were open, and the Romans poured in. As they ran through the streets of the city they killed every living being they encountered, and set fire to buildings. Many of the inhabitants succeeded in getting up on to the walls. But these offered no safety, and many of them hurled themselves in despair down from the battlements. The height was such that few escaped serious injury. The Roman soldiers below went round putting the maimed wretches out of their misery. (Browning 204)

The terse declarative sentences represent a modern mode that has its own kind of eloquence and allows the dreadfulness of an event to emerge from a simple narration.

Gibbon—following the same source, Ammianus Marcellinus—manages things quite differently. He too is concerned to create an atmosphere, but for very different ends.

Three chosen cohorts, advancing in a single file, silently explored the dark and dangerous passage; till their intrepid leader whispered back the intelligence that he was ready to issue from his confinement into the streets of the hostile city. Julian checked their ardour that he might ensure their success; and immediately diverted the attention of the garrison, by the tumult and clamour of a general assault. The Persians, who from their walls contemptuously beheld the progress of an impotent attack, celebrated, with songs of triumph, the glory of Sapor; and ventured to assure the emperor that he might ascend the starry mansion of Ormusd, before he could hope to take the impregnable city of Maogamalcha. The city was already taken. History has recorded the name of a private soldier, the first who ascended from the mine into a deserted tower. The passage was widened by his companions, who pressed forwards with impatient valour. Fifteen hundred enemies were already in the midst of the city. The astonished garrison abandoned the walls, and their only hope of safety; the gates were instantly burst open; and the revenge of the soldier, unless it were suspended by lust or avarice, was satiated by an undistinguishing massacre. (2:525–26)

No one could call that final sentence a whitewash, but it is very general indeed, even in the suggestion that a soldier would interrupt his killing just long enough to rob or rape someone. The modern historian reports more details, including the name of the chief tunneler, whereas Gibbon says that "history has recorded" the name of a soldier but doesn't bother to record it himself—the fact that an ordinary person's name has survived is interesting, but not the name itself. (It was Exsuperius, according to Ammianus.) The modern historian, in keeping with the mood of the mid-1970s when he was writing, dwells on the cruel sufferings of the civilian victims, and stresses visual images with a kind of cinematic urgency. Gibbon's attention is given mainly to the Roman soldiers, in their "ardour" and "impatient valour" and also in their intoxicated brutality after the victory. The telling detail for him is not the woman who was killed at her corn grinding before she could utter a cry, but the dramatic irony of the Persian victory songs. "The city was already taken."

All styles give their own versions of reality. The style of 1976, recounting the siege of a Persian town, is different from that of 1776 and necessarily has different ends in view. But however much Gibbon believed he was recreating reality in his tableaus, it is worth remarking that the plain style had been praised for at least a century and that Augustan parallelism was already an archaizing mode in which to narrate the past. In a lapidary style all things become lapidary, rape and murder included. For a final twentieth-century contrast, here is Gore Vidal's novelistic version of Julian's dying speech, adapted from Ammianus who said he had heard it:

For this good death, I thank Helios, since it is the fear of those in my place that we die ignobly by secret plots or, even worse, by some long illness. I am happy that I died in mid-career, victorious, and I am honored that the gods have found me worthy of so noble a departure from this world. For a man is weak and cowardly who wants not to die when he ought, or tries to avoid his hour when it comes. (417)

This simple eloquence seems positively relaxed by comparison with Gibbon's tightly managed clauses:

I now offer my tribute of gratitude to the Eternal Being, who has not suffered me to perish by the cruelty of a tyrant, by the secret dagger of conspiracy, or by the slow tortures of lingering disease. He has given me, in the midst of an honourable career, a splendid and glorious departure from this world; and I hold it equally absurd, equally base, to solicit, or decline, the stroke of fate. (2:543)

Gibbon's version may do justice to the philosopher-king's clarity of vision, but it also floats his painful death upon a current of Gibbonian rhetoric, gathering it into the rhythms of the *Decline and Fall* as a whole. The unsympathetic Walter Bagehot, while granting that Gibbon's history moves steadily forward as "a type of order and an emblem of civilisation," finds in its style a sort of willed limitation: "It is not a style in which you can tell the truth. . . . Truth is of various kinds—grave, solemn, dignified, petty, low, ordinary; and a historian who has to tell the truth must be able to tell what is vulgar as well as what is great, what is little as well as what is amazing" (2:32). Gibbon constantly insists upon his commitment to truth, but the truth of the nineteenth century, not to mention of the twentieth, is a very different thing.

The story of the siege of Maogamalcha may make one suspect that "philosophical" objectivity can serve as a cover-up. This is true not just of obvious bias, as in Gibbon's treatment of Christianity (which will be considered in the next chapter), but also in cases that betray an unacknowledged personal investment. The captain of the Hampshire grenadiers, self-ironizing or not, apparently relished martial heroism. Wars form an essential part of the life of nations, and "a philosophic mind" will therefore be interested in "the history of blood" (*Decline and Fall* 7:1). From this it is but a step to despising peoples who fail to be warlike. "Three hundred years of peace, enjoyed by the soft inhabitants of Asia, had abolished the exercise of arms, and removed the apprehension of danger. The ancient walls were suffered to moulder away, and all the revenue of the most opulent cities was reserved for the construction of baths, temples, and theatres" (1:284). Gibbon is openly disgusted by the "base advice" of "pusillanimous counsellors" who urge an emperor not to expose his person on the battlefield (5:82n). Happily, their advice is not heeded: "After a bloody conflict, which continued till the evening, the Romans prevailed in the assault, and a Persian of gigantic size was slain and thrown into the Sarus by the hand of the emperor himself" (5:91).

Since the imperial civilization is by definition good, anything that would weaken it is bad, and wars to protect it must necessarily be fought. But Gibbon often shrinks from a literal account of what this entails:

The signal combats of the heroes of history or fable amuse our fancy and engage our affections; the skilful evolutions of war may inform the mind, and improve a necessary though pernicious science. But, in the uniform and odious pictures of a general assault, all is blood, and horror, and confusion; nor shall I strive, at the distance of three centuries and a thousand miles, to delineate a scene of which there could be no spectators, and of which the actors themselves were incapable of forming any just or adequate idea. (7:199)

Is this the candor of an impartial judge who will not try to describe what was incomprehensible even to the participants? Is it the cool escapism of a narrator who knows that real battles are far more horrible than the exploits of fictional heroes, but who does not care to specify how? Or is it the bookish remoteness of a historian who cannot imagine what war is really like? Marc Bloch wrote not long before his execution, "I have many times read, and I have often narrated, accounts of wars and battles. Did I truly know, in the full sense of that word, did I know from within, before I myself had suffered the terrible, sickening reality, what it meant for an army to be encircled, what it meant for a people to meet defeat?" (44). The captain of the Hampshire Grenadiers was only playing at being a soldier.

Something of Gibbon's imaginative identification with his subject is suggested by a footnote a few pages later, summarizing a series of historians as if they had actually performed the actions they describe:

Ducas kills him [the emperor Constantine Palaeologus] with two blows of Turkish soldiers; Chalcondyles wounds him in the shoulder, and then tramples him in the gate. The grief of Phranza carrying him among the enemy escapes from the precise image of his death; but we may, without flattery, apply these noble lines of Dryden:

> As to Sebastian, let them search the field;
> And, where they find a mountain of the slain,
> Send one to climb, and looking down beneath,
> There they will find him at his manly length,
> With his face up to heaven, in that red monument
> Which his good sword had digg'd.
>
> (7:201n)

Buoyed by rhetoric, the ugly reality is heavily euphemized. And the account of the death-dealing historians suggests vicarious identification on Gibbon's part, as do the military metaphors that pervade his *Vindication*, where he describes "the repeated proofs which I have made of the weight and temper of my adversary's weapons. They have, in every assault, fallen dead and lifeless to the ground: they have more than once recoiled, and dangerously wounded the unskilful hand that had presumed to use them" (*English Essays* 276). Gibbon has not even had to fight: with godlike impunity, he looks on while his opponents are wounded on the rebound.

Identifying emotionally with the armies of civilization, Gibbon reserves his deepest contempt for their barbarian opponents. Although his account of the nomads rests on a theory of pastoral life (Pocock, "Gibbon and the Shepherds") this is pastoral without the usual positive values: "Their simplicity has been praised; yet they abstained only from the luxury they had never known; whatever they saw, they coveted; their desires were insatiate, and their sole industry was the hand of violence and rapine" (*Decline and Fall* 6:146–47). After describing the Huns' sadistic treatment of their captives, Gibbon comments, "Such were those savage ancestors, whose imaginary virtues have sometimes excited the praise and envy of civilised ages" (3:493). Even if he had known of it, Gibbon could never have accepted Vico's view that the energies of barbarism gave rise to civilization. Barbarism is simply a negative condition, neither socially effective nor subject to change over time. Meanwhile "the different characters that mark the civilized nations of the globe may be ascribed to the use, and the abuse, of reason" (3:74). Reason is always the norm, whether abused or properly exercised.

Pondering the notion that a new wave of invaders might someday terrorize Europe again, Gibbon defines its impossibility with remarkable complacency. "Europe is secure from any future irruption of Barbarians; since, before they can conquer, they must cease to be barbarous. Their gradual advances in the science of war would always be accompanied, as we may learn from the example of Russia, with a proportionable improvement in the arts of peace and civil policy; and they themselves must deserve a place among the polished nations whom they subdue" (4:179). It was left for a later age to discover that civilization and barbarism need not be contradictory terms, though Gibbon does observe that when passions are "indulged without control" during the sack of a city, "small, alas! is the difference between civilised and savage man" (7:205). But in modern times, he asserts, "the ordinary calamities of war" are moderated by "the prudence or humanity of the princes of Europe, who amuse their own leisure, and exercise the courage of their subjects, in the practice of the military art . . . and the peaceful citizen has seldom reason to complain that his life, or even his fortune, is exposed to the rage of war" (3:73). How far this cheerful vision is from Voltaire's in *Candide*!

It is notable that Burke, pleading for imperial unity in the 1775 *Speech on Conciliation with America*, sees the system of civilization as much more precarious than Gibbon does:

Many of the people in the back settlements are already little attached to particular situations. Already they have topped the Appalachian mountains. From thence they behold before them an immense plain. . . . Over this they would wander without a possibility of restraint; they would change their manners with the habits of their life; would soon forget a government by which they were disowned; would become hordes of English Tartars; and, pouring down upon your unfortified frontiers a fierce and irresistible cavalry, become masters of your governors and your counsellors, your collectors and comptrollers, and of all the slaves that adhered to them. (*Works* 3:63–64)

Gibbon was astonished by the advent of the French Revolution; Burke was not.

Gibbon's account of civilization and barbarism is sustained not only by a general acceptance of eighteenth-century cultural values, but also by specific assumptions about politics that are all the stronger for not being explicitly stated. He was, in fact, a conservative Whig who supported the status quo, voted in Parliament with Lord North, and admired the political writings of Hume and Burke (Dickinson 179). There is certainly a sense in which Gibbon is a spokesman for traditional culture; as a modern admirer puts it, "Gibbon, soaked in the values of his order, taught its members what they already accepted" (Curtis 79). Nevertheless, it would be too simple to conclude that "Gibbon tells us more about the mind of the eighteenth century than he does about the Roman Empire" (Gilmore ix). There is no single or simple "mind of the eighteenth century," whether conservative or radical. It would be truer to say that Gibbon invests his work, as any artist must, with his own deepest preoccupations, in which political and psychological attitudes interpenetrate.

Gossman's ground-breaking book explores many such preoccupations: Gibbon's identification with the patrician class and its nostalgia for a unified culture; his preference for "manly" authority over "feminine" resignation; his attraction to stories of good sons obedient to good fathers, and outrage at stories of rebellious sons, heartless mothers, and tyrannical fathers; his interest in masks and fictions as the necessary means by which society is held together. Specific mid-eighteenth-century themes of course emerge as well. Great anxiety was felt about royal control of a standing army, and Gibbon declares accordingly, "The army is the most forcible engine of absolute power" (*Decline and Fall* 2:477). His service in the militia takes on added significance in this context, since a militia formed by country gentlemen was the standard Tory alternative to a centralized army, and indeed was inseparable from civic humanism as Pocock describes it. In another place Gibbon comments, "A martial nobility and stubborn commons, possessed of arms, tenacious of property, and collected into constitutional assemblies, form the only balance capable of preserving a free constitution against the enterprises of an aspiring prince" (1:65). The assumptions of contemporary British politics are openly expressed; *commons, property,* and *constitution* are all sacred terms in that context.

Politics is power, and power must always excite resistance. Burrow (43) rightly remarks that Gibbon in Parliament was himself an oligarchic senator, albeit an unobtrusive one; and Gibbon exhibits an understanding of social control that is without illusions. "Most of the crimes which disturb the internal peace of society are produced by the restraints which the necessary, but unequal, laws of property have imposed on the appetites of mankind, by confining to a few the possession of those objects that are coveted by many" (*Decline and Fall* 1:93). Beyond that, the many must always labor so that "the select few, placed by fortune above that necessity, can . . . fill up their time by the pursuits of interest or glory, by the improvement of their estate or of their understanding, by the duties, the pleasures, and even the follies, of social life" (1:238). No wonder Gibbon handsomely expresses gratitude for his own good fortune: "When I contemplate the common lot of mortality, I must acknowledge that I have drawn a high prize in the lottery of life. The far greater part of the globe is overspread with barbarism or slavery; in the civilized world the most numerous class is condemned to ignorance and poverty; and the double fortune of my birth in a free and enlightened country, in an honourable and wealthy family, is the lucky chance of a unit against millions" (*Memoirs* 173).

Gibbon writes here as if he, as an individual, had been inserted entire and complete into a particular social context. He does not consider that he has been formed by it, has no conceivable existence apart from it, and can imagine the life of the past only through its time-bound imaginative structures. And he undoubtedly believes that his own age represents the happy culmination of history: "Within the ancient walls of Vindonissa, the castle of Habsburg, the abbey of Königsfeld, and the town of Bruck have successively arisen. The philosophic traveler may compare the monuments of Roman conquest, of feudal or Austrian tyranny, of monkish superstition, and of industrious freedom. If he be truly a philosopher he will applaud the merit and happiness of his own times" (*Decline and Fall* 4:112–13).

Gibbon manages his narrative in such a way that eighteenth-century political attitudes will seem to be confirmed by it, and even to arise from it of their own accord. This is indeed to control history, using it to enforce truths that are represented as being universal. Britain is implicitly congratulated for a fortunate constitution that preserves it from the horrors of Roman tyranny and that retains its metaphorical affinity with the human body: "Although the wounds of civil war appeared completely healed, its mortal poison still lurked in the vitals of the constitution" (1:133). Only positivist historians will complain that these symptoms of human involvement are incompatible with historical objectivity. "History has no choice in the matter," Lucien Febvre writes; "it systematically gathers in, classifies and assembles past facts in accordance with its present needs. It consults death in accordance with the needs of life" (41).

To be embedded in one's own time is the condition of all historiography. "Objectivity" can only mean that the historian seeks to present evidence fairly, but the selection of evidence—not to mention the identification of some things as "evidence" and others as irrelevant—will always be directed by personal and cultural presuppositions. In recent years this truth has been increasingly recognized, for instance in major reassessments of the historiography of the French Revolution which have shown how heavily modern orthodoxy has rested on analogies with Marxist (often Stalinist) experience. In British history, analogous tendencies are apparent in the redefinition of "the Civil War" as "the English Revolution," and in the close attention given to "the crowd" in the eighteenth century. It must be emphasized that studies based on these, or any other, assumptions are not therefore *wrong;* but they will certainly seem wrong to persons who do not share the assumptions. This has inevitably happened to significant elements of Gibbon's *Decline and Fall*; what is remarkable is that his story held up so well for so long, and that even today it contains much that modern readers can respond to. In certain respects, it speaks from a consensus that many people still inhabit, and Gibbon's ironic style—like Pope's and Fielding's—invites the qualified reader to join a community of like-minded spectators of human experience.

Control the past though he may, the historian can never control the present, let alone the future. The central theme of the *Decline and Fall* is the fact of change, and whatever may be said about the idea of progress in the Enlightenment, many people still found change profoundly disturbing. Most thinkers before the eighteenth century saw it as an unlucky consequence of imperfect structure; the ideal state would enjoy a static equilibrium, so that historical change would not need to occur. In Gibbon's usage, just as in most of the word's definitions in Johnson's *Dictionary*, a "revolution" is a revolving movement that returns to where it began. Johnson says in the *Journey to the Western Islands*, "Perhaps, in the revolutions of the world, Iona may be sometime again the instructress of the Western Regions" (153). Likewise Gibbon: "In the revolution of human events, a new ambuscade was concealed in the Caudine forks, the fields of Cannae were bedewed a second time with the blood of the Africans, and the sovereign of Rome again attacked or defended the walls of Capua and Tarentum" (*Decline and Fall* 6:175).

Eighteenth-century Britain now finds itself in the difficult position that Rome once occupied, imposing an empire on a restive world. The contemporary reference is unmistakable when Gibbon reviews the means by which Roman power was maintained:

There is nothing perhaps more adverse to nature and reason than to hold in obedience remote countries and foreign nations, in opposition to their inclination and interest. A torrent of barbarians may pass over the earth, but an extensive empire must be supported by a refined system of policy and oppression: in the centre, an absolute power, prompt in action and rich in resources; a swift and easy communication with the extreme parts; fortifications to check the first effort of rebellion; a regular administration to protect and punish; and a well-disciplined army to inspire fear, without provoking discontent and despair. (5:322)

Gibbon's first volume appeared in 1776, when it suddenly became apparent that the center might not hold, and the final one in 1788, only a year before the French Revolution which invigorated the young Romantics, but which Gibbon saw as a catastrophe so dire that a stronger noun was needed: "the revolution, or rather the dissolution, of the kingdom" (*Memoirs* 172).

The *Decline and Fall* is in every sense an ending. It recreates a lost past in order to explain why it was lost. It is also the life work of an author who loses a large part of himself when it is finished: "My pride was soon humbled, and a sober melancholy was spread over my mind by the idea that I had taken my everlasting leave of an old and agreeable companion, and that, whatsoever might be the future date of my History, the life of the historian must be short and precarious" (*Memoirs* 169). In the long view—and twenty years devoted to the *Decline and Fall* would encourage long views—even the strongest of human creations are transitory. At times Gibbon can sound like Thomas Browne: "The art of man is able to construct monuments far more permanent than the narrow span of his own existence; yet these monuments, like himself, are perishable and frail; and, in the boundless annals of time, his life and his labours must equally be measured as a fleeting moment" (7:316). But Gibbon would have been delighted to know that his interpretations would deeply influence historians for at least two centuries to come, "wrestling not only with 'Gibbon's problem,' but with Gibbon himself" (Lossky 1). There is an unintended compliment in Bagehot's sarcastic remark, "Perhaps when a Visigoth broke a head, he thought that that was all. Not so; he was making history; Gibbon has written it down" (2:29). The Greeks called the muses the daughters of memory; Gibbon wants to recover the fading traces of ancient civilization and reinscribe them in modern consciousness. The facts of Gibbon's own life have grown hazy, but even if he had kept a journal like Boswell's or had written gossip-filled letters like Horace Walpole, he would have had a continuous problem of selection and perspective. Just because the Visigoths lived so long ago, Gibbon can feel unconstrained in the task of reconstruction. If it matters that a Visigoth broke a head, Gibbon will say so, and in that case the Visigoth *did* make history.

The *Decline and Fall* is a constructed object in which the whole is made up of many thousands of discrete parts, and the portraits and episodes "are sketched on a vast canvas with tiny strokes" (Chapman 270). The work thus represents a remarkable marriage of empiricism with neoclassicism, joining facts to form, or explaining facts through form. And that is certainly the significance of neoclassicism for its more thoughtful admirers: not tidy packaging, but an attempt to locate significant structure in the chaos of experience. This is the point at which eighteenth-century history writing differs most fundamentally from its modern heirs. As historiography has gained in subtlety and self-awareness, it has come increasingly to recognize that while history is story and story implies art, the complexity and confusion of human experience resist the harmonious shape of traditional art. In Dale Porter's words, "The fact of discord in actual events explains why historical narratives often appear less satisfying than their fictional counterparts—why they have a problem with 'loose ends'" (137). Gibbon, like Fielding, offers a narrative structure more shapely and coherent than anything the participants could ever perceive, and *Tom Jones* and the *Decline and Fall* are twin monuments to the neoclassical ethos—terminal moraines, as someone has said of Joyce's *Ulysses*. Burke and Godwin, as we shall see, perceive the flow of history as open-ended and dangerous in a way that Gibbon repudiates; and it is perhaps a truism to say that for both Gibbon and Fielding, art quite nakedly compensates for the frustrations of life.

The gulf between Gibbon and modern historiography is revealed not so much in his selection of details or in his investment of personal feeling, as in his dismissive remark about meaningless battles. Gibbon's true subject is what Fernand Braudel calls *la longue durée*, the immense movement of a culture over time, but the model he has to work with is *l'histoire événementielle*, the narrative of discrete events. Such a model encourages a sense that (in Braudel's words) "history is nothing but a monotonous game, always changing yet always the same, like the thousand combinations of pieces in a game of chess—a game constantly calling forth analogous situations and feelings which are always the same, with everything governed by the eternal, pitiless recurrence of things" (11). But the unchangeable human nature in which Gibbon, Hume, and Johnson believed was thrown into doubt by the revolution of the 1790s and by a growing consciousness, which the revolution confirmed rather than created, that experience could be unique and change could be irreversible.

4

Hume, Gibbon, Johnson
The Fictions of Belief

ARGUMENTS AND BELIEFS

URING the eighteenth century the normal way of explaining mankind's place in the world was to invoke a religious context.
Even if the Christian myth was gradually losing its power as an
all-encompassing structure of interpretation, most writers continued to regard their writings as sustained by, and confirming, Christian values, even
while they felt compelled to integrate traditional beliefs with up-to-date
empiricism. Theological ideas, narrowly considered, represented a diminishing subdivision of experience. But religion in its largest implications
still lay at the center of symbolic world-making, and skeptical critiques
of its assumptions lie at the point of fracture between the old intellectual
world and the new.

By the middle of the century it was increasingly possible to imagine a
world in which Christian explanatory principles were irrelevant or even
mistaken. The modern paganism of the Enlightenment, as Peter Gay calls
it, was of crucial importance in shaping a modern world whose "reality"
is a product of two disparate factors: the sheer accumulated mass of facts,
and the psychological structuring that takes place in social groups and
in the private consciousness of individuals. Hume and Gibbon together
mounted the most sustained British assault on traditional ways of thinking
about religion. Hume was more radical in his exploration of the psychological bases of belief; Gibbon preferred to take these for granted and to
survey, with what he hoped was detached objectivity, their consequences
in historical experience.

Defining *belief* in his *Dictionary* of 1755, Johnson begins with "credit
given to something which we know not of ourselves, on account of the

authority by which it is delivered," and then "the theological virtue of faith, or firm confidence of the truths of religion." Only after establishing these traditional foundations of belief does Johnson mention "persuasion; opinion." In the culture as a whole, however, the role of authority was steadily dwindling in response to the notion that Johnson expresses elsewhere, that "belief ought to be proportioned to evidence or probability" (*Adventurer* No. 69). In effect empiricist philosophy was driving a wedge between belief and doctrine, as is evident in Hume's repeated identification of belief with the "vivacity" with which an idea is held. Belief is now a matter not of spiritual commitment but of psychological intensity, and this in turn is tied directly to the experience of the senses.

A poetical description may have a more sensible effect on the fancy than an historical narration. It may collect more of those circumstances that form a complete image or picture. It may seem to set the object before us in more lively colours. But still the ideas it presents are different to the *feeling* from those, which arise from the memory and the judgment. There is something weak and imperfect, amidst all that seeming vehemence of thought and sentiment, which attends the fictions of poetry. (*Treatise* 631)

Applied to religion, this formulation suggests the twin corollaries that religious belief is a poetical fiction inferior in truth-value to empirical experience, and that the proper way to understand the significance of religion is by "historical narration." From both points of view, religious convictions are increasingly seen to arise from human needs.

Hume's *Dialogues concerning Natural Religion*, written in the 1750s and published posthumously in 1779, has always been recognized as a polemical masterpiece. Historians of philosophy have tended to dwell on its sequence of arguments and to quarrel a bit over which of them are "Hume's." Perhaps more to the point, the work is a psychological drama that exposes the personal and cultural needs that arguments are invoked to shore up, and is profoundly modern in calling into question the traditional way of understanding the world that most people still hoped was self-evident. Each of the three speakers is genuinely a character—not a novelistic personality, but an embodied way of responding to experience. And each of the three represents one of the main directions in which belief was tending in the later eighteenth century: Demea reflects its privatization, Cleanthes its secularization, and Philo its marginalization.

Hume's purpose is to show that faith, if one has it at all, must be grounded entirely on non-naturalistic intuitions. He thinks of course that it cannot be so grounded and should therefore be dismissed, but he is willing to concede that others still insist on it; he thus prepares the way not only for agnostic naturalism but for Kierkegaardian existentialism as well. The *Dialogues* will repay a reading from this point of view: not as an argument against particular beliefs, but as a dramatization of the ways in which beliefs are entertained and defended.

Religious belief in the seventeenth century was generally fideistic, most famously in the "wager" or leap of faith of Pascal, and was explicitly distinguished from discursive reasoning. Dryden says in the preface to *Religio Laici* (1682) that he is "naturally inclined to skepticism in philosophy" and therefore insists on revelation as the sole foundation for belief: "They who would prove religion by reason, do but weaken the cause which they endeavour to support: 'tis to take away the pillars from our faith, and to prop it only with a twig." Hume's profound attack on causality would not have alarmed an occasionalist theologian, who would have held that the universe is sustained at every instant (or "occasion") by the arbitrary power of God. Even the urbane Robert South, in a sermon entitled *All Contingencies under the Direction of God's Providence*, remarks that we know nothing of the future, and "whether God will continue the world 'till tomorrow or no, we cannot know by any certain argument, either from the nature of God, or of the world" (1:280).

Half a century later, Hume's Demea is made to seem fussy and old-fashioned in clinging to this position. He finds himself in temporary alliance with Philo who has his own purpose for exposing the impotence of analogical reasoning, but he walks out in horror when he belatedly realizes that Philo's naturalistic skepticism is a diabolical parody of the Pascalian kind. Cleanthes meanwhile is the man in the middle, determined to defend his deism with analogies drawn from familiar experience: as a clock suggests a clockmaker, so the universe suggests a creator. "The religious hypothesis," Cleanthes maintains, is "founded on the simplest and most obvious arguments," and he praises Locke for defending "natural reason" against the cavils of both Catholics and Reformers. "Locke seems to have been the first Christian, who ventured openly to assert, that *faith* was nothing but a species of *reason*, that religion was only a branch of philosophy, and that a chain of arguments, similar to that which established any truth in morals, politics, or physics, was always employed in discovering all the principles of theology, natural and revealed" (138).

As Hume perceives, Lockean empiricism represents a crucial turning point in cultural history. An increasing number of people now take it for granted that naturalistic evidence is the only kind that counts, or else they have to assert an uneasy distinction between one kind of evidence for religion and another kind for everything else. Johnson, for instance, is deeply skeptical about Highlanders' claims to possess "second sight" or to have heard the original poems of Ossian, but he cannot afford to license the same skepticism in matters of faith, however much his temperament might incline him that way: "Every thing which Hume has advanced against Christianity had passed through my mind long before he wrote" (Boswell, *Life* 1:444). These are doubts that were natural to an intelligent person in the eighteenth century, and as Johnson sees clearly, "truth" has to be protected from them by a kind of quarantine. But if theists need to segregate the religious realm from the method of experience, this is a step which they are very reluctant to take.

Recognizing that the world around us does not clearly exhibit an all-powerful.and loving God, Demea accepts the doctrine of original sin according to which we inhabit a world that has been horribly mutilated through our own fault. His God is the unknown God of the Reformation and of Pascalian Jansenism, the *deus absconditus* in whom human beings must believe even if they can no longer communicate with him. Since in his opinion the visible universe is far from demonstrating anything comforting about God, Demea refuses to concede that we can prove anything about God's "nature," holding that it is enough to be certain of his "being" and to rely on revelation for the rest (*Dialogues* 141). This had long been the function of "natural religion": to confirm certain premises about God's existence, but not necessarily to explain how or why he acts as he does. Thus Duns Scotus argued that Aquinas' proofs of God, like those of his master Aristotle, prove the existence of an unmoved mover but not of an omnipotent and providential deity. And William of Occam, honing the instrument of reason still more keenly, denied even that God's existence, unity, and infinity could be proved. The Christian must therefore rely upon, rather than try to supplement, the convictions of faith.

But people in the eighteenth century were increasingly suspicious of fideism, and demanded that God's essential attributes be deduced from the world of phenomena. For Hume's Cleanthes, accordingly, to exclude the method of experience is simply to exclude truth. "In vain would the sceptic make a distinction between science and common life, or between one science and another. The arguments employed in all, if just, are of a similar nature, and contain the same force and evidence" (137). In Hume's philosophy, Demea's distinction between nature and being is meaningless. We cannot say that anything "is" unless we can also say something about its nature. Hume says in the *Treatise*, "The idea of existence is the very same with the idea of what we conceive to be existent. . . . Nothing is ever really present with the mind but its perceptions or impressions and ideas, and . . . external objects become known to us only by those perceptions they occasion" (66–67). When Demea produces a version of the classic ontological proof, Cleanthes brusquely dismisses it as empty a priori speculation. In keeping with the program of empiricism, he is committed to a posteriori reasoning: "Whence can any cause be known but from its known effects? Whence can any hypothesis be proved but from the apparent phenomena?" (199–200).

Seeing the logic of this position, Demea tries to step back into the seventeenth century, holding (as Johnson does in criticizing Pope's *Essay on Man*) that if Christianity takes Cleanthes' route it is lost: theodicies that argue the perfection of nature yield a God who is not superior to nature. Meanwhile Philo, Hume's spokesman, stands apart from the struggle between Demea and Cleanthes, encouraging each to press just those arguments that will weaken the other. It is essential to recognize that Philo does not attempt to prove that God does not exist, or even that God is not benevolent. There is no need to prove a negative, and a skeptic is in no position to take a definite stand one way or the other. The one time Philo finds himself in a difficult corner is when Cleanthes throws the burden of proof upon him: "If you can . . . prove mankind to be unhappy or corrupted, there is an end at once of all religion. For to what purpose establish the natural attributes of the Deity, while the moral are still doubtful and uncertain?" (199). Philo might indeed find it hard to prove this, but as William Capitan demonstrates, the dramatic situation rescues him: Demea intervenes with a traditional rationalization of evil, Cleanthes retaliates by asserting man's happiness, and the shoe is now on the other foot with Cleanthes obliged to prove the unprovable.

This maneuver is not just a sleight of hand on Hume's part. Philosophical positions derive from human needs, and it is a matter of temperament whether one or another argument is felt to satisfy them. For this reason the modern scholarly debate about the cogency of Hume's arguments in the *Dialogues*, not to mention about the extent to which they are fully "his" rather than Philo's or Cleanthes', in a way misses the point. Certainly Hume identifies with Philo more than with Cleanthes. But part of his purpose is to show how deeply each character needs to insist on certain positions, since an entire world view rests upon them, whether or not they can be adequately defended against the objections of someone who occupies a different position. In an age when different and incompatible world views are beginning to be available as genuine options, representations of reality—even in philosophical argument—can no longer hide their fictive basis, and Hume's *Dialogues* is overtly a fiction about human fictions.

Against Cleanthes' claim that human life is essentially happy, Philo retorts with a very Johnsonian appeal: "But this is contrary to every one's feeling and experience; it is contrary to an authority so established as nothing can subvert" (201). The only escape from despair, Philo says, is to assert truths that lie outside the evidence of experience.

> Why is there any misery at all in the world? Not by chance surely. From some cause then. Is it from the intention of the Deity? But he is perfectly benevolent. Is it contrary to his intention? But he is almighty. Nothing can shake the solidity of this reasoning, so short, so clear, so decisive; except we assert that these subjects exceed all human capacity, and that our common measures of truth and falsehood are not applicable to them. (201)

With evident irony, Philo here pretends to embrace the orthodox position that Demea represents, covertly implying that it is high time to repudiate the fideistic illogic that clings to the Christian God in the face of actual experience. But reasoning analogically from experience is precisely what Cleanthes is committed to. "If we abandon all human analogy, as seems your intention, DEMEA, I am afraid we abandon all religion, and retain no conception of the great object of our adoration" (203).

Cleanthes is therefore vulnerable to Philo's freewheeling alternatives to the Christian world picture. Analogy might well lead us to conclude, Philo suggests, that the world "was only the first rude essay of some infant Deity, who afterwards abandoned it, ashamed of his lame performance; it is the work only of some dependent, inferior Deity, and is the object of derision to his superiors; it is the production of old age and dotage in some superannuated Deity, and ever since his death has run on at adventures, from the first impulse and active force which it received from him" (169). These conjectures, if playful, are far from frivolous. That there is order in the universe, Philo freely acknowledges, but he will not concede that it bears any definite analogy with human intelligence. The universe might just as well be compared to an animal or a vegetable, "and when CLEANTHES asks me what is the cause of my great vegetative or generative faculty, I am equally entitled to ask him the cause of his great reasoning principle" (179).

To suggestions like these, Cleanthes wearily replies that he cannot keep up with Philo's "fertility of invention" (181). But that is exactly Philo's point: "a thousand more of the same kind" are perfectly plausible so long as analogy is accorded a privileged position (169). These are the products of fancy rather than reason, since reason is helpless here and Hume will not concede any mode of spiritual knowing higher than reason. And fancy, for Hume as much as for Johnson, is a purely arbitrary faculty. Philo even calls it "she" as if to emphasize its ludic otherness from himself:

After [a man] opens his eyes, and contemplates the world as it really is, it would be impossible for him, at first, to assign the cause of any one event; much less, of the whole of things or of the universe. He might set his fancy a rambling; and she might bring him in an infinite variety of reports and representations. These would all be possible; but being all equally possible, he would never, of himself, give a satisfactory account for his preferring one of them to the rest. Experience alone can point out to him the true cause of any phenomenon. (145–46)

If experience is allowed to supply its data, the fictions by which the mind interprets them will have a more or less reliable connection with a shared reality. But if fancy operates with complete freedom, its fictions will be connected with nothing at all.

Argument having failed, Cleanthes summons rhetoric to persuade Philo that the universe proclaims its maker, proposing an analogy that poignantly embodies a dying metaphor:

Suppose, therefore, that an articulate voice were heard in the clouds, much louder and more melodious than any which human art could ever reach. Suppose, that this voice were extended in the same instant over all nations, and spoke to each nation in its own language and dialect. Suppose, that the words delivered not only contain a just sense and meaning, but convey some instruction altogether worthy of a benevolent Being, superior to mankind. Could you possibly hesitate a moment concerning the cause of this voice? (152)

Of course not. But that is exactly what is at issue: God no longer speaks compellingly from the sky in articulate language, let alone with an unmediated presence as when he walked with Adam and Eve in the cool of the evening. As Addison puts it in his ode "The spacious firmament on high" (first published in the *Spectator* in 1712), the planets move "in solemn silence" through the heavens, though they continue to proclaim their divine maker. In this demythologized universe there is no longer any pretense, as there had been in Renaissance poetry, that the physical ear might hear the music of the spheres. Only in "reason's ear" can the glorious voice be perceived, and God's message is now "published" in the endless cycles of the Newtonian heavens.

For many people, a vague understanding of Newton's achievement helped to guarantee a continued belief in God's creation. Thus Pope:

> Nature, and nature's laws lay hid in night;
> God said, Let Newton be! and all was light.

But a profound mathematician like Pascal was well aware of how much was lost when the old symbolic order broke down: "Le silence éternel de ces espaces infinis m'effraie" (*Pensées* No. 392). Hume grasped as Pope did not that by "admitting no principles but such as were founded on experiment," Newtonian science limited its aims and renounced metaphysical explanation. "While Newton seemed to draw off the veil from some of the mysteries of nature, he showed at the same time the imperfections of the mechanical philosophy; and thereby restored her ultimate secrets to that obscurity in which they ever did and ever will remain" (*History of England* 6:329).

Empiricist philosophy was still more destructive to traditional religion than Newtonian physics was, since it reduced experience to epistemology and ultimately to psychology. "All the sciences," Hume says in the *Treatise*, "have a relation, greater or less, to human nature. . . . Even *Mathematics, Natural Philosophy, and Natural Religion*, are in some measure dependent on the science of MAN; since they lie under the cognizance of men, and are judged of by their powers and faculties" (xix). Pope proclaims that "the proper study of mankind is man" but grounds the *Essay on Man* on received religious and metaphysical ideas; Hume's lifelong project is to reverse the sequence. An inspired misprint in Kemp Smith's edition of the *Dialogues* makes Philo say, "What peculiar privilege has this little agitation of the rain which we call thought, that we must thus make it the model of the whole universe?" (148). It should be *brain,* of course, not *rain,* but the two nouns express the same mechanist universe, in which the jostling of percepts in the mind is similar in every way to the ceaseless rain of atoms through the void. Naturalistic explanation must account for everything, not just some things, and "the experimental reasoning itself" is nothing more than "a species of instinct or mechanical power" (*Inquiry . . . Understanding* 115–16).

At the very end of the *Dialogues*, Philo notoriously seems to back down and acknowledge the truth of religion, but (some incidental ironies apart) he does so entirely by limiting religion to a minimal position which no traditional theist could accept: "one simple, though somewhat ambiguous, at least undefined proposition, *that the cause or causes of order in the universe probably bear some remote analogy to human intelligence*" (227). This is a religion so fully natural—if indeed it qualifies as "religion" at all—that Philo disavows atheism only by asking "whether the rotting of a turnip, the generation of an animal, and the structure of human thought be not energies that probably bear some remote analogy to each other" (218). It is perfectly obvious that the universe exhibits order, but no one can say why it does or what, if any, should be the implications for human life. One may even argue that Hume regards this minimal belief in order as irrational on his own part, the result perhaps of early education and habits of thought which even the most resolute skeptic cannot overcome (Penelhum, *Hume* 189–96).

At all events the skeptic is precluded from decisive opinions of any kind, difficult though it may be for human nature to give up wanting them. Whenever arguments present themselves that "run wide of common life" like those of natural religion, "the mind must remain in suspense between them; and it is that very suspense or balance, which is the triumph of scepticism" (*Dialogues* 135–36). For this reason Hume writes severely in his *History of England* about the so-called skeptic Hobbes, whose destructive dogmatism is in fact the very reverse of true skepticism (5:440). The *philosophes* in Paris, Gibbon says similarly, "laughed at the skepticism of Hume, preached the tenets of atheism with the bigotry of dogmatists, and damned all believers with ridicule and contempt" (*Memoirs* 136).

In the study of visible nature, however, a skeptical suspense would be just as inappropriate as misplaced dogmatism, as Hume goes on to say. "It was remarked, that no physician in Europe, who had reached forty years of age, ever, to the end of his life, adopted Harvey's doctrine of the circulation of the blood, and that his practice in London diminished extremely, from the reproach drawn upon him by that great and signal discovery. So slow is the progress of truth in every science, even when not opposed by factious or superstitious prejudices!" (*History* 5:440–41). Hume is perfectly willing to speak of "truth" in such contexts as this, but he rejects it as meaningless in the context which, for traditional believers, is the ultimate one that informs every other.

In religion as in medicine, people believe what they want to believe. For the orthodox, religion is an existential fact that underlies and guarantees all other experience. For Hume, it is an anomaly that calls for explanation: beneath the reasoned arguments in the *Dialogues* lie temperamental needs that the arguments exist to satisfy, or to shore up. At the beginning of the crucial Part X, Demea quite openly grounds his faith on feelings of anxiety and guilt:

It is my opinion, I own, replied DEMEA, that each man feels, in a manner, the truth of religion within his own breast; and from a consciousness of his imbecility and misery, rather than from any reasoning, is led to seek protection from that Being on whom he and all nature is dependent. So anxious or so tedious are even the best scenes of life, that futurity is still the object of all our hopes and fears. . . . Wretched creatures that we are! What resource for us amidst the innumerable ills of life, did not religion suggest some methods of atonement, and appease those terrors with which we are incessantly agitated and tormented? (193)

Demea's appeal fails to move Cleanthes simply because he does not *feel* it. "I can observe something like what you mention in some others, replied CLEANTHES, but I confess I feel little or nothing of it in myself, and hope that it is not so common as you represent it" (197).

The logical next step, in which Hume participates in the program of the Enlightenment at large, is to develop a natural history of religion. Theology resolves into psychology in the individual case, and into historical anthropology in the general. Guilty fears like Demea's are diagnosed as self-perpetuating, since they project an impossibly high religious ideal that imposes, in turn, an impossibly harsh abnegation of self. Johnson begins a *Rambler* with the grim observation,

That to please the Lord and Father of the universe is the supreme interest of created and dependent beings, as it is easily proved, has been universally confessed; and since all rational agents are conscious of having neglected or violated the duties prescribed to them, the fear of being rejected or punished by God has always burdened the human mind. The expiation of crimes, and renovation of the forfeited hopes of divine favour, therefore constitutes a large part of every religion. (No. 110)

Hume would agree that (modern) religion dwells on guilt and expiation, but he would reject every one of Johnson's premises—that God is a father, that he prescribes duties, that human beings will be punished for disobeying them, and that each of these claims can be "easily proved."

If most eighteenth-century people still agree with Johnson, Hume diagnoses their situation in the terms he gives to Philo in the *Dialogues*: having conquered all his natural enemies, man invents "*imaginary* enemies, the daemons of his fancy, who haunt him with superstitious terrors and blast every enjoyment of life" (195). The source of a guilt like Johnson's must lie in a painful psychogenesis. Moreover, it is not just a matter of private spirituality. A religion of fear and punishment promotes "virtues" that are actually antisocial vices, since the postulate of an infinitely superior God operates "to sink the human mind into the lowest submission and abasement, and to represent the monkish virtues of mortification, penance, humility, and passive suffering as the only qualities which are acceptable to him" (*Natural History of Religion* 52).

By replacing man firmly in the natural world, Hume, like the *philosophes* with whom he was allied, issues a challenge to free the mind from needless self-abasement. In a naturalized universe the present life is the only one there is, and to degrade it by adoring a remote and demanding

God is far worse than to adopt the charming fictions (as Hume sees them) of classical polytheism.

> The fables of the pagan religion were, of themselves, light, easy, and familiar; without devils, or seas of brimstone, or any object that could much terrify the imagination. Who could forbear smiling, when he thought of the loves of MARS and VENUS, or the amorous frolics of JUPITER and PAN? In this respect, it was a true poetical religion; if it had not rather too much levity for the graver kinds of poetry. We find that it has been adopted by modern bards; nor have these talked with greater freedom and irreverence of the gods, whom they regarded as fictions, than the ancients did of the real objects of their devotion. (61)

Poetry is fiction, fiction is fanciful, and a "true poetical religion" is attractive for its abdication of serious truth claims like those of Christianity. "Hume does not object to the spirit becoming flesh, as long as it is the flesh of a worldly Jupiter and not of an unworldly Jesus" (Siebert 392).

Still more to the point, Hume thinks he sees plenty of evidence that even for those who profess Christianity, it has in fact dwindled into a fiction that may be convenient but is no longer firmly held. Hume's critique is devastating because it appeals to what people do rather than to what they say:

> We may observe that notwithstanding the dogmatical, imperious style of all superstition, the conviction of the religionists, in all ages, is more affected than real, and scarcely ever approaches, in any degree, to that solid belief and persuasion which governs us in the common affairs of life. Men dare not avow, even to their own hearts, the doubts which they entertain on such subjects: they make a merit of implicit faith, and disguise to themselves their real infidelity by the strongest asseverations and most positive bigotry. But nature is too hard for all their endeavours, and suffers not the obscure, glimmering light, afforded in those shadowy regions, to equal the strong impressions made by common sense and by experience. The usual course of men's conduct belies their words, and shows that their assent in these matters is some unaccountable operation of the mind between disbelief and conviction, but approaching much nearer to the former than to the latter. (*Natural History* 60)

Or as Hume says even more trenchantly later on, "Hear the verbal protestations of all men: nothing so certain as their religious tenets. Examine their lives: you will scarcely think that they repose the smallest confidence in them" (75). If most people still claim to believe in Christianity, that may be due to an assumption that it remains useful to social order, whether or not it still satisfies spiritual needs. "If I thought Deism the true religion," Dr. Pringle says superbly in Boswell's *London Journal*, "I would not say so to my wife" (278).

As matters now stand, therefore, many people enjoy religion as nothing more than an aesthetic experience, and they may even relish Johnsonian fears in this artificial context.

We may add . . . that in matters of religion men take a pleasure in being terrified, and that no preachers are so popular as those who excite the most dismal and gloomy passions. In the common affairs of life, where we feel and are penetrated with the solidity of the subject, nothing can be more disagreeable than fear and terror; and 'tis only in dramatic performances and in religious discourses that they ever give pleasure. In these latter cases the imagination reposes itself indolently on the idea; and the passion, being softened by the want of belief in the subject, has no more than the agreeable effect of enlivening the mind and fixing the attention. (*Treatise* 115)

Far from resting upon belief, then, eighteenth-century religion is characterized by want of belief. In the case of art, no one pretends that the unreal is real; "the least reflection dissipates the illusions of poetry, and places the objects in their proper light" (123). But the poet himself, perhaps, sometimes temporarily achieves a willing suspension of disbelief: "In the warmth of a poetical enthusiasm, a poet has a counterfeit belief, and even a kind of vision of his objects" (123). Religious "enthusiasm," by implication—one thinks of Methodism as satirized in eighteenth-century novels—is a similarly willed illusion, but one whose votaries are reluctant to see it exposed.

Hume undoubtedly thought that so far as argument went, he had delivered a fatal blow to natural religion. But beyond the boundaries of argument, he recognized that belief is both psychologically and culturally conditioned. As has often been remarked, his skepticism functions mainly to demolish extravagant claims for reason, while ordinary life continues to rest securely on instinctual guarantees which "nature" provides. If language is a game, Hume recognizes that his three characters are playing by different rules. Philo may win in Hume's opinion, but he certainly fails to convince Cleanthes, let alone Demea. And their young auditor Pamphilus declares at the end, as many an eighteenth-century reader might, "Upon a serious review of the whole, I cannot but think that PHILO's principles are more probable than DEMEA's, but that those of CLEANTHES approach still nearer to the truth" (228). This is usually regarded as a red herring intended to distract attention from Hume's own identification with Philo. But it may also represent his recognition that arguments can be found to support any position, and that no argument will overcome entrenched resistance.

Hume remarks in the *Treatise*, "Belief is more properly an act of the sensitive, than of the cogitative part of our natures" (183), and he does not hesitate to represent his own beliefs in this light: "Can I be sure that in leaving all established opinions I am following truth; and by what criterion shall I distinguish her, even if fortune should at last guide me on her footsteps? After the most accurate and exact of my reasonings, I can give no reason why I should assent to it; and feel nothing but a *strong* propensity to consider objects *strongly* in that view, under which they appear to me" (265). Demea's orthodoxy, Cleanthes' deism, and Philo's skepticism all rest on strong propensities, and exemplify the psychological basis of the "reality" that each person inhabits.

Disbelief, William James observes in *The Principles of Psychology*, is a matter not of mental inaction but of believing "something else which contradicts the first thing." The opposite of belief is doubt, not disbelief (2:914). Hume is professionally committed to doubt, but he is well aware that the mind *wants* to believe, and that it is eager to find grounds for belief in psychological associations that have little to do with argument and proof.

A man, whose memory presents him with a lively image of the *Red Sea*, and the *Desert*, and *Jerusalem*, and *Galilee*, can never doubt of any miraculous events which are related either by *Moses or the Evangelists*. The lively idea of the places passes by an easy transition to the facts, which are supposed to have been related to them by contiguity, and increases the belief by increasing the vivacity of the conception. The remembrance of these fields and rivers has the same influence on the vulgar as a new argument; and from the same causes. (*Treatise* 110–11)

James, who quotes this passage (2:931), emphasizes the chain of associations by which a person's structure of beliefs depends upon personal experience and temperament: "Our requirements in the way of reality terminate in our own acts and emotions, our own pleasures and pains. These are the ultimate fixities from which . . . the whole chain of our beliefs depends, object hanging to object, as the bees, in swarming, hang to each other until, *de proche en proche,* the supporting branch, the Self, is reached and held" (2:939). But such "fixities" would not have looked very fixed to Milton or Johnson. Empiricism, even when it claimed to confirm the religious basis of existence, was systematically demolishing the vertical dimension that had connected the world of phenomena with a metaphysical structure of meaning through which they might be organized and understood.

Speaking for a modern pragmatism, Hilary Putnam says, "If philosophy which simply scorns our intuitions is not worth the candle, philosophy which tries to preserve *all* of them becomes a vain attempt to have the past over again" (29). This is what eighteenth-century deists like Cleanthes are doing: accepting the canons of evidence that modern science demands, but claiming that this kind of evidence substantiates the Christian world picture. Philo has Cleanthes in a bind because both disputants accept the modern premise that William James states in *Pragmatism*:

The truth of "God" has to run the gauntlet of all our other truths. It is on trial by them and they on trial by it. Our *final* opinion about God can be settled only after all the truths have straightened themselves out together. Let us hope that they shall find a *modus vivendi*! (79)

This is Cleanthes' hope, but Philo (and Hume) believe it to be illusory.

Hume would agree with James that "all our theories are *instrumental*, are mental modes of *adaptation* to reality, rather than revelations or gnostic answers to some divinely instituted world-enigma" (127). Hume is therefore willing to grant a hearing to "the religious hypothesis" because, as James says, "on pragmatic principles we cannot reject any hypothesis if consequences useful to life flow from it" (177). Demea holds to the old revelation of divinely instituted enigma, and Hume grants that this belief does produce useful consequences *for Demea*. But he denies that Cleanthes' much more limited religious hypothesis really works— that it guarantees or explains anything that is not already secured on other grounds. Demea, in a word, needs his faith; Cleanthes is nostalgic for a faith that he would like to retain but does not actually need or use.

One might well ask why religious beliefs, since some people certainly hold them strongly, are not just as unassailable as "natural beliefs" about the physical world. The answer seems to be that "the causes of religious beliefs are pathological and, with luck, education and reflection can overcome them; so religious belief is not inescapable in the way natural belief is" (Penelhum, "Natural Belief" 166). So if in one sense the *Dialogues* points forward to Kierkegaard, in another it is very much a product of the Enlightenment. It is no wonder that the Continental tradition of philosophy has had little use for Hume, who rejected as empty the puzzles about ontology that have so preoccupied phenomenology and existentialism, and that continue to preoccupy poststructuralist thinkers like Derrida who, as Giles Gunn points out, pursue a "transcendence beyond negativity" in language that sounds, and perhaps is, religious (50).

The burden of Hume's critique, of which twentieth-century "ordinary language philosophy" is a lineal descendant, is to decline the seductive appeal of metaphysics, which seeks to understand the nature of being and regards the inability to understand it as a profound revelation. In Stanley Cavell's words, "It is a departure from ordinary language to say either that I do or that I do not believe there are material objects; so to that extent, it would be incoherent to provide a 'defense' of such a 'belief' " (186). From this point of view Hume's critique of religion, like Gibbon's, might seem to imply a betrayal of his own premises: if people behave as if the doctrines of Christianity are true, then one cannot ask for further proofs of their belief. But in fact that is precisely Hume's point: whatever may have been the case in the first century A.D., people do *not* behave any longer as if they really believed in Christian doctrine.

So the *Dialogues* offers both a psychology of belief and a critique of belief, and the critique works not so much by argument as by assaulting the psychology. Very similarly, when Candide stands weltering in blood and exclaims, "If this is the best of all possible worlds, what can the rest be like?" (Voltaire 37), Voltaire knows that he has not refuted Leibnizian optimism, whose premise is that it is impossible for human beings to grasp the infinite considerations that led God to create the particular world we live in. Voltaire's intention, as Peter Kivy says, is "to 'confound' the optimist by putting his belief system under stress" (222). This is exactly what Philo does to the belief systems of Demea and Cleanthes. One may add that Johnson's horror of Hume, and Boswell's fascinated attraction to Hume, reflect the way in which traditional belief systems were under stress throughout the culture of the eighteenth century.

RELIGION AS HISTORICAL EXPERIENCE

Hume studies the natural history of religion, Gibbon its political history. Both writers investigate a major phenomenon of culture, but if Hume's interpretation is psychological and anthropological, Gibbon's is sociological. And whereas Hume's psychological explanation of belief is relatively sympathetic—he takes pains to portray the Demea temperament fairly—Gibbon focuses on the trouble that religion can cause. Reconstructing religious fictions, Hume tries to see them from the inside, even while making it clear that some insides look more satisfactory than others. Gibbon, in keeping with his program of commanding the past, sees them from outside or above.

Hume deploys dramatic irony to indicate that people inhabit separate worlds: Demea imagines that he and Philo are saying the same thing, but the reader appreciates that language is profoundly contextual, so that an identical sequence of words can have radically different implications for different people. Gibbon insists on maintaining control to such an extent that his famous ironies are usually sarcasms, dismissing in advance any possible authority on the part of the voices being mocked. In *Childe*

Harold's Pilgrimage Byron speaks of Gibbon as "the lord of irony," "sapping a solemn creed with solemn sneer" (3.107). But it is important to remember that Gibbon is first and foremost a historian, not a satirist. His aim is to expose the historical foundations of religion, and the play of rhetoric is intended to support the exposition, not to take its place.

Behind the asserted objectivity of Gibbon's treatment of religion, as Hume might have predicted, lurks submerged personal feeling. In his youth he was briefly drawn to Catholicism, but unlike the young Boswell, who was briefly intoxicated by its aesthetic features, Gibbon says that he responded intellectually. "The blind activity of idleness urged me to advance without armour into the dangerous mazes of controversy, and at the age of sixteen I bewildered myself in the errors of the Church of Rome" (*Memoirs* 84). Looking back in maturity, he sees only absurdity, a wish to believe rather than belief itself. "To my actual [i.e., *actuel*, present] feelings it seems incredible that I could ever believe that I believed in Transubstantiation!" (85). Burke remarks in passing that "our education is in a manner wholly in the hands of ecclesiastics, and in all stages from infancy to manhood" (*Reflections* 198). Both Hume and Gibbon are reacting against a central element in their early mental experience; Gibbon was tutored both by William Law (whose *Serious Call* made Johnson serious about religion) and by a Calvinist pastor in Switzerland.

As the repeated starts in Gibbon's drafts show, he has trouble understanding the extent of his boyhood commitment. In Carnochan's words, he first describes himself as a "passive plaything of fate," later as a "lost pilgrim," and finally as an "adolescent hero" fighting with inadequate intellectual armor (*Gibbon's Solitude* 146). Throughout the *Decline and Fall* the tendency of religions to seek converts is described with particular animus. Looking back ruefully at his own experience, Gibbon emphasizes the ways in which belief is conditioned, or perhaps even created, by social forces that stimulate that vivacity of conception that Hume identifies as its basis. So he says of the pagan philosopher-king Julian, whom on the whole he admires, "The acquisition of new proselytes gratified the ruling passions of his soul, superstition and vanity." Gibbon adds in a footnote, "Under the reign of Lewis XIV his subjects of every rank aspired to the glorious title of *Convertisseur,* expressive of their zeal and success in making proselytes. The word and idea are growing obsolete in France; may they never be introduced into England!" (2:476).

Even when Gibbon is willing to concede that religious feeling may grow from worthy roots, he still regards it as deluded. This is the burden of his portrait of Mohammed:

The energy of a mind incessantly bent on the same object would convert a general obligation into a particular call; the warm suggestings of the understanding or the fancy would be felt as the inspirations of heaven; the labour of thought would expire in rapture and vision; and the inward sensation, the invisible monitor, would be described with the form and attributes of an angel of God. From enthusiasm to imposture the step is perilous and slippery; the daemon of Socrates affords a memorable instance, how a wise man may deceive himself, how a good man may deceive others, how the conscience may slumber in a mixed and middle state between self-illusion and voluntary fraud. (5:400–401)

Gibbon considers it impossible that reason might condone spiritual vision, let alone aspire to it, and if Mohammed is not a deliberate deceiver, that is only because he is self-deceived.

Not only Christians, but Neoplatonic philosophers too are derided in the *Decline and Fall*: "Consuming their reason in these deep but unsubstantial meditations, their minds were exposed to illusions of fancy" (1:423). The fundamental fault of Neoplatonic thought is that it is "removed beyond the senses and the experience of mankind" (2:21). As for less intellectual forms of devotion, they are dismissed in the materialist terms of Swift's *Mechanical Operation of the Spirit*, for example the navel-gazing meditations of the monks of Mount Athos: "This light, the production of a distempered fancy, the creature of an empty stomach and an empty brain, was adored by the Quietists as the pure and perfect essence of God himself" (6:529). Petrarch's Greek friend Barlaam, Gibbon says, "rashly provoked the swarms of fanatic monks by attempting to substitute the light of reason to that of their navel" (7:124).

The vulgar will always be drawn to one form or another of superstition, whether pagan or Christian, but in ancient Rome the upper classes were able to pay lip service to traditional religion without having to believe that they believed. "On public occasions the philosophic part of mankind affected to treat with respect and decency the religious institutions of their country; but their secret contempt penetrated through the thin and awkward disguise" (2:59). As in Hume's philosophy, the goal is social harmony, not doctrinal assent: "The various modes of worship which prevailed in the Roman world were all considered by the people as equally true; by the philosopher as equally false; and by the magistrate as equally useful. And thus toleration produced not only mutual indulgence, but even religious concord" (1:31). Gibbon is perfectly explicit about the condescension of a philosophical upper class that engaged in devout practices without any devotion at all. "Viewing with a smile of pity and indulgence the various errors of the vulgar, they diligently practised the ceremonies of their fathers, devoutly frequented the temples of the gods;

and, sometimes condescending to act a part on the theatre of superstition, they concealed the sentiments of an Atheist under the sacerdotal robes" (1:34). Fictions work best when the right people know they are fictions.

Roman public religion, as Gibbon idealizes it, was charmingly social and generous, celebrating "hospitable deities" who symbolized "the genial powers of fecundity" and the other forces of nature (2:18–19). Unlike Christianity or Islam, Roman religion was not propositional, and Gibbon says in his *Vindication* that "Pagan worship was a matter, not of *opinion,* but of *custom*" (*English Essays* 285). Gossman underlines the point: "That social activity might be directed toward nothing or founded on nothing and yet be productive of something was perhaps a paradox for the philosopher, but for the practical magistrate and the empirical student of history and society, it was abundantly demonstrable. All history, in a sense, was the product of absurd or illusory beliefs and motives" (*Empire* 73). Such a recognition may seem comfortable so long as one's concern remains sociological, as Gibbon's does, but for philosophically inclined persons it is the trapdoor to an abyss of skepticism, and even Enlightenment thinkers might hesitate to step through it. If justice should turn out to be merely a function of human conventions, Usbek says in Montesquieu's *Lettres persanes,* "this would be such a terrible truth that we would have to hide it from ourselves" (Letter No. 82).

Augustine—whom Gibbon always treats with suspicion—denounced paganism not only because he saw it as the worship of demons, but also because it encouraged a theatrical pretence of belief that reflected existential bad faith. "Seneca, who had been, as it were, emancipated by the philosophers, but who was also an illustrious senator of the Roman people, worshipped what he criticized, performed acts which he reprehended, venerated what he condemned. . . . Because of the laws of the country and the accepted customs, he learnt that without playing an actor's part in theatrical fictions, he should imitate such a performance in the temple" (251). Gibbon, like many thinkers of the Enlightenment, has no commitment to sincerity in the Augustinian or Rousseauvian sense. One goes along with the customs of one's country, but inward assent, if it exists at all, is nobody's business but one's own. Gibbon wrote memoirs, not confessions, and although he concedes to Augustine "a strong, capacious, argumentative mind" (*Decline and Fall* 3:431), he has little sense of Augustine's imaginative genius, or of his theology as a response to the collapsing civilization that is Gibbon's own subject. Theology itself is surveyed at length in the *Decline and Fall,* but as a weird nest of intellectual conundrums, not as a system of compelling paradoxes. Having read through Augustine's *City of God*, with its vehement and tireless probing of the meaning of experience, Gibbon comments condescendingly, "His learning is too often borrowed, and his arguments are too often his own; but the whole work claims the merit of a magnificent design, vigorously, and not unskilfully, executed" (3:223n).

Christianity, by contrast with civic paganism, is in Gibbon's view a religion of negation, ridiculous when not dangerous. Like Hume, Gibbon believes that an antihumane asceticism is implicit in Christianity, even if not always given full expression. "Pleasure and guilt are synonymous terms in the language of the monks" (4:72). "The lives of the primitive monks were consumed in penance and solitude, undisturbed by the various occupations which fill the time, and exercise the faculties, of reasonable, active, and social beings" (4:76). Gibbon admires Mohammed's "carnal paradise" (5:374) and says approvingly, "Perfumes and women were the two sensual enjoyments which his nature required and his religion did not forbid" (5:402). The formulation is reminiscent of Dryden's lines on patriarchal polygamy in *Absalom and Achitophel*—"When nature prompted, and no law denied, / Promiscuous use of concubine and bride" (ll. 5–6)—and of Boswell's fantasy of "promiscuous concubinage." As for Christian denial of the flesh, it strikes Gibbon as both hypocritical and unrealizable. In a footnote he quotes a passage from Hume's *History of England* on a Norman lord who had a group of clergy castrated for choosing a bishop without his consent, "and made all their testicles be brought him in a platter." Gibbon adds slyly, "Of the pain and danger they might justly complain; yet, since they had vowed chastity, he deprived them of a superfluous treasure" (7:225n).

The fifteenth chapter of the *Decline and Fall* is filled with brisk ironies at the expense of the early church, which (as in Hume's critique of miracles) insisted on believing the unbelievable. Throughout that chapter and the next, Gibbon explains the success of Christianity by its appeal to the dispossessed classes. But the less famous forty-seventh chapter gives a richer analysis of the power of the new faith, elaborately surveying the dispute over the doctrine of the incarnation. It begins with a glimpse of the historical Jesus: "The familiar companions of Jesus of Nazareth conversed with their friend and countryman, who, in all the actions of rational and animal life, appeared of the same species with themselves. His progress from infancy to youth and manhood was marked by a regular increase in stature and wisdom; and, after a painful agony of mind and body, he expired on the cross" (5:105). For prudential reasons Gibbon is not prepared to declare openly that Christ was only a man and that his death on the cross was final, but there are asides elsewhere in the *Decline and Fall* that sufficiently indicate his views. A footnote quite early in the work carries a superbly insinuating parenthesis: "Apollonius of Tyana was born about the same time as Jesus Christ. His life (that of the former) is related in so fabulous a manner by his disciples, that we are at a loss to discover whether he was a sage, an impostor, or a fanatic" (1:328n). And there is a devastating note on allegations that the northern barbarians worshiped a she-goat: "I know but of one religion in which the god and the victim are the same" (5:9).

In Gibbon's opinion there can be no such thing as the incarnation, which has not prevented its establishment as a tenet that modern Europeans continue to hold. "*They* established, and *we* still embrace, the substantial, indissoluble, and everlasting union of a perfect God with a perfect man" (5:113). This result was achieved by interminable quarrels fought inside "the theological labyrinth" (5:114), whose windings Gibbon delights in recounting to modern Christians who are "ignorant or careless of their own belief concerning the mystery of the incarnation" (5:135), and whose assent to "supernatural truths is much less an active consent than a cold and passive acquiescence" (2:33).

One might well argue that in stressing the doctrinal content of belief, Gibbon shows himself ignorant of the psychological basis of faith. To the extent that he is concerned with the consciousness of individuals, this is essentially true; Gibbon is concerned not just to describe the Christian religion as a historical phenomenon but to embarrass it as a factor in eighteenth-century culture. Like Hume, he seeks to discredit Christianity by showing that modern Christians "believe," in the sense of paying lip service to, doctrines that they cannot possibly *believe,* or would not believe if they actually understood them.

Once faith has been discredited at the level of specific doctrines entertained by individual minds, it can be placed in a more comprehensive context as a social movement. "Our curiosity is naturally prompted to inquire by what means the Christian faith obtained so remarkable a victory over the established religions of the earth" (2:2). Augustine saw the progress of Christianity as a movement made up of individual souls; Gibbon sees it as a movement centered in dispossessed classes for whom it had profound worldly as well as otherworldly appeal. This is very much a question of the collective and political use of belief, and Gibbon's analysis is prescient at many points of the *mentalité* postulated by modern historiography. In Lucien Febvre's terms, a shared complex of emotions gives a group security and power, and the emotions thereby become "a sort of institution" (15).

It becomes clear that in Gibbon's view, doctrine serves as an agency of power, and that he is really talking about ideology rather than theology. Sainthood is a worldly reward, not a spiritual state; Cyril of Alexandria was one of the winners, "and the title of *saint* is a mark that his opinions and his party have finally prevailed" (5:114). What strikes Gibbon as significant about Cyril is not his "seven verbose folios," which "now peaceably slumber by the side of their rivals" (5:114), but the political power which religious authority allowed him to wield:

A rumour was spread among the Christians that the daughter of Theon was the only obstacle to the reconciliation of the praefect and the archbishop; and that obstacle was speedily removed. On a fatal day, in the holy season of Lent, Hypatia was torn from her chariot, stripped naked, dragged to the church, and inhumanly butchered by the hands of Peter the Reader and a troop of savage and merciless fanatics; her flesh was scraped from her bones with sharp oyster shells, and her quivering limbs were delivered to the flames. The just progress of inquiry and punishment was stopped by seasonable gifts; but the murder of Hypatia has imprinted an indelible stain on the character and religion of Cyril of Alexandria. (5:117)

Violence becomes the normal recourse of the ecclesiastical parties as they struggle for supremacy. " 'May those who divide Christ be divided with the sword, may they be hewn in pieces, may they be burnt alive!' were the charitable wishes of a Christian synod" (5:130).

The mob, which Gibbon despises just as Swift and Pope did, seizes upon convenient symbols for rivalry, and religious symbols serve as well as any. "The people of Constantinople was devoid of any rational principles of freedom; but they held, as a lawful cause of rebellion, the colour of a livery in the races, or the colour of a mystery in the schools" (5:139). Religious wars are political wars in disguise, and often represent nothing more than mob rule, fomented by cynical leaders to gain their own ends.

Day and night they were incessantly busied either in singing hymns to the honour of their God or in pillaging and murdering the servants of their prince. . . . The statues of the emperor were broken, and his person was concealed in a suburb, till, at the end of three days, he dared to implore the mercy of his subjects. . . . These furious but transient seditions were encouraged by the success of Vitalian, who, with an army of Huns and Bulgarians, for the most part idolaters, declared himself the champion of the Catholic faith. In this pious rebellion he depopulated Thrace, besieged Constantinople, exterminated sixty-five thousand of his fellow-Christians, till he obtained the recall of the bishops, the satisfaction of the pope, and the establishment of the council of Chalcedon. . . . And such was the event of the *first* of the religious wars which have been waged in the name, and by the disciples, of the God of peace. (5:140–41)

Gibbon's finely controlled rhetoric, like Voltaire's in *Candide*, throws a cool but powerful light on the hypocrisies embedded in a politicized Christianity.

As for doctrinal issues, they eventually resolved themselves along with the political settlement. "Before the end of the seventh century, the creed of the incarnation, which had been defined at Rome and Constantinople, was uniformly preached in the remote islands of Britain and Ireland; the same ideas were entertained, or rather the same words were repeated, by all the Christians whose liturgy was performed in the Greek or the Latin tongue" (5:153). A creed is nothing but words, and after the chaos and cruelty are finished, it can settle down into comfortable rote repetition because the hegemony that imposed it is secure. When Gibbon condemns "the spiritual despotism which shackles not only the actions but even the thoughts of the prostrate votary" (5:181), there is no doubt that he means political despotism as well.

Gibbon does not deny that Christianity made important contributions to culture; he says that at its best it taught the barbarians literacy, law, and mercy (4:86). What interests him is that it was able to do this by establishing itself as a successful ideology, driving out others that lacked its organizational abilities. And for all of its internal vitality, Christianity seems to Gibbon to have sapped the vitality of the empire. During the first centuries A.D. "the enemies of Rome were in her bosom—the tyrants, and the soldiers" (1:211). It is not surprising that tyrants would find the new religion a useful ally: "The throne of the emperors would be established on a fixed and permanent basis, if all their subjects, embracing the Christian doctrine, should learn to suffer and to obey" (2:314). Johnson says very differently of Constantine, in a legal memorandum written for Boswell's use, "Truth took possession of imperial power" (*Life* 3:60).

Julian's short-lived attempt to restore paganism is clearly attractive to Gibbon, but he does not idealize Julian, as writers like Shaftesbury and Voltaire had done, as a champion of toleration against religious persecution. For Julian was just as superstitious as the Christians, and Gibbon's grasp of the function of ideology helps him to recognize that the old religion was seriously lacking in competitive skills. "The genius and power of Julian were unequal to the enterprise of restoring a religion which was destitute of theological principles, of moral precepts, and of ecclesiastical discipline; which rapidly hastened to decay and dissolution, and was not susceptible of any solid or consistent reformation" (2:472). All three of these factors—doctrines, ethical orientation, and organization—were crucial in the worldly triumph of Christianity, which proclaimed that a better world awaited the faithful, insisted on rigid virtue, and enforced its beliefs with "that irresistible weight which even a small band of well-trained and intrepid volunteers has so often possessed over an undisciplined multitude, ignorant of the subject, and careless of the event of the war" (2: 57–58).

As a way of dramatizing the changes that occurred between the third and fifth centuries, Gibbon invokes the legend of the Seven Sleepers of Ephesus, who awoke in a world they could no longer recognize (3:439). It is interesting that Peter Brown, who uses the same legend to launch *The Making of Late Antiquity*, starts out from an investigation of the idea of the holy, a concept virtually invisible to Gibbon. Brown sees the myriad expressions of supernaturalism, whether Christian or pagan, as attempts to bring down "into the dubious and tension-ridden world beneath the moon a clarity and a stability associated with the unchanging heavens" (17). The quotations Brown chooses from religious writers, accordingly, sound very different from Gibbon's. The tranquil and regular movements of the stars "shone out, Eusebius said, as light streaming from the outer doors of the great palace of Heaven; little wonder that Eusebius would emphasize the manner in which Constantine showed himself on his coins, his eyes raised to that steady and perceptible light" (17). There is no room for this kind of poetry in the *Decline and Fall*, though Brown's analysis is just as unsentimental as Gibbon's, locating this highly structured religious consciousness in an age of ambition and competitiveness, in which otherworldly forces were called in as potent allies.

No eighteenth-century "philosophical historian," of course, would have been likely to think about religious ideas in these ways. But Gibbon's procedure is not the only possible one. A striking contrast to his externalized treatment of religion is suggested by a passage in Hume's *History of England* that describes a demented figure during the time of the Puritan Commonwealth:

James Naylor was a Quaker noted for blasphemy, or rather madness, in the time of the protectorship. He fancied that he himself was transformed into Christ, and was become the real saviour of the world, and in consequence of this frenzy he endeavoured to imitate many actions of the Messiah related in the evangelists. As he bore a resemblance to the common pictures of Christ, he allowed his beard to grow in a like form; he raised a person from the dead; he was ministered unto by women; he entered Bristol, mounted on a horse, I suppose from the difficulty in that place of finding an ass; his disciples spread their garments before him, and cried, "Hosannah to the highest! holy, holy is the Lord God of Sabaoth!" When carried before the magistrate, he would give no other answer to all questions than "Thou hast said it." What is remarkable, the Parliament thought that the matter deserved their attention. Near ten days they spent in inquiries and debates about him. They condemned him to be pilloried, whipped, burned in the face, and to have his tongue bored through with a red-hot iron. All these severities he bore with the usual patience. So far his delusion supported him. But the sequel spoiled all. He was sent to Bridewell, confined to hard labour, fed on bread and water, and debarred from all his disciples, male and female. His illusion dissipated, and after some time he was contented to come out an ordinary man, and return to his usual occupations. (5:431)

Hume obviously thinks that Naylor was a fanatic, and he has fun with his deadpan account, in which it is as easy to raise someone from the dead as to be ministered unto by women. But Hume also thinks that the Puritan regime was more dangerously fanatical than Naylor. The unhappy man needed therapy, not torture, and there really is something Christlike in the way he endured his suffering. What Hume is representing in this story is a national delusion, or cultural illness, from which England was fortunate to wake up as Naylor did and "return to its usual occupations." Gibbon emphasizes the narrowly political significance of supernatural belief: "The lame walked, the blind saw, the sick were healed, the dead were raised, daemons were expelled, and the laws of Nature were frequently suspended for the benefit of the Church" (*Decline and Fall* 2:74). Hume handles the same theme with similar ironic economy, but with sympathy as well.

Still, one ought not to conclude, as Trevelyan does, that " 'the age of common sense' had forgotten what a revolutionist or a religious fanatic was really like" (88). Whether or not Gibbon really knows what a fanatic is, he cannot afford to concede anything to "fanaticism." Hayden White says that in a historical narrative "the systems of meaning-production peculiar to a culture or society are tested against the capacity of any set of 'real' events to yield to such systems" ("The Question of Narrative" 21). In part Gibbon is engaged in a reconstructive act, testing the system of early Christianity against the "reality" of his own culture. But beyond that he is engaged, like Hume, in a polemic that tests eighteenth-century religious beliefs against their own reality system. His point about Christians who do not understand their own beliefs is that they do not actually *believe* those beliefs. From one point of view the *Decline and Fall* defies the majority consensus of its culture; from another point of view it seeks to encourage a developing consensus toward which that culture is or should be moving. In tracing the fall of empire Gibbon speaks to the community of British readers whose own empire, still growing, must one day decline and fall. In tracing the rise of Christianity he postulates an audience which in one sense is narrower, since most of his readers are still "believers," but in another sense is broader, since he tempts them to join the Enlightenment community of irony against religion. The *Decline and Fall*—rather like *Paradise Lost* with its "fit audience though few"—implies a true community of intelligent readers, and invites each individual reader to deserve to be within it.

THE DEFENSIVE REACTION

Cultural history tends to have a Whig coloration, placing its emphasis on those tendencies that seem to point forward into the future. But just as political radicalism was long resisted in Britain, so also was the religious critique of the Enlightenment; if the old fictions were increasingly revealed to be fictions, the strength of the conservative reaction shows how deeply many people still needed them. And as Johnson and Hume have been placed in dialogue throughout this book, it will be instructive to look briefly at the stratagems by which Johnson defended his beliefs against the empiricist assault.

When a companion praised, much as Hume or Gibbon might have done, "the candour and good humour" with which the ancient philosophers disputed, Johnson responded with a statement of great interest, lucidly reported by Boswell:

Sir, they disputed with good humour, because they were not in earnest as to religion. . . . Accordingly you see in Lucian [that] the Epicurean, who argues only negatively, keeps his temper; the Stoic, who has something positive to preserve, grows angry. Being angry with one who controverts an opinion which you value, is a necessary consequence of the uneasiness which you feel. Every man who attacks my belief diminishes in some degree my confidence in it, and therefore makes me uneasy; and I am angry with him who makes me uneasy. Those only who believed in Revelation have been angry at having their faith called in question; because they only had something upon which they could rest as matter of fact. (*Life* 3: 10–11)

In Hume's (then unpublished) *Dialogues*, Demea shows just this kind of anger in the face of a fundamental threat, while the skeptical Philo can well afford to be candid and agreeable.

The problem for Johnson, as for many of his contemporaries, is that he is deeply committed to the empiricist philosophy whose logic threatens the foundations of Christian belief. Fredric Bogel remarks shrewdly, "What is remarkable is not that Hume or Franklin or the *philosophes* appealed so often to common experience and seemed to insist that there was little or nothing else to appeal to, but that a figure like Johnson, to whom the implications of such a view were profoundly disturbing, conducted his campaign of defiant resistance with little more than the materials of that very experience" (*Literature and Insubstantiality* 71). One reason is that Johnson deliberately confines himself to arguments that his audience will find convincing, but another is that he wants very badly to find them adequate. As Robert Walker shows in "Johnson and the 'Age of Evidences,'" he followed earlier apologists in relying on "external" arguments from miracles and prophecies, and resisted the growing emphasis on "internal" conviction of faith. Discussing Hume with Boswell, Johnson declared, "We have as strong evidence for the miracles in support of Christianity as the nature of the thing admits" (*Life* 1:445).

Two quite distinct areas of debate are implicated here: the deduction of divine attributes from the evidence of nature, and the support of Christian doctrine by the evidence of miracles and prophecies. It was because the first kind of deduction looked shaky, as Hume demonstrates so decisively in the *Dialogues*, that the second kind of evidence came to seem crucial. Pope writes in the *Essay on Man*,

> Through worlds unnumbered though the God be known,
> 'Tis ours to trace him only in our own.
>
> (1.21–22)

On this Pope's editor Warburton—later a bishop—comments just as Hume's Cleanthes might: "We can *reason only from what we know*, and as we *know* no more of *Man* than what we see of his station here; so we know no more of *God* than what we see of his dispensations in this station; being able to trace him no further than to the limits of our own system" (Warburton 6). This is dangerously close to Philo's position in the *Dialogues* that "we have no *data* to establish any system of cosmogony. Our experience, so imperfect in itself and so limited both in extent and duration, can afford us no probable conjecture concerning the whole of things" (177). To carry sufficient weight for conviction, therefore, God's "dispensations in this station" need confirmation by the biblical record.

That record in turn rests on two separate bases. One is the documentary reliability of its testimony, which Johnson and others considered to be at least as secure as other historical data. The other is the intrinsic plausibility, or even possibility, of the miracles that the testimony describes. In *An Apology for Christianity* (1776), addressed to Gibbon, Richard Watson concedes that miracles cannot be demonstrated from sense experience, so that in Lockean terms "we cannot then, philosophically speaking, be said to know that a miracle has ever been performed." But if the defense must rest on probability rather than on demonstration, it has to face the Humean objection that human testimony can never sustain a position contrary to uniform experience. Watson retorts, "Whose experience do you mean? You will not say, your own; for the experience of an individual reaches but a little way; and no doubt you daily assent to a thousand truths in politics, in physics, and in the business of common life, which you have never seen verified by experience." Since our entire knowledge of past experience rests on the testimony of history, to disqualify historical accounts of miracles because they "contradict the experience of all ages and nations" is to "beg the very question in debate" (91–93). Very similarly Johnson's friend William Adams argues in an *Essay on Mr. Hume's Essay on Miracles* (1751) that whereas Hume tells us to judge of testimony by experience, "it is more certain that we must judge of the experience of men by their testimony" (19). Hume had observed that we do not doubt Caesar's death in the senate house (*Treatise* 83), and Johnson on his deathbed told William Windham that "with respect to evidence . . . we had not such evidence that Caesar died in the Capitol, as that Christ died in the manner related" (Hill 2:384).

But however reliable the documents may be, miracles might still fail as evidence, for as Boswell rather nervously notes, Johnson's kind of empiricist skepticism could easily threaten them just as it threatens the data of secular history.

Talking of Dr. Johnson's unwillingness to believe extraordinary things, I ventured to say, "Sir, you come near Hume's argument against miracles, 'that it is more probable witnesses should lie, or be mistaken, than that they should happen.'" JOHNSON. "Why, Sir, Hume, taking the proposition simply, is right. But the Christian revelation is not proved by the miracles alone, but as connected with prophecies, and with the doctrines in confirmation of which the miracles were wrought." (*Life* 3:188)

Christianity rests on a whole complex of arguments and "evidences," and whenever one of them starts to look weak, the focus is shifted to one of the others.

Johnson said he had thought most of Hume's doubts but resisted them, and Hume interestingly confesses a similar anxiety in a letter in 1751 to a friend who had been reading the manuscript of the *Dialogues*:

You would perceive by the sample I have given you, that I make Cleanthes the hero of the dialogue. Whatever you can think of to strengthen that side of the argument will be most acceptable to me. Any propensity you imagine I have to the other side crept in upon me against my will; and 'tis not long ago that I burned an old manuscript book, wrote before I was twenty, which contained, page after page, the gradual progress of my thoughts on that head. It begun with an anxious search after arguments to confirm the common opinion; doubts stole in, dissipated, returned, were again dissipated, returned again; and it was a perpetual struggle of a restless imagination against inclination, perhaps against reason. (*Letters* 1: 153–54)

Probably Hume never really supposed that Cleanthes was the hero of the *Dialogues* or that his doubts went against reason, but this account suggests that those doubts may once have been as disturbing as Johnson's were. So does the revelation that in a fever in 1748 Hume talked deliriously, "with much seeming perturbation, of the Devil, of Hell, and of damnation" (Mossner 217). The difference between Hume and Johnson here is that Hume dispelled his doubts by taking them all the way, pressing empiricism farther than most people were willing to do, while Johnson sought to quell them by doggedly reasserting truths that no longer seemed quite self-evident.

The final line of defense against Hume was that even if he could not be proved wrong, it was unendurable to imagine that he might be right. James Beattie's *Essay on Truth*, which Reynolds depicted in a famous painting as victorious over Hume, and which Hume himself denounced as "a horrible large lie in octavo" (Mossner 581), openly rests on emotional and social needs. Let skepticism once be countenanced, Beattie declares, and "the fatal fermentation" will transform the whole of knowledge "into rottenness and poison" (496–97). The consequence of Hume's speculations, if widely adopted, would be catastrophic: "Suppose these opinions established in the world, and say, if you can, that the good of mankind would be promoted by them. To me it seems impossible for society to exist under the influence of such opinions" (494–95). Since Hume's views would demolish society they are ipso facto inadmissible. (In response to such a view, Hume and Gibbon both emphasize that one can be a deist—"infidel" is the usual term for Gibbon in Boswell's journals—and still be a social and political conservative.)

The doubts Johnson resists are by no means confined to points of doctrine. Far more profoundly, as Max Byrd argues in "Johnson's Spiritual Anxiety," they require the suppression of his intuitions of contingency, uncertainty, and a "vacuity" that amounts to existential emptiness. In an empiricist world, human beings find that their senses somehow fail to report existence adequately, which leads Rasselas to the almost Blakean insight that "man has surely some latent sense for which this place affords no gratification, or he has some desires distinct from sense which must be satisfied before he can be happy" (*Rasselas*, chap. 3). So Johnson finally endorses the position that the life of faith must be "regulated not by our senses but our belief" (*Rambler* No. 178), and he divorces belief from the senses in a way that empiricism was committed never to do. Johnson does not deny, however, that faith in the invisible can seem tempting only if what is visible fails to satisfy: "None would have recourse to an invisible power, but that all other subjects had eluded their hopes. None would fix their attention upon the future, but that they are discontented with the present" (*Idler* No. 89). Whether or not revelation can be proven to be true, Johnson feels it to be indispensable. The point of the Bible for believers, after all, is not to validate a theology but to tell a story that makes sense of suffering in human terms.

Different temperaments need different fictions. Perceiving a grim world, Johnson needs a traditional theology to explain and justify it. Hume, perceiving an agreeable one, can do without it. Similarly, morality for Hume is natural, while for Johnson it must be based on revelation, and beneficence is the best that can be expected of a species not much given to benevolence (Voitle 52–53). "Pity is not natural to man," Johnson declares roundly; "children are always cruel. Savages are always cruel. Pity is acquired and improved by the cultivation of reason" (*Life* 1:437). Similarly, Johnson's and Hume's views on freedom and necessity are expressions of their world views in the deepest sense. Committed to skepticism as to knowledge and proof, Hume is in danger of confronting a chaotic universe, so he is naturally drawn to a determinism that asserts the inevitable concatenation of every event that has ever happened. Like Hobbes before him and Godwin after him, Hume gets rid of a superintending Providence and replaces it with Necessity. Johnson, very differently, fears determinism in himself, so he affirms a loving God who can save him from the concatenation of causes that a compulsive personality finds especially painful. Hume wants determinism because it liberates the self to act according to the natural order. Johnson wants free will because it liberates the self to act in opposition to the (debased) natural order.

In the end, fictions work because their users need them to work, as a memorable passage in Boswell's *Tour to the Hebrides* illustrates:

We spoke of Death. . . . I mentioned Hawthornden's *Cypress-grove*, where it is said that the world is a mere show; and that it is unreasonable for a man to wish to continue in the show-room after he has seen it. Let him go cheerfully out, and give place to other spectators. JOHNSON. "Yes, sir, if he is sure he is to be well, after he goes out of it. But if he is to grow blind after he goes out of the show-room, and never to see any thing again; or if he does not know whither he is to go next, a man will not go cheerfully out of a show-room. No wise man will be contented to die, if he thinks he is to go into a state of punishment. Nay, no wise man will be contented to die, if he thinks he is to fall into annihilation; for however unhappy any man's existence may be, he yet would rather have it, than not exist at all. No; there is no rational principle by which a man can die contented, but a trust in the mercy of God, through the merits of Jesus Christ."—This short sermon, delivered with an earnest tone, in a boat upon the sea, which was perfectly calm, on a day appropriated to religious worship, while every one listened with an air of satisfaction, had a most pleasing effect upon my mind. (*Tour* 5:179–80)

The dying Hume claimed to be prepared for annihilation; Johnson denies that anyone can face such a prospect, and fears moreover—as he tells his old Oxford tutor—that he may be "sent to Hell, and punished everlastingly" (*Life* 4:299). So for him Christian doctrine is the essential "rational principle," whereas for Hume it is fundamentally irrational. Johnson has not actually provided arguments against annihilation, but has simply asserted its imaginative unacceptability. And Boswell, listening with the others in the boat on the peaceful sea, has turned Johnson's "short sermon" into a fiction of consolation for himself and his readers. The foundation of Hume's philosophy, meanwhile—and its modernity— lies in its rejection of any argument that claims to rise above the experience of our common world. Hume's paganism is a rejection of fictions not rooted in the world of the senses, imperfect and ultimately unknowable though that world may be.

5

Gilbert White
Enlightenment Science,
Conservative Myth

THE LIFE OF NATURE
AND THE LITERARY ARTIST

The Natural History of Selborne (1789) by Gilbert White at once participates in the intellectual world of the late eighteenth century and yet manages to ignore many of its preoccupations as if they did not exist. White gives the impression of inhabiting a world of social and natural harmony which, even for conservatives such as Fielding and Goldsmith and Burke, was normally regarded with nostalgia but contrasted with actual life. In this sense he was a survivor from an earlier age who escaped the generalized anxiety that many of his contemporaries experienced. On the other hand, White's studies in natural history, though predicated on an old-fashioned physicotheology, were entirely up to date and in some ways highly original. He was no casual or sentimental lover of little creatures; in his unassuming way he speculated deeply on ecological adaptation and the nature of instinct, and had an appreciation of life as process that brings him closer to the adventurous Diderot than to the taxonomist Linnaeus. Moreover, he wrote with great intelligence and grace, and his *Selborne* has always been regarded as a "minor classic" of English literature, particularly by readers who have shared its emotional and ideological commitments. Attempting to identify a reality independent of human preconceptions, White participates in the ideal of "science" that has preoccupied Western culture since the Renaissance. But because of his intellectual naiveté and his ideological assumptions, his vision of that reality is pervaded by imaginative categories in a way that illustrates, however unconsciously, the central themes of the present study.

Few lives could be less eventful than White's. After graduating from Oxford in 1743 he remained an absentee fellow of Oriel, returning once in 1752–53 to serve as university proctor. Further academic advancement never materialized, and he settled down to a clerical life in his native Selborne in Hampshire, a village of seven hundred inhabitants which his most recent biographer describes as "on the road to nowhere" (Mabey 17). For most of the next forty years he was curate of a neighboring parish, since the Selborne living belonged to a different college from his own; in 1784, when he was in his mid-sixties, a new incumbent chose not to live at Selborne and White became curate in his stead. He never married, but enjoyed the visits of an ever-growing host of nephews and nieces, and was clearly a sociable man; he even turns up in a modern footnote to Boswell's *Life of Johnson* as an inimitable teller of stories (2:443n).

White's passion was the observation of nature, and his correspondence with two prominent investigators, Thomas Pennant and Daines Barrington, grew at last into *The Natural History and Antiquities of Selborne*, published in his sixty-eighth year (by his publisher brother) to immediate acclaim. It was a time when natural histories were highly popular; one of his contemporaries wrote to Linnaeus that "they sell the best of any books in England" (Keith 41). *Selborne* (normally reprinted, as in the Penguin edition used here, without the *Antiquities*) is cheerfully unsystematic, using the device of "letters" to Pennant and Barrington to suggest the accretive process by which knowledge is acquired. A multitude of observations on specific themes—crickets, swallows, the distillation of dew— are drawn together in the context of the village and countryside which White knew by heart. Localization of scope produces precision of detail: "Men that undertake only one district are much more likely to advance natural knowledge than those that grasp at more than they can possibly be acquainted with: every kingdom, every province, should have its own monographer" (125). Equally important is a willingness to search and consider over an entire lifetime. "It is now more than forty years that I have paid some attention to the ornithology of this district, without being able to exhaust the subject: new occurrences still arise as long as any inquiries are kept alive" (231).

Unquestionably, White's images of nature are colored by a kind of pastoral patina, in part deliberately intended and in part activated by the nostalgia of later generations. One of his epigraphs is a speech of Odysseus on the sweetness of his native Ithaca, and another is a quotation from Horace which may be translated, "In the manner and custom of the Matinian bee, I gather pleasing things through much labor" (*Odes* 4.2.27–30). Some of his admirers have emphasized the honey rather than the labor. According to James Russell Lowell, "The book has the delightfulness of absolute leisure. Mr. White seems never to have had any harder work to do than to study the habits of his feathered fellow-townsfolk, or to watch the ripening of his peaches on the wall. . . . It is positive rest only to look into that garden of his" (1–2). But if *Selborne* suggested pleasant escapism to a poet, it offered the vision of a lifetime's work to the young Charles Darwin. "From reading White's *Selborne*, I took much pleasure in watching the habits of birds, and even made notes on the subject. In my simplicity I remember wondering why every gentleman did not become an ornithologist" (1:32). White emphasizes birds because they abound at Selborne, "a very abrupt, uneven country, full of hills and woods, and therefore full of birds" (*Selborne* 33).

White's conception of the naturalist's work was omnivorous; he lived in an age when one could still hope to be well informed in many branches of knowledge. Nothing subhuman was alien to him. Like his correspondent Pennant, whom Johnson praised as a travel writer for observing "more things than any one else does" (Boswell, *Life* 3:274), White is eminent for an accuracy of attention that is a function of alert intelligence. Always he insists on veracity, believing nothing that he has not seen for himself—his "own autopsia" (122) as he calls them, in the eighteenth-century sense defined in Johnson's *Dictionary*: "Ocular demonstration; seeing a thing one's self."

It is one thing to recommend observation, and another to practice it successfully. The villagers of Selborne are a valuable source of information and suggestions, but White is careful not to trust their casual observation and inherited folk wisdom.

It is the hardest thing in the world to shake off superstitious prejudices: they are sucked in as it were with our mother's milk; and growing up with us at a time when they take the fastest hold and make the most lasting impressions, become so interwoven into our very constitutions, that the strongest good sense is required to disengage ourselves from them. No wonder therefore that the lower people retain them their whole lives through, since their minds are not invigorated by a liberal education, and therefore not enabled to make any efforts adequate to the occasion. (184)

It may be easy for modern readers to resent, on behalf of "the lower people," White's claims for the superiority of a liberal education, and we will return to his social views later. But one should not overlook the two points which this passage makes very strongly: that observation is biased by preconceptions, and that deliberate "efforts" are necessary to overcome them. *The Natural History of Selborne* is founded on an extraordinary ability to see and understand what others miss, experts included. For example, the Italian naturalist J. A. Scopoli "advances some false facts; as when he says of the *hirundo urbica* that '*pullos extra nidum non nutrit.*' This assertion I know to be wrong from repeated observations this summer, for house-martins do feed their young flying, though it must be acknowledged not so commonly as the house-swallow; and the feat is done in so quick a manner as not to be perceptible to indifferent observers" (80).

The heart of White's writing is its testimony to the vivid *haeccitas*, the inscape as Hopkins would call it, of natural phenomena. In his journal, the storehouse of material for *Selborne*, White continually labored to achieve descriptions that should be at once precise and expressive.

Vast swagging rock-like clouds appeared at a distance. . . . Spitting fog, dark & cold. . . . Wood-larks hang suspended in the air, and sing all night. . . . A man brought me a common sea-gull alive: three crows had got it down in a field, and were endeavouring to demolish it. . . . The ground as hard as iron. . . . Soft wind. The wood-pecker laughs. (*Journals* 8, 46, 120, 133, 169, 379)

In *Selborne* observations like these are amplified into masterly paragraphs in which rhetoric may add charm but is always intended to enhance accuracy of observation.

Published accounts like Scopoli's must be tested against the phenomena themselves, and they are most likely to go wrong when one author merely borrows from another. In his first letter to Barrington, White declares with pride that he is "an out-door naturalist, one that takes his observations from the subject itself, and not from the writings of others" (109). And his interest is always behavioral rather than taxonomic. "Faunists, as you observe, are too apt to acquiesce in bare descriptions, and a few synonyms: the reason is plain, because all that may be done at home in a man's study; but the investigation of the life and conversation of animals is a concern of much more trouble and difficulty, and is not to be attained but by the active and inquisitive, and by those that reside much in the country" (136). Hume's confidence in the replicability of knowledge from one text to another is met, in this specialized arena, by a skepticism deeper than his own.

Observation can be accurate, however, without being dispassionate; indeed White might well say that it is his passion for nature that makes him observe it so closely. He certainly strives for objectivity in the sense of accuracy, but not in the sense that Raymond Williams attributes to him in *The Country and the City*: "While Cobbett and Jane Austen, in their different ways, were absorbed in a human world, Gilbert White was watching the turn of the year and the myriad physical lives inside it: nature in a sense that could now be separated from man" (119). If for White "nature" is distinct from human life, the two remain intimately continuous. "Every species of bird has a mode of nidification peculiar to itself; so that a schoolboy would at once pronounce on the sort of nest before him" (*Selborne* 243).

Boys hunt for birds' eggs; adults need to know the particular properties of stone (13–14), timber, and soil:

As the parish still inclines down towards Wolmer-forest, at the juncture of the clays and sand the soil becomes a wet, sandy loam, remarkable for timber, and infamous for roads. The oaks of Temple and Blackmoor stand high in the estimation of purveyors, and have furnished much naval timber; while the trees on the freestone grow large, but are what workmen call *shakey*, and so brittle as often to fall to pieces in sawing. Beyond the sandy loam the soil becomes an hungry lean sand, till it mingles with the forest; and will produce little without the assistance of lime and turnips. (9)

"Freestone," incidentally, is an old term that refers to use rather than to geological type: it is any sedimentary rock that can be cut "freely" in all directions.

This is the twin vision of *Selborne*: the integrity of nature, but also the emotional, intellectual, and practical responses of human beings to nature. Natural history is fascinating in itself, but beyond that, "the botanist that could improve the sward of the district where he lived would be an useful member of society; to raise a thick turf on a naked soil would be worth volumes of systematic knowledge; and he would be the best commonwealth's man that could occasion the growth of 'two blades of grass where one alone was seen before'" (210). White's modern editors seem not to have recognized the allusion, and one of them comments with some surprise, "This passage of White's on production for use might (in implication but not style) have been written by Karl Marx!" (Fisher 288n). The speaker is in fact the King of Brobdingnag in *Gulliver's Travels*: "He gave it for his opinion, that whoever could make two ears of corn, or two blades of grass to grow upon a spot of ground where only one grew before, would deserve better of mankind, and do more essential service to his country, than the whole race of politicians put together" (2.7).

White is a naturalist of genius because he knows how hard it is to understand what one sees and hears. "The language of birds is very ancient, and, like other ancient modes of speech, very elliptical: little is said, but much is meant and understood" (*Selborne* 216). At the same time, these mysterious sounds carry an aesthetic charge, and (true to empiricist theory) the response of a human listener must be founded on association of ideas: "Swifts are no songsters, and have only one harsh screaming note; yet there are ears to which it is not displeasing, from an agreeable association of ideas, since that note never occurs but in the most lovely summer weather" (171). Or again,

Sounds do not always give us pleasure according to their sweetness and melody; nor do harsh sounds always displease. We are more apt to be captivated or disgusted with the associations which they promote than with the notes themselves. Thus the shrilling of the field-cricket, though sharp and stridulous, yet marvelously delights some hearers, filling their minds with a train of summer ideas of everything that is rural, verdurous, and joyous. (226)

Like his contemporaries whom we have been considering, White combines factual accuracy with a recognition of the mental fictions that pervade all of life. And like them he uses the resources of rhetoric to evoke experience. "Rural, verdurous, and joyous" is not the language of objectified description.

White's favorite means of accomplishing the evocation of the actual, just as in eighteenth-century nature poetry, is the potent epithet. Many of John Aikin's examples from Thomson in *An Essay on the Application of Natural History to Poetry* (1777) work in the same way that White's prose does:

> Faint, underneath, the household fowls convene;
> And in a corner of the buzzing shade,
> The house-dog, with the vacant greyhound, lies
> Outstretched and sleepy.

A striking instance of the extraordinary effect of a well-chosen epithet in adding life and force to a description, is shown in the expression *buzzing shade*. It is by means of such bold comprehensive touches as these, that poetry is frequently enabled to produce more lively representations than painting, even of sensible objects. (Aikin 72–73)

Aikin says elsewhere that "the descriptive poet, who does not habituate himself to view the several objects of nature minutely, and in comparison with each other, must ever fail in giving his pictures the congruity and animation of real life" (11). As it happens, White's own poetic imitations of Thomson sag with halting rhythms and lugubrious Latinisms; descriptive prose rather than verse is his true language of feeling.

As observer, White recognizes the cruelty and suffering inherent in nature, the strong compulsion of instinct. With great penetration he proposes that bird song, however pleasing to the human ear, reflects territorialism rather than merriment: "The two great motives which regulate the proceedings of the brute creation are love and hunger; the former incites animals to perpetuate their kind, the latter induces them to preserve individuals. . . . Most of the singing and elation of spirits of that time [the winter] seem to me to be the effect of rivalry and emulation: and it is to this spirit of jealousy that I chiefly attribute the equal dispersion of birds in the spring over the face of the country" (137). But as a writer for human beings, White describes bird song in human terms, though he is aware that the description may bear little relation to the bird's own strange, indeed unknowable, mode of experience. Sometimes he will cast a little drama in mock epic language, as when a yardful of hens attacks a captured hawk: "The exasperated matrons upbraided, they execrated, they insulted, they triumphed" (219). More often it is simply a matter of conveying meaning by a gently humanizing touch. When young swallows are fed they utter "a little quick note of gratitude and complacency" (157). "Rooks, in the breeding season, attempt sometimes in the gaiety of their hearts to sing, but with no great success" (216–17).

Anthropomorphism, often deplored by modern writers on nature, reflects the view that all creatures, including man, occupy interdependent places in the chain of being (a term White occasionally uses). It is notable that the arch-skeptic Hume exhibits attitudes that are quite naively anthropomorphic: " 'Tis plain that almost in every species of creatures, but especially of the nobler kind, there are many evident marks of pride and humility. The very port and gait of a swan, or turkey, or peacock show the high idea he has entertained of himself, and his contempt of all others" (*Treatise* 326). White's descriptions are quite different from this: they center on observation that does not depend on human feelings, though it may well appeal to them.

The swift is almost continually on the wing; and as it never settles on the ground, on trees, or roofs, would seldom find opportunity for amorous rites, was it not enabled to indulge them in the air. If any person would watch these birds of a fine morning in May, as they are sailing round at a great height from the ground, he would see, every now and then, one drop on the back of another, and both of them sink down together for many fathoms with a loud piercing shriek. This I take to be the juncture when the business of generation is carrying on. (167)

This passage is founded on close observation; indeed, White was the first naturalist to realize that swifts mate in the air. In describing the fact, he uses two kinds of diction. Boswell would have appreciated the "amorous rites" and would have projected himself into a fantasy of aerial delights, like the union of angels. But White knows that what is happening can be described equally well as "the business of generation." He looks on with interest but also detachment, and "amorous rites" has a playful tone, just as in another passage a technical Latin name is joined with anthropomorphic reflections: "The *alauda pratensis* of Ray was the poor dupe that was educating the booby of a cuckoo mentioned in my letter of October last" (133).

The issues raised by White's combination of anthropomorphism and accuracy remain alive today because they reflect the inescapable influence of the observer's imagination. Stephen Jay Gould has recently written, "The standard tradition in natural history tries to capture organisms as they 'are' in nature—and it favors the beautiful and pleasant, rather than the disturbing or ugly. Its conceit is factuality and separation from human concerns—nature as she is, away from the corruptions of civilization. Its twin claims are *objectivity* and *beauty*" (11). In some ways White fits this description closely: he is responsive to beauty even while striving for objectivity. Unlike the naturalists of a later era, however, his objectivity is filtered through the twin beliefs that a loving creator is responsible for every organism (so that ugliness should, as it were, be forgiven) and that human existence is comfortably merged in the rhythms of nature.

Proto-Romantic attacks on civilization were already widespread in White's time, but *Selborne* assumes a vital interchange between civilization and nature, not a gulf separating them. Accordingly, White's writing is more amenable to a modern position than that of many scrupulously "scientific" naturalists in the nineteenth and twentieth centuries. Gould goes on to say, "I believe that organisms have, through their evolution, an irreducible and inalienable status in and for themselves. But we can only speak of them in terms of their meaning for us; culture and mind permeate our world of discourse" (11). White, while giving (naive) expression to the fictions of nature and mind, holds to a philosophical position that accords deep respect to the inalienable status of living things "in and for themselves."

PHYSICOTHEOLOGY AND SCIENCE

"We remember a little girl," White says in an account of the "pleasing murmur" of rooks, "who, as she was going to bed, used to remark on such an occurrence, in the true spirit of physico-theology, that the rooks were saying their prayers" (250). The mention of physicotheology, though rarely invoked so openly as here, warns us not to forget that *Selborne* is conceived in a specific intellectual tradition. That tradition has not been treated kindly by historians of ideas who emphasize its didactic aspect, the sometimes naive claim that every detail in nature illustrates divine planning, but its strength lies in its systematic observations rather than in its homiletic explanations. White's fellow townspeople get things wrong because they see without understanding what they see; if nature is a text written by God, the text is full of mysteries that demand to be solved.

The central physicotheological work is John Ray's *The Wisdom of God Manifested in the Works of the Creation* (1691), a deliberately popular book by the author of several important technical treatises. Ray takes his epigraph from Psalm 104, "How manifold are thy works, O Lord! In wisdom hast thou made them all." Ray is a preacher, and at times he does propose explanations of the kind satirists like Voltaire would later deride. "I cannot but look upon the strange instinct of this noisome and troublesome creature a louse, of searching out foul and nasty clothes to harbour and breed in, as an effect of divine Providence, designed to deter men and women from sluttishness and sordidness, and to provoke them to cleanliness and neatness. God himself hateth uncleanliness and turns away from it, as appears by Deut. xxii. 12, 13, 14" (309). But even this passage occurs in a context of refuting theories of spontaneous generation —lice do lay eggs—that exhibits careful observation and shrewd reasoning. Ray's book is filled with examples of what Darwinians would call purposive adaptation, for instance the structure of the eye, the hollowness of bones, the hedgehog's armor, whose accuracy is in no way diminished by attributing their origin to God's wisdom rather than natural selection. White similarly examines the breathing apertures in a deer's head and finds "a new instance of the wisdom of God in the creation" (*Selborne* 57).

Ray's profoundest influence on White lies in his appreciation of living behavior. Providence is asserted throughout, but it is identified not in acts of special intervention but in a repetitive force of instinct that is "a kind of Fate" operating upon living creatures (Ray 128). The scientist is committed to close study of the facts and to extreme skepticism about careless superstition, like the popular notion (which White praises Ray for refuting) that little frogs drop from rain (*Selborne* 50). As in the sermons of the latitudinarian divines, God remains the first cause while the investigator is free to examine connections among second causes. "Thus is instinct," White remarks, "a most wonderful unequal faculty; in some instances so much above reason, in other respects so far below it!" (150). Like Henri Fabre a century later, White was repeatedly struck by the inflexibility of instinct, adding further examples to Ray's observations on the blindness of the nesting drive. "Thus is instinct in animals, taken the least out of its way, an undistinguishing, limited faculty; and blind to every circumstance that does not immediately respect self-preservation, or lead at once to the propagation or support of their species" (*Selborne* 160). White remarks that a hen, "when the fury of incubation is on her," will sit on a stone if her eggs have been removed (121).

After reading a draft of *Selborne*, White's friend John Mulso wrote, "You have happily grounded ethics on a stable and beautiful basis, the works of God; and your figures formed from naked and genuine beauty, beat every finical composition that would fascinate the judgement by adventitious ornament" (Mulso 258). But that is to read into Selborne the beliefs that sustain it, rather than to define an argument that it actually asserts. The physicotheological tradition culminated in William Paley's *Natural Theology* of 1802, a work intended to deduce "the personality of the Deity, as distinguished from what is sometimes called nature, sometimes called a principle" (34). For Paley the phenomena of nature are ammunition for a polemic that reduces the creator to an artificer not greatly different from human beings, though as Leslie Stephen sarcastically remarked, "superior to Watt or Priestley in devising mechanical and chemical contrivances" (*History* 1:349). White, on the other hand, far from marshaling evidence to support orthodox religion, scarcely acknowledges that orthodoxy is under attack. His book is expressive of nature's complexity, not its metaphysical utility, though he would doubtless agree with William Derham's claim in *Physico-Theology* that the creator is as much an artist as a mechanic. Turning to that favorite topic of both Ray and White, the "nidification" of birds, Derham exclaims that the "architectonic skill" of these "poor untaught creatures" exceeds all human art. And their superbly fashioned bodies, like their shapely nests, are the work of "that infinite Artist" to whom is due "all imaginable honour and praise" (231). No part of their anatomy, Derham says, is "unartificially made" (367), for in God's universe the natural is artificial. Physicotheology is self-authenticating: every new evidence of order further proves the glory of God.

Virginia Woolf comments acutely in her essay on White, "Providence about 1760 was in its prime; it sets all doubts at rest, and so leaves the mind free to question practically everything" (125). White's indifference to controversy enables him to participate in the great project of Enlightenment science while ignoring its radical implications. His passion for accurate observation is perfectly congruent with the new emphasis on detail and suspicion of mathematical abstraction. "The book of nature is written in mathematical characters," Galileo had declared (Gillispie 46); now Diderot, siding with Buffon and against d'Alembert, was abusing mathematics in *De l'Interprétation de la nature* as a realm of purely mental constructions (Diderot 178). Enlightenment scientists distrusted abstract theory unless, as Cassirer has said, it could be deduced from "direct contact with the specific welter of phenomena and individual instances of the forms of nature" (76). "Now we are no longer comparing nature with our concepts but, as it were, with itself; we see how each of nature's operations dovetails with other operations and how, finally, they are joined in the totality of one activity" (78). In keeping with the movement from physics to biology, White pursues "natural history" rather than "natural philosophy," a distinction that suggests temporal experience rather than timeless laws. But like Ray and Derham, who describe a magnificent order from the solar system down to earwax, White sees Cassirer's "totality of nature" as informed by the wisdom of God.

Diderot's speculations led to a searching inquiry into the nature of life. How, he asks d'Alembert in the *Entretien entre d'Alembert et Diderot*, does life get inside an egg? The answer is materialist: *sensibilité* is a property of matter itself, and affords no evidence for religious belief. "Voyez-vous cet oeuf? c'est avec cela qu'on renverse toutes les écoles de théologie et tous les temples de la terre" (274). But Diderot's fascination with life leads to an uneasy compromise between materialism and vitalism, the former atheistic, the latter verging on Spinozan pantheism. Carl Becker observes, "Diderot stumbled over all the elements essential to the Darwinian theory of evolution; but the point is that he stumbled over them as if they were obstacles instead of stepping-stones" (97). Diderot studies biology and worries about the problem of life. White studies natural history and worries about the problems of behavior; for him there is no problem of life.

In keeping clear of the larger theoretical issues, White manages to participate in the study of nature while retaining the old faith that looks backward to medieval Aristotelianism, with its purposive function, and preserves that moral structure of reality that Sedgwick would later rebuke Darwin for demolishing: " 'Tis the crown and glory of organic science that it *does*, through *final cause*, link material to moral. . . . You have ignored this link; and, if I do not mistake your meaning, you have done your best in one or two pregnant cases to break it" (Gillispie 350). In Darwin's theory the richness of functional adaptation is explained without reference to any presiding intelligence, and only the fittest survive. In

White, for whom all species have survived just as Adam first beheld them, the possibility cannot arise. All are fit, having been so designed by their affectionate maker, though his reasons may sometimes be impenetrable: "When one reflects on the state of this strange being [an old pet tortoise], it is a matter of wonder to find that Providence should bestow such a profusion of days, such a seeming waste of longevity, on a reptile that appears to relish it so little as to squander more than two-thirds of its existence in joyless stupor, and be lost to all sensation for months together in the profoundest of slumbers" (233).

For Hume, the phenomena of nature are evidence for religious skepticism.

Look round this universe. What an immense profusion of beings, animated and organized, sensible and active! You admire this prodigious variety and fecundity. But inspect a little more narrowly these living existences, the only beings worth regarding. How hostile and destructive to each other! How insufficient all of them for their own happiness! How contemptible or odious to the spectator! The whole presents nothing but the idea of a blind nature, impregnated by a great vivifying principle, and pouring forth from her lap, without discernment or parental care, her maimed and abortive children. (*Dialogues* 211)

In the next century this line of thinking would lead to Darwin's morally neutral evolution and to Nietzsche's contempt for "natural" existence:

You desire to *live* "according to Nature"? . . . Imagine to yourselves a being like Nature, boundlessly extravagant, boundlessly indifferent, without purpose or consideration, without pity or justice, at once fruitful and barren and uncertain: imagine to yourselves *indifference* as a power—how *could* you live in accordance with such indifference? To live—is not that just endeavouring to be otherwise than this Nature? (Nietzsche 388)

Hume, as we have seen, continued to postulate "nature" as the benevolent guarantor of human experience, but eighteenth-century orthodoxy was right to perceive the radical implications of his philosophy.

As an astute observer of the natural world, White knows very well that it is not a happy family. "Magpies sometimes, I see, perch on the backs of sheep, and pick the lice and ticks out of their wool; nay, mount on their very heads; while those meek quadrupeds seem pleased and stand perfectly still, little aware that their eyes are in no small danger; and that their assiduous friends would be glad of an opportunity of picking their bones" (*Journals* 133). But writers like Hume, if White was aware of them at all, must have seemed to him like Hamlet obsessed with the earth as a sterile promontory and unable to appreciate its beauty. Physicotheology, while denying none of the observed facts, controlled their implications within an emotionally protective framework of explanation.

From a historical point of view, science can be seen as the third term in a progression that began with myth and moved on to theology. When a gap began to be felt between the human and the divine worlds, theology developed to explain the gap and to assert that the continuity between the two was not lost. Science goes still further, rendering the mythic and theological explanations marginal if not irrelevant. In such a development, the word *nature* has utterly different implications for a skeptic like Hume than it has for a traditionalist like White. As Cassirer describes the new philosophy:

All knowledge, no matter what its content, is "natural" so long as it springs from human reason alone and does not rely on other foundations of certainty. "Nature" therefore does not so much signify a given group of objects as a certain "horizon" of knowledge, of the comprehension of reality. . . . The "realm of nature" is thus opposed to the "realm of grace." (39)

Science was ceasing to reinforce religion and was beginning to devour it, but White remained innocent of the danger.

Yet there is a sense in which any description of nature other than mathematical abstraction must retain its roots in older, metaphorical modes of thought. White's appeal to the familiar everyday world remains appealing for the reason that William James gives in *The Principles of Psychology*: "Witness the obduracy with which the popular world of colors, sounds, and smells holds its own against that of molecules and vibrations. Let the physicist himself but nod, like Homer, and the world of sense becomes his absolute reality again" (2:930). James's aside "like Homer" is a nice touch: scientific theories are works of art in the end, and like other works of art they address the imagination as well as the intellect.

"The peculiarity of the scientific method," Marc Bloch writes, "is that it deliberately abandons the observer in order to know more about the thing observed. To the natural sciences, the connections which our mind weaves between things appear arbitrary; they deliberately break them in order to reestablish a diversity which seems to them more authentic" (150–51). But White, although reticent, is ubiquitous in *The Natural History of Selborne* as the individual whose interests and affection call his subject into being, and from whose single perspective everything is seen. The casual and anecdotal quality of the book makes it a "natural history" in an unusual and important sense. Science, taking for granted the indefinite replicability of its findings, tends to represent natural objects as noncontextual and ahistorical. In *Selborne*, the newts and ravens are actual individuals which he has repeatedly observed, and the anecdotal (rather than conspective) mode of presentation gives them a kind of biographical status.

Because we know that poems are intended as fictive utterances, Barbara Herrnstein Smith suggests, "we recognize that the contexts we infer from them are also fictive: unfixable, unlocatable, in the natural universe—as unreal as the sky we seem to see above the painter's oak tree" (55). It might be more accurate to say that this is one way of *using* a painting, engaging in aesthetic appreciation rather than pursuing possible lines of referentiality. The specificity of the painted oak would be greatly increased if it were identified—either by the painter or by some commentator—as a particular tree, perhaps with topographical or historical interest. And one can easily think of genres of painting whose historical specificity is their fundamental premise. A portrait by Reynolds is obviously meant to represent a particular person. In this instance as in *Selborne*, the devices of the fictive (painterly techniques, emotive language, and so forth) are summoned to represent the real.

IDEOLOGY

At the heart of *Selborne* is a man at home in a specific place. *The Naturalist's Summer-Evening Walk*, a poem which White inserted in the book, is weakest when condemning "man's prying pride" in the language of Pope and strongest when testifying to familiar experience in the manner of Gray or Goldsmith.

> While deep'ning shades obscure the face of day,
> To yonder bench, leaf-sheltered, let us stray,
> Till blended objects fail the swimming sight,
> And all the fading landscape sinks in night;
> To hear the drowsy dor come brushing by
> With buzzing wing, or the shrill cricket cry;
>
> . . .
>
> Each rural sight, each sound, each smell combine;
> The tinkling sheep-bell, or the breath of kine;
> The new-mown hay that scents the swelling breeze,
> Or cottage-chimney smoking through the trees.
>
> (67)

The leisurely catalogue in which each object gets its deserved weight is reminiscent of *The Deserted Village* (though White may have written his poem before Goldsmith's was published). But *The Deserted Village* is filled with nostalgia for a lost Eden and with rage against social change.

> These were thy charms—But all these charms are fled.
> Sweet smiling village, loveliest of the lawn,
> Thy sports are fled, and all thy charms withdrawn.

Typically the eighteenth-century writer went up to London as soon as he was able, and returned to his childhood home with a sense of loss. But White settled permanently in Selborne as a young man and resisted all temptations to leave; when he chose as epigraph a description of Ithaca, it was with the gratitude of a man who had never been exiled from home.

Here is an important source of *Selborne*'s appeal: the penetrating observation of nature, tactfully colored by the piety of the old physicotheologians, is based in a rural life that calls forth deeply traditional associations. A social historian remarks that White happened to live in "a fortunate corner of England" (Dorothy Marshall 171). Within this little world he moved at ease among his neighbors and parishioners in a life undisturbed by major calamity. As self-perceived, his life corresponds to a perennial ideal, from Chaucer on down, of the rural parson who is "to all the country dear, / And passing rich with forty pounds a year" (*Deserted Village*, ll. 141–42).

Loss and death do of course occur in Selborne, but always in a context of seasonal recurrence and rebirth.

In the centre of the village, and near the church, is a square piece of ground surrounded by houses, and vulgarly called The Plestor. In the midst of this spot stood, in old times, a vast oak, with a short squat body, and huge horizontal arms extending almost to the extremity of the area. This venerable tree, surrounded with stone steps, and seats above them, was the delight of old and young, and a place of much resort in summer evenings; where the former sat in grave debate, while the latter frolicked and danced before them. Long might it have stood, had not the amazing tempest in 1703 overturned it at once, to the infinite regret of the inhabitants, and the vicar [White's grandfather], who bestowed several pounds in setting it in its place again: but all his care could not avail; the tree sprouted for a time, then withered and died. (10)

"Sitting under the oak, / Among the old folk, / They laugh at our play" —here is the world of Blake's Innocence, with Experience held at bay. In this scene of immemorial age ("Plestor" derives from the Anglo-Saxon for "play place"), White was once one of the children on the green. To the end of his life he marks the arrival of spring by noting in his journal that boys are playing at taws on the Plestor, and he remarks in the mood of Gray's *Elegy*: "Our forefathers in this village were no doubt as busy and bustling, and as important, as ourselves: yet have their names and transactions been forgotten from century to century, and have sunk into oblivion; nor has this happened only to the vulgar, but even to men remarkable and famous in their generation" (*Antiquities* 284). Unlike the Cambridge don Gray, White is himself a part of that village world.

White was an unpolitical man, but the French Revolution, which erupted just after his book was published, deeply threatened his Burkean sense of continuity. "Of all these strange commotions," he wrote to a friend, "the sudden overthrow of the French despotic monarchy is the most wonderful—a fabric which has been now erecting for near two centuries, and whose foundations were laid so deep, that one would have supposed it might have lasted for ages to come: yet it is gone, as it were, in a moment!" (Holt-White 2:210–11). In 1793 he wrote to another friend,

You cannot abhor the dangerous doctrines of levellers and republicans more than I do! I was born and bred a gentleman, and hope I shall be allowed to die such. The reason you have so many bad neighbours is your nearness to a great factious manufacturing town. Our common people are more simple-minded and know nothing of Jacobin clubs. (Mabey 213)

Selborne rests upon a conservative ideology that is all the more powerful for not being articulated explicitly. In this ideal, as Lucy Maddox has shown, all of nature cooperates harmoniously in the way that eighteenth-century British society was supposed to cooperate, and gentlemen of leisure (particularly Anglican clergymen like White) are the best guides to rational wisdom.

An index to the tranquillity or complacency of White's social vision is furnished by the topic of hunting, which in the older "locodescriptive" poetry like Denham's *Cooper's Hill* and Pope's *Windsor-Forest* had symbolized the violent passions of man. White agrees that "there is such an inherent spirit for hunting in human nature, as scarce any inhibitions can restrain," and goes on to deplore the depredations of the poachers known as Waltham Blacks (*Selborne* 23). But instead of being an insight into human turbulence or political unrest, this leads to a genre piece of genial reminiscence. "Our old race of deer-stealers are hardly extinct yet: it was but a little while ago that, over their ale, they used to recount the exploits of their youth" (24).

As for the disasters of nations, White regards them with horror but does not pretend to analyze them, and in his journal they alternate with the seasonal changes that still command his full attention.

Jan. 21. Thrush sings, the song-thrush: the missle-thrush has not been heard. On this day Louis 16th late king of France, was beheaded at Paris, and his body flung into a deep grave without any coffin, or funeral service performed.

Jan. 28. Bees come out, and gather on the snowdrops.

Feb. 1. The Republic of France declares war against England and Holland.

Feb. 3. A strong gust in the night blew down the rain-gauge, which by the appearance in the tubs, must have contained a considerable quantity of water. (*Journal* 422)

Whatever *The Natural History of Selborne* may provide for its readers, its function for White was almost exactly inverse to that of Boswell's compulsive journalizing: it affords a reliable refuge not only from history, but also from the self. As a resident of Selborne, the childless White merges into the generations that have gone before; as a resident of nature, he explores the lives of beings that obey laws of behavior quite different from his own. *Selborne* betrays almost nothing of White's private feelings, and neither do his laconic journals. As Woolf says, "The story of Selborne is a vegetable, an animal story. The gossip is about the habits of vipers and the love interest is supplied chiefly by frogs. Compared with Gilbert White the most realistic of novelists is a rash romantic" (123).

If modern preoccupations tend to focus on the fictions in *Selborne*, for White the appeal of natural history lies in its resistance to fiction. By virtue of thinking and writing as a "natural historian" he commits himself to methods and assumptions which, as J. G. A. Pocock observes, are more rigorous and predictable than those governing less structured forms of intellectual work. "The scientific community is formally constituted by the paradigms of intellectual inquiry of a specific sort, and by the concept of that inquiry itself acting as a paradigm. A man is a member of the scientific community only because he has assumed the *persona* of one engaged in that form of inquiry and acknowledging the authority of its paradigms" (*Politics* 16). The self-effacing White no doubt finds a particular satisfaction in disappearing into a persona, and the device of printing a (one-sided) correspondence with Barrington and Tennant helps to establish the sense of a scientific community that shares observations in order to build up a collective picture of reality. White's critical allusions to Ray, Scopoli, and the others extend that community to the world of scientific books, where personality is supposed to count for nothing, and argument based on evidence is the test of success.

White's *Selborne* concludes with a journeyman compilation (omitted in most subsequent editions) of the *Antiquities of Selborne*. A chance remark in this section of the book, referring to the gradual destruction of medieval buildings, suggests how much has been left out:

Wantonness, no doubt, has had a share in the demolition; for boys love to destroy what men venerate and admire. A remarkable instance of this propensity the writer can give from his own knowledge. When a schoolboy, more than fifty years ago, he was eye-witness, perhaps a party concerned, in the undermining a portion of that fine old ruin at the north end of Basingstoke town, well known by the name of Holy Ghost Chapel. Very providentially the vast fragment, which these thoughtless little engineers endeavoured to sap, did not give way so soon as might have been expected; but it fell the night following, and with such violence that it shook the very ground, and, awakening the inhabitants of the neighbouring cottages, made them start up in their beds as if they had felt an earthquake. The motive for this dangerous attempt does not so readily appear: perhaps the more danger the more honour thought the boys; and the notion of doing some mischief gave a zest to the enterprise. As Dryden says upon another occasion, "It looked so like a sin it pleased the more." (*Antiquities* 347–48)

Is "perhaps a party concerned" a coy hint at White's involvement, or an honest confession that he recalls the depredation but is no longer sure whether he actually took part? At all events, this is a scene of significant transgression, like the orchard-robbing episode in Augustine's *Confessions*, and White's quotation from Dryden shows that he knows it. But his own emotions are kept carefully out of sight, and *Selborne* contains no other revelations of this kind. Instead, as Raymond Williams says, "his customary mode of attention was outward: observing, inquiring, annotating, classifying" (*The Country and the City* 119), even if the nonhuman world is best understood, in White's enabling fiction, in humanized terms.

Hume comments with reference to his *Treatise*, "Authors have this privilege in common with lovers, and founded on the same reason, that they are both besotted with a blind fondness of their object" (*Letters* 1:27). White, however, seeks to displace this narcissistic infatuation by redefining the "object" as the things he writes about rather than the thing he writes. If he can encourage his readers to love the object as he does, he apparently hopes that his own personality will become irrelevant. Of course exactly the opposite turns out to be the case: many readers have enjoyed *Selborne* who have little interest in "natural history" as ordinarily practiced, and White's personality, which pervades the book, gains a good deal of its much-remarked "charm" from being agreeably covert. As so often in the British tradition, self-deprecation is the best form of self-recommendation.

In his emphasis on factual accuracy and deductive reflection, White obeys Johnson's prescription in *Rambler* No. 5 for the study of nature as an escape from psychology. Those who cannot bear their own company, Johnson says, should examine "the volume of nature," which offers variety, morality, utility, and liberation from the self:

There are animals that borrow their colour from the neighbouring body, and, consequently, vary their hue as they happen to change their place. In like manner it ought to be the endeavour of every man to derive his reflections from the objects about him; for it is to no purpose that he alters his position, if his attention continues fixed to the same point. . . . He has always a certain prospect of discovering new reasons for adoring the sovereign author of the universe, and probable hopes of making some discovery of benefit to others, or of profit to himself. . . . He that enlarges his curiosity after the works of nature, demonstrably multiplies the inlets to happiness.

From what little biographical information survives, it appears that White turned to natural history at a time of uncertainty and depression in a life that seemed to be going nowhere (Mabey, chap. 5). Obscurity, though White eventually embraced it comfortably, was probably not his original goal. And his own *Advertisement* to *Selborne* states clearly that he values the writing for taking him out of himself: "If [the author] should not have been successful in any of these his intentions, yet there remains this consolation behind—that these his pursuits, by keeping the body and mind employed, have, under Providence, contributed to much health and cheerfulness of spirits, even to old age" (4).

This is an altogether Johnsonian prescription for mental health, and, to translate it into the terms of the present study, it produces a fiction whose power rests on fidelity to the external reality that it both invokes and recreates. In so doing, it conceals from itself its fictive status, which historical hindsight enables us to see clearly, and which would have been at least partly apparent to many of White's contemporaries. If, as Clifford Geertz says, "man is an animal suspended in webs of significance he himself has spun" (5), White is the one writer considered in this book who has almost no suspicion of that condition. His ideology is deeply implicated in the social world of the eighteenth century and in a consensus which —as he begins to suspect only at the time of the French Revolution—is quite capable of breaking down. His scientific vision, sustained in an unacknowledged way by that ideology, is intended to locate truths that are simply true, depending not on consensus but on the nature of things.

In the ultimate sense it may be the case that there can be no nature of things independent of ideology, and that "scientific" and "political" attitudes differ more in their claims than in their practice. "Science defines the structure of situations in such a way as to promote an attitude of disinterestedness toward them, whereas ideology defines them in a manner that elicits an attitude of commitment" (Gunn 103). White, in a way, does both: his ideology is so unreflective that it *feels* disinterested, and his scientific observations, though scrupulously accurate, are motivated by affection. To put it another way, his physicotheology fits in easily with a social ideology that ratifies the patriarchal status quo, but it also promotes a genuine humility toward nature that is very different from the imperial ambitions that have characterized mainstream science ever since Bacon, who vowed to extort nature's secrets by placing "her" on the rack of experimentation. White seeks with passionate avidity to know how the nonhuman world *is,* and his unselfconsciousness frees him to unriddle the puzzles of nature with a naive attentiveness that achieves remarkable results. *The Natural History of Selborne* is deeply imbued with the spirit of its time and place, which no doubt accounts for its survival as a "minor classic," but it reminds us as well that to identify an ideology is not always to discredit the observations that are made under its auspices. And even if social and scientific ideology have more in common than they want to admit, they are still far from identical. There remains a significant difference between asserting that the Church of England ought to be established by law and that harvest mice build spherical nests.

6

Burke
The Breakdown of Consensus

POLITICS AND EXPERIENCE

THE EMPHASIS of this book until now has been primarily epistemological rather than political. The final two chapters will reverse that priority, reflecting the ways in which eighteenth-century culture grew increasingly political in the deep sense of that term. Burke and Johnson quarreled in the 1770s about the respective merits of Lord North's Tories and the Rockingham Whigs; Burke and Paine quarreled in the 1790s about the respective merits of aristocratic monarchy and popular democracy. These two disagreements were different in kind, not just in degree: Johnson and Burke shared important assumptions about the nature of society, if not about practical politics, while Paine and Burke were profoundly opposed. But from another point of view it was Paine and the radicals who agreed with Burke on a fundamental point: the conservative fiction of reality was coming apart, and now that it could no longer be accepted simply as given, its only hope of preservation lay in winning an open war between fictive systems. From this perspective Johnson and Hume are comfortable in a secure paradigm of social and linguistic consensus, while Burke perceives himself as fighting for his life and for that of his culture.

At this moment of decisive paradigm shift, Burke's mission was the defense of the social and ideological order that people like Gilbert White had been taking for granted, and his tactic was to reinvigorate the shared rhetoric that used to guarantee consensus. Modern scholars sometimes lament that "Burke interpretation has been, to a distressing degree, a function of the ideologies of different historical periods" (Wilkins 10). But this is distressing only if one believes that interpretation can be ideologically innocent. Burke, who certainly does not believe that, deliberately invites ideological attention by the dogmatic energy with which he pushes his own positions as far as they will go, or farther. In his opinion no society can subsist without ideology, and in a time of unprecedented change it is especially important to define the ideology that makes one's own society work. By the same token, Burke sees historical change in ideological terms: what happens is inseparable from what people think is happening. He therefore stresses both the psychological basis and the temporal specificity of communities of belief. His writing is overtly rhetorical because he is openly pleading with his readers not to let the existing community collapse, and his often strident rhetoric reflects a feeling that a lot of people just aren't listening anymore (whereas Johnson, in his political writings, loftily despises anyone who disagrees with him).

In *Thoughts on the Cause of the Present Discontents* Burke defines the politician as "the philosopher in action" (*Works* 2:335), and during nearly thirty years as a member of Parliament (1766–94) he constantly proclaimed the interdependence of principles and practice. Indeed he was as much as a facilitator as a theorist, involved with quotidian politics as Hume and Johnson never were—or even Gibbon, whose brief (and mute) term in Parliament overlapped with his. Burke's career began as a behind-the-scenes advisor and speechwriter for William Gerard Hamilton; one observer called him Hamilton's "jackal" and another his "genius" (Cone 1:51). After six years he broke with Hamilton on the grounds that he was permitted too little time for his own pursuits ("for a drudge, disobedient," Goldsmith calls him in the comic poem *Retaliation*, adding that he "gave up to party what was meant for mankind"). Shortly afterward Burke formed his connection with the Whig group led by the marquis of Rockingham, which led to two brief periods in office punctuating three decades in the parliamentary opposition. Throughout that time, in addition to preparing his own speeches and publications, Burke was "the practical politician who undertook the management of votes and men, the party secretary who was concerned with an infinite variety of details, and even the party hack" (Cone 1:74).

But it is a fact of fundamental importance that even as Burke claimed to speak for England (or for that vaguer concept, Britain), he was almost continuously excluded from the center of power. Boswell heard him say, "I believe in any body of men in England I should have been in the minority; I have always been in the minority" (*Life* 3:235). In addition, the contrast between Burke's magisterial discourse and the confused exigency of his private affairs was often remarked; acting in daily competition with hardheaded political manipulators, he could not hope to sustain the Olympian elevation of "the Rambler" or of "the historian of the Roman Empire." Burke, of course, always claimed that being an Irish outsider enabled him to see the value of the English inside more clearly, embracing what in the late *Letter to a Noble Lord* he calls "this my adopted, my dearer, and more comprehensive country" (*Works* 8:40). And his whole career embodies the belief that in a time of turbulent historical change, philosophy must be acted out in the arena of political power.

Burke constantly invokes "principles," and just as constantly declares that these are empirical, deduced from the collective experience of the ages. The foundation of his thought is a recognition that "circumstances (which with some gentlemen pass for nothing) give in reality to every political principle its distinguishing colour and discriminating effect" (*Reflections* 90). In *A Letter to a Member of the National Assembly* (1791) he asserts, "I must see with my own eyes, I must, in a manner, touch with my own hands, not only the fixed, but the momentary circumstances, before I could venture to suggest any political project whatsoever" (*Works* 6:53). Social consensus is a stream fed by millions of individual tributaries, a partnership "between those who are living, those who are dead, and those who are to be born" that holds at bay "an unsocial, uncivil, unconnected chaos of elementary principles" (*Reflections* 194–95).

Just as in Hume's philosophy, the assumptions that sustain human life are necessarily collective. Hume could well endorse Burke's statement that "we are afraid to put men to live and trade each on his own private stock of reason; because we suspect that this stock in each man is small, and that the individuals would do better to avail themselves of the general bank and capital of nations and of ages" (*Reflections* 183). It would be easy to dilate on the way capitalist metaphors are embedded here in Burke's thinking; more significant is his implicit rejection of the monadic individual of capitalist theory. Reason is inadequate in any single person and can be effective only when it is merged with that of others. The shared assumptions of British culture, Burke says, "are so worked into my mind, that I am unable to distinguish what I have learned from others from the results of my own meditation" (*Reflections* 197).

As with Hume, feeling is the mechanism by which consensus is held together. In an early notebook Burke writes, "Metaphysical or physical speculations neither are, nor ought to be, the grounds of our duties, because we can arrive at no certainty in them. They have a weight when they concur with our own natural feelings; very little when against them" (*Notebook* 71). Imagination, just as in Hume and Johnson, is the private extravagance by which consensus is threatened. The "mild and indulgent" rule of the ecclesiastical states in Germany, Burke says, has permitted their subjects "to think lightly of their governments, and to judge of grievances, not by feeling, but by imagination" (*Thoughts on French Affairs*, *Works* 7:27). It is frequently remarked that Burke tended to aestheticize life, but less often recognized that he proposes an aesthetics of shared feeling rather than of private contemplation.

Language fascinates Burke, as it does Hume and Johnson, because it is the medium in which these feelings are stimulated, communicated, and reinforced. Burke says in the *Philosophical Enquiry* that "*descriptive* poetry operates chiefly by *substitution;* by the means of sounds, which by custom have the effect of realities" (173). As in Johnson's usage, *realities* is plural: we do not perceive a single intelligible order, but rather the myriad of particulars that link our senses to the world of experience. The function of language, whether organized in art or used more casually in conversation, is to summon and reinforce the shared associations by which a culture builds up its meanings, and in a sense Burke looks forward to the Wittgensteinian view that "what matters in semantics is not the mental or physical apparatus behind the word but the situation of its use" (Land 47). He is quite prepared to say that most of our experience is not immediate at all, but mediated through socially based preconceptions: "The influence of most things on our passions is not so much from the things themselves, as from our opinions concerning them; and these again depend very much on the opinions of other men, conveyable for the most part by words only" (*Philosophical Enquiry* 173).

The social context of feeling is confirmed by the phenomenon of "general words" to which no definite ideas are attached:

It is hard to repeat certain sets of words, though owned by themselves unoperative, without being in some degree affected, especially if a warm and affecting tone of voice accompanies them, as suppose,
    Wise, valiant, generous, good and great.
These words, by having no application, ought to be unoperative; but when words commonly sacred to great occasions are used, we are affected by them even without the occasions. (166)

Johnson defines *operative* in the *Dictionary* as "having the force of acting; having forcible agency." Lacking distinct links with "ideas," words like these ought to be "unoperative," but it is perfectly obvious that they do operate, especially if spoken in "a warm and affecting tone of voice." Burke's example happens to be a slightly irregular poetic line, "wise, váliant, génerous, góod and gréat"—an apparently casual list that unobtrusively summons the rhythms of art.

Understanding language in this way, Burke implicitly has a philosophical reply to the often-heard criticism that he "asserted rather than proved his arguments, leaving it to the reader to react according to his instincts and emotions" (Cone 1:294). That is precisely Burke's point: emotions make sense of life. In the *Reflections* he speaks with concise precision of "the nakedness and solitude of metaphysical abstraction" (90). It is solitary because it argues with purported logic from purported principles, instead of allying itself with the collective wisdom of the race. And it is naked because it claims to eschew metaphors and emotive rhetoric— the "dress of thought," in Pope's often-echoed phrase—in favor of an impossibly purified ideal of statement and proof.

Burke's chosen arena, at least until the late tracts, was the parliamentary speech, and he seems to have regarded printed language as a kind of speaking (Faulkner 1756). In Johnson's famous tribute, "his stream of mind is perpetual" (Boswell, *Life* 2:450); for Burke the function of writing, as of speaking, was to influence the larger current of which that stream was a part. Empiricist psychology, political experience, and rhetorical eloquence combine in a single structure of feeling, at once sustained by the social order and committed to preserving that order from attack. As he explains in the *Speech on the Economical Reform*, a good politician is both a spokesman for his society and an expert who helps it to know what it needs:

The people are the masters. They have only to express their wants at large and in gross. We are the expert artists; we are the skilful workmen, to shape their desires into perfect form, and to fit the utensil to the use. They are the sufferers, they tell the symptoms of the complaint; but we know the exact seat of the disease, and how to apply the remedy according to the rules of art. (*Works* 3:344)

In Burke's pragmatic metaphors the politician is both craftsman and physician, and his labor would be in vain if it did not confirm the larger tendencies of society as a whole. The politician can cure but he cannot invent.

Boswell reports that in 1777 Johnson ridiculed Burke's definition, in his recently published *Letter to the Sheriffs of Bristol on the Affairs of America*, of a free government: "For any practical purpose, it is what the people think so." Johnson retorted, "I will let the King of France govern me on those conditions, for it is to be governed just as I please" (*Life* 3:187). Johnson's sarcasm depends on believing (or pretending to believe) that Burke submits the definition of liberty to the judgment of each individual. "When Dr. Taylor talked of a girl being sent to a parish workhouse, and asked how much she could be obliged to work, 'Why (said Johnson) as much as is reasonable: and what is that? as much as *she thinks* reasonable.' " Burke's position is travestied here because in fact it rests on an understanding of "the people" as much more than a sum total of individual persons. Johnson does tend to think of society as individuals, and for him "subordination" is the lid placed on their greed and ambition.

Shortly after the passage Boswell quotes, Burke denounces those who "have split and anatomised the doctrine of free government, as if it were an abstract question concerning metaphysical liberty and necessity" (3:183), and he declares that "social and civil freedom, like all other things in common life, are variously mixed and modified, enjoyed in very different degrees, and shaped into an infinite diversity of forms, according to the temper and circumstances of every community. The *extreme* of liberty (which is its abstract perfection, but its real fault) obtains nowhere, nor ought to obtain anywhere. . . . Liberty must be limited in order to be possessed" (3:185). In this disagreement, Johnson insists on reducing freedom to a question of individual status and then repudiates it as incompatible with the good of the whole. As he puts it in *Taxation No Tyranny*, a 1775 pamphlet written in support of the ministry Burke was attacking, "If choice of evil be freedom, the felon in the galleys has his option of labour or of stripes. The Bostonian may quit his house to starve in the fields; his dog may refuse to set, and smart under the lash, and they may then congratulate each other upon the smiles of liberty" (*Political Writings* 417). From Burke's very different point of view, taxation of the Americans *is* tyranny simply because the whole community perceives it so.

The central message of Johnson's *Taxation No Tyranny* is that "all government is ultimately and essentially absolute," so that "an English individual may by the supreme authority be deprived of liberty, and a colony divested of its powers, for reasons of which that authority is the only judge" (422–23). The central message of Burke's *Letter to the Sheriffs of Bristol* is that consensus is the final measure of political reality: "The completeness of the legislative authority of parliament over this kingdom is not questioned; and yet many things indubitably included in the abstract idea of that power, and which carry no absolute injustice in themselves, yet being contrary to the opinions and feelings of the people, can as little be exercised as if parliament in that case had been possessed of no right at all" (*Works* 3:179). Johnson's society is a collection of individuals who must accept their places in a particular social order simply because that is where they happen to find themselves, and what keeps them in those places is power. Burke believes that in order for power to be effective, it must be internalized in the minds of those who submit to it, and while he rejects any historical (and therefore reversible) social contract, he endorses a spirit of communal assent that very much resembles Rousseau's *volonté générale*. On the concept of community, Burke is closer to Rousseau than to Johnson; where he differs from Rousseau is in identifying that community with the status quo. In modern literary jargon, the Burkean state is always already in existence.

The famous phrase "art is man's nature" occurs in the *Appeal from the New to the Old Whigs* during a discussion of the artifices of society, which include the development of the aristocracy that embodies its best impulses:

> The state of civil society, which necessarily generates this aristocracy, is a state of nature; and much more truly so than a savage and incoherent mode of life. For man is by nature reasonable; and he is never perfectly in his natural state, but when he is placed where reason may be best cultivated, and most predominates. Art is man's nature. (*Works* 6:218)

As in the thought of Swift and Pope, aristocracy in this sense means something more than arbitrary privilege. It is the old Renaissance ideal of the nobleman whose education has prepared him to represent the needs of the nation as a whole.

Although Burke believes that the status quo is beneficial for everyone in British society, he cannot deny that it is built upon inequalities that might easily give rise to rebellious thoughts. His goal, accordingly, is to identify and reinforce the benign fictions that preserve the existing consensus in the face of individualist alternatives like the "monstrous fiction" (*Reflections* 124) of the Rights of Man. There is no such thing as *the* people. In human societies, individuals are joined together in collective groups, each of which is *a* people and is literally a fiction: "It is wholly artificial, and made like all other legal fictions by common agreement." When the "covenant" of a particular society is broken up, there is no longer a people at all, but merely "a number of vague, loose individuals, and nothing more" (*Appeal from the New to the Old Whigs*, *Works* 6:211).

As in Johnson's thought, religion is the force that guarantees this order and protects mankind from a Hobbesian chaos of force against force. "We know, and what is better we feel inwardly, that religion is the basis of civil society" (*Reflections* 186). Atheism, on the other hand, reduces all rights to a question of might. Hence the strong statement in the *Appeal from the New to the Old Whigs*: "I allow that if no supreme ruler exists, wise to form, and potent to enforce, the moral law, there is no sanction to any contract, virtual or even actual, against the will of prevalent power. On that hypothesis, let any set of men be strong enough to set their duties at defiance, and they cease to be duties any longer" (*Works* 6:205). But atheists are mistaken, for God is "the Author of our place in the order of existence" and has "subjected us to act the part which belongs to the place assigned us" (6:206). As in Pope's *Essay on Man*, arguments for "man's" place in the chain of being are easily translated into arguments for the place of individual men and women in the contemporary social order.

Burke's espousal of this mode of conservatism is made precarious by a second commitment which older conservatives like Dryden or Swift would have regarded as utterly incompatible with religion and aristocracy: in scores of places he praises the automatic operation of the market and rejects any interference with it. In his later writings this position hardens, uniting laissez-faire economics with traditional religious fatalism. *Thoughts and Details on Scarcity* (1795), written during a famine, urges private charity toward the poor but warns their rulers "manfully to resist the very first idea, speculative or practical, that it is within the competence of the government, taken as government, or even of the rich, as rich, to supply to the poor those necessaries which it has pleased the Divine Providence for a while to withhold from them. We, the people, ought to be made sensible that it is not in breaking the laws of commerce, which are the laws of nature, and consequently the laws of God, that we are to place our hope of softening the Divine displeasure to remove any calamity under which we suffer, or which hangs over us" (*Works* 7:404).

By Burke's time, C. B. Macpherson says, "the capitalist order *had in fact been* the traditional order in England for a whole century" (63), and it is Burke's determination to identify the commercial with the aristocratic order that drives him to extreme statements about providential supervision. But this is not to say that he ignores the artificiality of any economic system, reflecting as it does the artificiality of the culture of which it is a part. "Even commerce and trade and manufacture, the gods of our oeconomical politicians, are themselves perhaps but creatures; are themselves but effects, which, as first causes, we choose to worship" (*Reflections* 174). Blake would say that human beings must learn to stop worshiping their own creations; Burke would reply that any attempt to do so leaves a vacuum which worse objects soon fill up.

In support of the traditional fictions, Burke rather defiantly extols "prejudice," probably recalling the Latin *praejudicium,* a judgment based on previous decisions and experiences (Wilkins 110). Prejudice undergirds morality and indeed merges with it: "The moral sentiments [are] so nearly connected with early prejudice as to be almost one and the same thing" (*Appeal from the New to the Old Whigs, Works* 6:256). Or as Burke puts it during the trial of Warren Hastings, "Man, in his moral nature, becomes, in his progress through life, a creature of prejudice—a creature of opinions—a creature of habits, and of sentiments growing out of them. These form our second nature, as inhabitants of the country and members of the society in which Providence has placed us" (*Works* 16:117). Just as Johnson in the *Rambler* insists on the necessity of developing right habits, so Burke sees duty and subordination as habits that can be learned and then lived. "Prejudice renders a man's virtue his habit, and not a series of unconnected acts. Through just prejudice, his duty becomes a part of his nature" (*Reflections* 183).

At the same time, however, Burke has to claim that any emotions and habits he dislikes are somehow *mistaken*. We look up to kings with awe and to aristocrats with respect "because when such ideas are brought before our minds, it is *natural* to be affected; because all other feelings are false and spurious" (*Reflections* 182). "Ideas," in the empiricist sense, are "brought before" the inner spectator, and "natural" feelings then come into play unless they have somehow been perverted. This is not only to place feeling at the heart of the moral and political system, but also to reserve the right to define which kinds of feeling are eligible and which are not. No wonder Burke places great reliance on the customary rituals and conventions that make up "the decent drapery of life" and cover "the defects of our naked shivering nature" (*Reflections* 171).

The French Revolution goaded Burke to passion on this theme, but it was one that had preoccupied him ever since his twenties, when he recorded a story in which Diogenes said he didn't care if his dead body were to be devoured by beasts. Burke comments,

It is not easily conceived what use funeral ceremonies (for my story led me to think) are to mankind. Trifling as they may seem, they nourish humanity, they soften in some measure the rigour of death, and they inspire humble, sober and becoming thoughts. They throw a decent veil over the weak and dishonourable circumstances of our nature. What shall we say to the philosophy that would strip it naked? (*Notebook* 91)

Bruce Smith, calling attention to the term *defects* in the passage in the *Reflections*, remarks that "Burke's teaching is to be understood not as being in 'conformity to nature,' but rather as an effort to again close the curtain of forgetfulness around a defective nature" (138). That is certainly true, and not by accident. Like Swift and Johnson, and in explicit opposition to Rousseau, Burke believes that (fallen) nature is so defective that the best protection against it is to live according to a set of sedulously inculcated habits, for which "the decent drapery of life" is a convenient term.

Burke *agonistes*, striving in Parliament and in published writings to sustain the old consensus, speaks for an idealized nation that is somehow greater than its parts. In a speech in 1782 attacking proposals to reform the House of Commons he clearly expresses his fear and rejection of individualism, including the collectivity of individuals postulated by one-man-one-vote radical theory. "The individual is foolish. The multitude, for the moment, is foolish, when they act without deliberation; but the species is wise, and when time is given to it, as a species, it almost always acts right" (*Works* 10:97). What Johnson concedes to literary value judgments, Burke allows for the entire range of values and assumptions that a society lives by.

This pronouncement is followed by what Isaac Kramnick calls "a virtuoso rendition of self-deprecating, deferential Burke" (125), disclaiming any desire for more power than the social order countenances for someone of his rank.

I know that if I possessed all the talents of the gentlemen on the side of the House I sit, and on the other, I cannot by Royal favour, or by popular delusion, or by oligarchical cabal, elevate myself above a certain very limited point, so as to endanger my own fall, or the ruin of my Country. I know there is an order that keeps things fast in their place; it is made to us, and we are made to it. Why not ask another wife, other children, another body, another mind? (10:104–5)

In this rich passage Burke rejects all three of the possible avenues by which an obscure Irishman might hope to rise to ministerial status: direct action by the crown, demagogic encouragement of "popular delusion," or the manipulations of an oligarchy such as the "Rockingham connection" whose servant he is. If he were ever to rise above his allotted place, he must expect to fall; but since he cannot rise, he will never be guilty of "the ruin of my Country," like the "Cromwell guiltless of his country's blood" in Gray's *Elegy*.

So Burke embraces his lot, strangely joining, as he does so, two very different kinds of inadmissible desires. No man can hope to have a different body or mind, but he could certainly have had a different wife and different children. Burke thus couples choices that might have easily been altered with conditions of existence that escape all choice. Choosing not to choose, he represses his own rebellious impulses and relies on the hierarchical system to keep him in his place.

AMERICA AND INDIA: CONSENSUS REINFORCED

If Burke's career began and ended with ambitious treatises, most of his other publications were printed versions of the spoken word. The House of Commons was a debating society in which he excelled in living discourse, and those speeches that he printed depend for effect on an always-apparent echo of the original occasion. The *Speech on American Taxation* (1774), which occupied two hours in delivery and was one of his first triumphs, is representative of his achievement as an orator-in-print, and illustrates the way Burke appeals to, and simultaneously seeks to guide, the consensus that sustains social experience.

The *Taxation* speech is addressed to the vacillating policy of Lord North's ministry, which had bowed to pressure and repealed five of six duties that had been imposed on American trade, but for symbolic reasons had retained the objectionable duty on tea. Burke's immediate aim is to expose the folly of this partial exaction, which inflamed American resistance while virtually confessing the impossibility of enforcement. The immediate issue is economic, and Burke accordingly gives close attention to commercial considerations. But he is unwilling to grant them primacy. Whatever the connection of ideology with its material basis may be, Burke claims that its role is to shape the way people perceive the sociopolitical world, rather than to reflect politics at second hand. Reality is inseparable from ideas about reality, and when people's ideas begin to alter, so does their reality. This, of course, is precisely the hope and goal of the Continental Enlightenment; Burke's counterrevolutionary goal is to keep change at bay unless it can be channeled within the structures of existing ideas—in which case, from the radical point of view, it isn't really change at all.

The speech begins in answer to a challenge. A former ally has cast aspersions on the actions of the Rockingham group in the 1760s, and it is therefore appropriate to place the crisis in historical context. This is something very different from Gibbon's Olympian and remote kind of history, for Burke is addressing the participants themselves and inviting them to remember—actually, to reimagine—the decisions that led them to be "lashed round and round this miserable circle of occasional arguments and temporary expedients" (*Works* 2:350). One of Burke's opponents has made the plausible suggestion that it is useless (and, perhaps, politically risky) to go over the events of the past, so that it would be best simply to resolve the present crisis as expediently as possible. But from Burke's point of view, the present is a product of the myriad events of the past, and no solution can succeed that ignores or suppresses them. "He asserts that retrospect is not wise; and the proper, the only proper subject of inquiry, is 'not how we got into this difficulty, but how we are to get out of it.' In other words, we are, according to him, to consult our invention and to reject our experience" (2:352).

The ministry, Burke goes on to say, "never had any kind of system, right or wrong; but only invented occasionally some miserable tale for the day, in order meanly to sneak out of difficulties into which they had proudly strutted" (2:361). These are the conventional fictions of politics, ad hoc stories that are hastily invented to mask blunders and scandals and are put about by paid hacks. "Sir, this vermin of court reporters, when they are forced into day upon one point, are sure to burrow in another, but they shall have no refuge; I will make them bolt out of all their holes" (2:413). In his campaign to recover what he believes to be the facts, Burke counters evasiveness with directness. "By such management, by the irresistible operation of feeble councils, so paltry a sum as three-pence in the eyes of a financier, so insignificant an article as tea in the eyes of a philosopher, have shaken the pillars of a commercial empire that circled the whole globe" (2:361). The inaction and folly of Parliament have permitted feebleness to seem irresistible, and a threepenny duty on tea has been allowed to assume major symbolic importance.

It is not that tea is trivial in itself, considered in purely economic terms. "Tea is perhaps the most important object, taking it with its necessary connections [with the East India trade], of any in the mighty circle of our commerce. If commercial principles had been the true motives to the repeal, or had they been at all attended to, tea would have been the last article we should have left taxed for a subject of controversy" (2:360). It is in a *philosophical* context that tea is trivial: just because it has economic importance, it should never have been allowed to become the occasion for a constitutional crisis that centers on Britain's right to tax her colonies.

It was far from clear at that time, and Burke thinks it best to leave it unclear, whether Parliament has the right to tax the colonies as well as to regulate their trade. The tea duty has become a test case when test cases are precisely what Burke wants to avoid. It was only when a particular tax was discontinued and then reinstated, Burke says, that the colonists "quarreled with the old taxes as well as the new; then it was, and not till then, that they questioned all the parts of your legislative power, and by the battery of such questions have shaken the solid structure of this empire to its deepest foundations" (2:354). In modern terms, a movement has been set in motion in which ideology and praxis are visibly re-forming, like a storm cloud growing around a seed crystal. The Americans could pay the tea duty easily enough, but they will not: "No commodity will bear three-pence, or will bear a penny, when the general feelings of men are irritated, and two millions of people are resolved not to pay" (2:364). In the same way, Burke adds, John Hampden resisted the ship money exactions of Charles I, and that resistance led to the disaster of the civil war.

Burke's intention in the *Taxation* speech is to reaffirm the adequacy of the old consensus by showing that the crisis has arisen from avoidable human blunders rather than from the current of history or the nature of things. So he proceeds to narrate the course of events in which the legislation was passed, repealed, and reinvoked; he recalls how individuals in Parliament argued for or against it, and how expectations gradually developed that can no longer be ignored. At one point he actually offers to stop, and receives fresh authorization from an offstage voice or voices: "I hope I am not going into a narrative troublesome to the House. [A cry of, go on, go on.]" (2:401). Then, after this judicious review, Burke rises again to heated rhetoric against those who have been misrepresenting the past, using the language of Augustan satire: "Thus are blown away the insect race of courtly falsehoods! Thus perish the miserable inventions of the wretched runners for a wretched cause, which they have fly-blown into every weak and rotten part of the country, in vain hopes that when their maggots had taken wing, their importunate buzzing might sound something like the public voice!" (2:416). This is not argument; it is not even persuasion. Rather, it is invective, intended to give pleasure to Burke's allies, to annoy the ministry and its supporters, and to provoke a recovery of recent history from those who have coopted and reinvented it for their own ends.

The *Speech on American Taxation* has other set pieces, notably the account of the Chatham coalition as "a cabinet so variously inlaid, such a piece of diversified mosaic, such a tesselated pavement without cement," in which the dead metaphor of the "cabinet" is made to yield up a flow of ironic delight. Burke then abruptly shifts the metaphor and arrives at a ludicrous image of ministers who had never before met "pigging together, heads and points, in the same truckle-bed" (2:420). But it would be a mistake to overemphasize purple passages and anthology pieces. Burke is not a satirist, though he is often satirical. His purpose is to recall the details of events that have become blurred in memory, including a repeal of the Stamp Act that followed "the fullest, most impartial, and least garbled body of evidence that ever was produced to this House" (2:403). He aspires in fact to embody the qualities he ascribes to the late Charles Townshend, "officially the re-producer of this fatal scheme," who knew better than anyone "how to bring together within a short time all that was necessary to establish, to illustrate, and to decorate that side of the question he supported" (2:422). Illustration and decoration follow upon the establishment of a version of the truth, "that side of the question" that the speaker believes to be true. In Humean terms, truth is psychological and its expression rhetorical, but belief is a fact even if absolute truth is not.

Resisting any suggestion that the course of history is inevitable and irreversible, Burke holds that ideas and personalities motivate events. But the great men who occupy center stage are prone to error, as Burke declares in his summation of Townshend's career: "He was truly the child of the House. He never thought, did, or said any thing, but with a view to you. He every day adapted himself to your disposition, and adjusted himself before it as at a looking-glass" (2:426–27). Boswell once described his private journal as a mirror for adjusting character; Burke belongs to a class of "senators" (the term was frequently used) whose ideal of virtue makes their behavior public in a Roman or Renaissance sense. Despite his gifts, Townshend lacked the larger perspective that would have permitted him to see beyond the temporary and shifting demands of the political mirror, which in this case was composed of the very politicians who are now the audience for Burke's words. "To please universally was the object of his life; but to tax and to please, no more than to love and to be wise, is not given to men. However he attempted it" (2:426). Townshend's was a misplaced love, a political passion that encouraged the communal narcissism of the Commons as self-reflexive mirror, and he exemplifies what Burke laments throughout the entire business, "the mischief of not having large and liberal ideas in the management of great affairs" (2:360).

Arguments can always be found to justify change, but change feeds on itself and will eventually overturn all arguments.

I am not here going into the distinctions of rights, not attempting to mark their boundaries. I do not enter into these metaphysical distinctions; I hate the very sound of them. Leave the Americans as they anciently stood, and these distinctions, born of our unhappy contest, will die along with it. . . . Be content to bind America by laws of trade; you have always done it. Let this be your reason for binding their trade. Do not burden them by taxes; you were not used to do so from the beginning. Let this be your reason for not taxing. These are the arguments of states and kingdoms. Leave the rest to the schools; for there only they may be discussed with safety. (2:432–33)

Philosophical enquiries are academic projects better suited—as Hume admits of his own meditations—to theoretical recreation than to actual living. As for the tea duty, it exists only as a negative symbol, an incentive to rebellion that no longer enjoys any positive status at all. "You are therefore at this moment in the awkward situation of fighting for a phantom;

a quiddity; a thing that wants, not only a substance, but even a name; for a thing which is neither abstract right nor profitable enjoyment" (2: 365–66).

The crux, then, is what the Americans believe to be true, which thereby becomes the truth *for them.*

Reflect how you are to govern a people who think they ought to be free, and think they are not. Your scheme yields no revenue; it yields nothing but discontent, disorder, disobedience; and such is the state of America that after wading up to your eyes in blood, you could only end just where you begun; that is, to tax where no revenue is to be found, to—my voice fails me; my inclination indeed carries me no farther—all is confusion beyond it. (2:435)

The Americans may be free, but they think they are not, and Burke breaks down histrionically as he imagines the consequences of defying this psychological fact. Unless Britain and America can once again think alike—in Humean terms, believe alike—the course of events will rapidly enact the chaotic discord that Burke's speech seeks to avert. "After this, are you surprised that Parliament is every day and everywhere losing (I feel it with sorrow, I utter it with reluctance) that reverential affection which so endearing a name of authority ought ever to carry with it; that you are obeyed solely from respect to the bayonet; and that this House, the ground and pillar of freedom, is itself held up only by the treacherous underpinning and clumsy buttresses of arbitrary power?" (2:373). Many Continental thinkers, and (as we shall see) Godwin in England, held that the exposure of that basis is both necessary and desirable. Burke holds very differently that an ideology is a living structure of belief, not just a mask for exploitation, and by "reverential affection" he means something in addition to hegemony: he means a sense of common values that can be willingly shared by the colonists, the British, and the parliamentary system in which authority must finally rest. Hume holds that life rests on feeling, but discusses it calmly and rationally; Burke brings feeling into the open.

In his speeches on America, Burke could take it for granted that America and Britain formed a single cultural body united, as he says in the *Speech on Conciliation*, by "the close affection which grows from common names, from kindred blood, from similar privileges, and equal protection" (3:123). His speeches on India, very unusually for their time, confront the radically dissimilar traditions of "a people for ages civilized and cultivated; cultivated by all the arts of polished life, whilst we were yet in the woods" (*Speech on Fox's East India Bill*, 4:18). No doubt Burke idealizes Hindu civilization as a "polemical utopia" (Janes 9) that contrasts with British corruption, but at any rate he takes immense pains to learn what Indian culture is like, and he insists that it is both impossible and wrong for an imperial power to impose its own social fictions from without. As he puts it during the trial of Warren Hastings for corruption in the administration of India, "God forbid we should pass judgment upon people who framed their laws and institutions prior to our insect origin of yesterday. . . . They have stood firm on their ancient base—they have cast their roots deep in their native soil" (*Works* 13:70).

The broad outline of the story may be briefly sketched. By the middle of the eighteenth century the British East India Company had taken advantage of the fragmentation of the Mughal Empire to establish a position of extraordinary power, acting as a de facto government over huge areas of the subcontinent. As Burke describes it in the 1783 speech on Fox's bill, it controlled the lives of thirty million persons, commanded an army of sixty thousand men, and received an annual revenue of seven million pounds (4:10). The crucial *Ninth Report from the Select Committee* (1783), an exhaustive document written entirely by Burke, makes plain the Company's political role: "The English are a people who appear in India as a conquering nation; all dealing with them is therefore, more or less, a dealing with power" (11:145). As an instance of the unjust use of economic power, Burke notes that in the year following a terrible famine in Bengal the produce of opium was doubled: the Company was compelling farmers to plant poppies for the China trade rather than grain for consumption.

The India problem was doubly vexed because the relationship between the Company and the British government was ambiguous, and because the financial and territorial stakes were immense. Always preferring to rely on established precedents, Burke is daunted, as he says in a footnote to a 1784 speech, by their absence in this case: "It is a very anomalous species of power and property which is held by the East India company. Our English prerogative law does not furnish principles, much less precedents, by which it can be defined or adjusted" (4:161). Burke's immediate conclusion is that only Parliament has the authority to define this literally unprecedented situation. But the deeper implication is that novelty is ipso facto dangerous, allowing greed and corruption to invade areas of life where no boundaries are yet in place. With respect to India such novelty is still more alarming because the power involved is incommensurately vast: "The East-India company governs an empire through all its concerns, and all its departments, from the lowest office of economy to the highest councils of state—an empire to which Great Britain is in comparison but a respectable province" (4:170). Above all, the Company is a political entity disguised as a trading firm, as Burke observes during the Hastings trial: "The East India Company in Asia is a state in the disguise of a merchant. . . . The whole external order and series of the service is commercial; the principal, the inward, the real, is almost entirely political" (13:29).

Burke's position in the 1770s was that the British government had a right to regulate the affairs of the Company but not to take control of it; he saw in the Indian question, as in many others, a threat of unreasonable extension of the power of the crown. In later years he reversed this view, when a deeper understanding of Indian affairs led him to believe that the Company had abused its trust and that its chartered rights were therefore abrogated. And even if the threat to the British constitution were real, circumstances dictated that one set of principles must give way to another. "If I am not able to correct a system of oppression and tyranny that goes to the utter ruin of thirty millions of my fellow-creatures and fellow-subjects, but by some increase to the influence of the crown, I am ready here to declare that I, who have been active to reduce it, shall be at least as active and strenuous to restore it again" (*Speech on Fox's East India Bill*, 4:114–15).

It is not irrelevant, as Burke's opponents regularly noted, that members of his family had huge holdings in East India Company stock, involving him in what would certainly be seen today as conflict of interest, and that from 1778 onward his kinsman and close friend Will Burke was employed in India and had strong opinions as well as a financial stake. (It might well appear that in seeking to correct "abuses" in the Company administration, Burke's aim was to protect his family's investments.) Burke's often-reiterated defense of his conduct was that personal involvement was not incompatible with moral concern and might indeed stimulate it. In fact it is for his emotional rather than financial investment that he has been most often criticized, as if a dispassionate objectivity would have made him understand India better. On this point a modern Indian economist, reprinting Burke's *Ninth Report*, remarks dryly that "the critics seem to forget that no political philosopher can be detached; of course he can pretend to be" (Sen 1). In Burke's view of human experience, facts gain their life from feeling, and the first paragraph of his speech on Fox's bill states as much: "I have felt, with some degree of sensibility, the natural and inevitable impressions of the several matters of fact" (*Works* 4:3).

In 1781 Burke was elected to a parliamentary select committee that investigated charges of Company abuses in Bengal, and he began the heavy course of reading that made him an expert on Indian affairs, focusing on the extensive powers exerted by Warren Hastings, the governor of Bengal. It would be a mistake, however, to concentrate entirely on the trial of Hastings, who seemed to many people (including Johnson and Boswell) to have exercised necessary authority in a fluid and dangerous situation, and who was ultimately acquitted. Burke's concern for India runs far deeper than the malversation of individuals, though in the political arena his analysis naturally emphasizes that, and addresses the profound dislocations that occur when cultures collide. In seeking to reconstruct events, however recent, that had taken place in a far-off land, Burke was acting essentially as a historian, and the otherness of India encouraged him to develop what Gibbon and the Enlightenment historians lacked, a sense of the uniqueness of cultural contexts.

At the beginning of the speech on Fox's bill Burke issues this challenge: "If Parliament, Sir, had nothing to do with this charter [of the East India Company] we might have some sort of Epicurean excuse to stand aloof, indifferent spectators of what passes in the company's name in India and in London. But if we are the very cause of the evil, we are in a special manner engaged to the redress" (*Works* 4:12). Later in the speech Burke paints a memorable picture of the welcome extended at home to the "wave after wave" (4:40) of Britons who have despoiled India:

Arrived in England, the destroyers of the nobility and gentry of a whole kingdom will find the best company in this nation, at a board of elegance and hospitality. Here the manufacturer and husbandman will bless the just and punctual hand that in India has torn the cloth from the loom, or wrested the scanty portion of rice and salt from the peasant of Bengal, or wrung from him the very opium in which he forgot his oppressions and his oppressor. They marry into your families; they enter into your senate; they ease your estates by loans; they raise their value by demand; they cherish and protect your relations which lie heavy on your patronage; and there is scarcely a house in the kingdom that does not feel some concern and interest that makes all reform of our eastern government appear officious and disgusting; and, on the whole, a most discouraging attempt. In such an attempt you injure those who are able to return kindness, or to resent injury. If you succeed, you save those who cannot so much as give you thanks. (4:42)

India is not just a remote dependency; it is the scene where fortunes are made by people who are deeply rooted in British government and society. To argue on behalf of the Indian people is therefore a direct challenge to the whole nexus of wealth and privilege which Burke is normally committed to defend.

Thus considerations that are as much moral as political compel Burke to dwell on the disagreeable subject, and the only way he can hope to sway his hearers is by means of a compelling feat of imagination. The British will not care about the plight of India unless they can be brought to sympathize with the Indians. There is plenty of vivid rhetoric in Burke's India speeches, but he knows that rhetoric by itself will not convert people who have strong personal and financial reasons to resist it. Conviction must flow from facts, and he therefore describes himself as one who "thought himself obliged, by the research of years, to wind himself into the inmost recesses and labyrinths of the Indian detail" (4:6). Only thus can the gulf be bridged that separates Britain from its far-off dominion: "The cries of India are given to seas and winds, to be blown about, in every breaking up of the monsoon, over a remote and unhearing ocean" (4:41). In his speech on the third day of the Hastings trial (1788) Burke tells his hearers: "It is not from this district, or from that parish, not from this city, or the other province, that relief is now applied for: exiled and undone princes, extensive tribes, suffering nations, infinite descriptions of men, different in language, in manners, and in rites—men, separated by every barrier of nature from you, by the providence of God are blended in one common cause, and are now become suppliants at your Bar" (13:16). If the act of imaginative recreation could produce sufficient "vividness" in the Humean sense, then it would be as if the whole of India had come to life at the bar of the House of Lords.

Rather than surveying Burke's highly charged denunciations of Hastings, it will be more useful to consider the powerful *Speech on the Nabob of Arcot's Debts* (1785), in which he uses all of his resources of argument and rhetoric to give life to a topic that is manifestly obscure. Mohammed Ali Khan, the Nabob (or Nawab) of Arcot in the southeastern region known as the Carnatic, had long been useful to the Company both as a client prince—in 1777 he helped to engineer a convenient revolution in Madras—and as a conduit for laundering the personal wealth of Company officials. The so-called debts were huge sums, made even greater by extravagant interest, which the Nabob purportedly owed to these persons. The heart of Burke's case is that "there is strong reason to suspect that the body of these debts is wholly fictitious, and was never created by money *bona fide* lent" (4:187). The very title of the speech therefore alludes to the thing that is not. "The system of concealment is fostered by a system of falsehood. False facts, false colours, false names of persons and things, are its whole support" (4:207).

In the *Advertisement* to the printed version of the speech Burke relates that the Company's directors in England had long demanded an inquiry into the question of the Nabob's debts, but that a recently constituted board had countermanded this policy, had admitted all the debts "without any investigation whatever," and had established a fund for paying them out of the revenues of the Carnatic (4:191). Public money was thus to be used to enrich British officials, under color of reimbursing them for personal funds which they had supposedly lent to the Nabob. Facts had been covered up by fictions, of which the Nabob himself might be said to be the most outrageous, and tribute was paid "not to a real potentate, but to a shadow, a dream, an incubus of oppression" (4:292). Burke's goal is to penetrate the "shades of eternal night" (4:206) that cover "the conversion of a department of British government into an Indian mystery" (4:207), in order to reveal "that the Nabob of Arcot and his creditors are not adversaries, but collusive parties, and that the whole transaction is under a false colour and false names" (4:216).

In a sense Burke and his allies seem to have been fiction makers themselves, as a modern historian sternly reports, developing "the myth of the secret influence wielded over the ministry by the Nawab of Arcot" (Sutherland 323). The Nabob, who had in fact no money at all at this time, was supposed to have purchased control of eight seats in Commons and to be directly influencing the government through bribes. But this is to take too narrow a view of the subject. Burke's point is not that the Nabob is a monster, but that he serves members of the Company as a useful conduit for corruption. It is indisputable that a number of members of Parliament were obedient to certain officials of the Company who had spent huge sums "in the purchase of lands, in the buying and building of houses, in the securing quiet seats in parliament, or in the tumultuous riot of contested elections" (4:212).

This power is real enough, extending through the whole network of influence of the country gentry, and it is a matter of indifference whether it is exerted literally by the Nabob or by those whose rise to incredible wealth is concealed behind the fiction of his "debts." As Burke puts it, "treasures equal to the revenues of a respectable kingdom" have been amassed in a few years by "a small number of slight individuals, of no consequence or situation, possessed of no lucrative offices, without the command of armies or the known administration of revenues, without profession of any kind, without any sort of trade sufficient to employ a pedlar" (4:211–12). Such individuals could never have operated so invisibly at home, where their countrymen would have known how to penetrate their schemes; it is because they batten on India, whose riches are popularly supposed to be limitless, that they can return to Britain with the fruits of injustices that nobody thinks to question. "During the deep, silent flow of this steady stream of wealth which set from India into Europe, it generally passed on with no adequate observation; but happening at some periods to meet rifts of rocks that checked its course, it grew more noisy and attracted more notice" (4:209).

Still more to the point, these persons could never have achieved success without the connivance of others in high places. More than once in the speech Burke alludes directly to the collusion of the prime minister, the younger Pitt, and permits himself the most extravagant of analogies: "Never did Nero, in all the insolent prodigality of despotism, deal out to his praetorian guards a donation fit to be named with the largess showered down by the bounty of our chancellor of the exchequer on the faithful band of his Indian sepoys" (4:243). Sepoys are Indian natives serving in the British army; the corrupt officials of the East India Company are the sepoys of William Pitt.

To emphasize his adversarial posture, Burke prefaces the printed version of the speech with an epigraph in Greek from the *Epistles* of the Emperor Julian, which asks (in modern translation) whether a student of Plato and Aristotle should look on indifferently "while the wretched people were being betrayed by thieves," and concludes that to "desert my post" would be disgraceful, "especially when God is fighting on my side, for it was indeed he who posted me here" (Julian 3:13). Burke presents himself as a lonely sentry at an exposed outpost, resisting thieves in high places on behalf of the wretched of the earth. That he had unacknowledged psychological motives for this crusade is likely enough, particularly in the "near maniacal obsession" (Kramnick 127) of his vendetta against Hastings. But insofar as he can, he seeks to persuade the reader that his account of India, though necessarily fictive in building up a story from the testimony of others, is more nearly real than the shameless fictions of his opponents. Burke offers himself, with all of his rhetorical and oratorical gifts, as the vehicle of truth. The *London Journal* is Boswell's fiction of the self, in which everything in the surrounding world gets translated into the terms of his own life; Burke's speeches are fictions of the other, in which the self—like the persona of Augustan satire—dwindles into a specialized and conventionalized spokesman for morality and truth.

At the end of the *Advertisement* Burke reports that when Fox called for a renewed inquiry into the scandal, the question "passed in the negative by a very great majority" (4:193). At its initial hearing the speech was therefore a failure, and in printing it Burke appeals to a wider audience than the original one, just as the Hastings trial, a battle he knew he would lose, served as a "theatrical drama" (O'Gorman 95) to bring India's sufferings to light. Rhetoric and metaphor are an important part of Burke's appeal, but at bottom it must rest on those facts which have been hidden under the veil of fictions, and Burke undertakes to go further than others have done "into the detail of the subject" (4:194). He insists that the facts are not in themselves unintelligible: "I beg leave to assure you that there is nothing in the Indian detail which is more difficult than in the detail of any other business" (4:199). The problem is a double one, that certain persons have an interest in keeping the facts muddled, and that India's remoteness allows them to hide their actions under a cloud of obfuscating terms, *jagirs* and *soucars* and *bannians* and *zemindars*.

As so often, language is used to obscure rather than to express, and Burke's goal is to overcome the indifference that is the best ally of duplicity. "Terms of art, indeed, are different in different places, but they are generally understood in none. The technical style of an Indian treasury is not one jot more remote than the jargon of our own exchequer from the train of our ordinary ideas, or the idiom of our common language. The difference, therefore, in the two cases is not in the comparative difficulty or facility of the two subjects, but in our attention to the one, and our total neglect of the other" (4:200). The reality of India can emerge from the fog of obscurity only when Burke recasts it in "the idiom of our common language." This process of exposure is analytical as well as descriptive, a detective story (too complex to recount here) in which Burke retraces the conflicting accounts of Indian affairs in order to deduce the truth. "Clandestine and collusive practice can only be traced by combination and comparison of circumstances. To reject such combination and comparison is to reject the only means of detecting fraud" (4:314).

Far from acting as a responsible commercial institution, the Company has steadily impoverished its territories for the personal profit of its officials. True commerce would be a reciprocal relationship between Britain and India, not an exploitation of Indian workers by British overlords. In a passage in the *Reflections on the Revolution in France* that defends the right of capitalists—Burke is thinking of the owners of rural estates, including himself—to appropriate the profit of labor, he states a concomitant moral obligation:

In every prosperous community something more is produced than goes to the immediate support of the producer. This surplus forms the income of the landed capitalist. It will be spent by a proprietor who does not labour. But this idleness is itself the spring of labour; this repose the spur to industry. The only concern of the state is, that the capital taken in rent from the land should be returned again to the industry from whence it came; and that its expenditure should be with the least possible detriment to the morals of those who expend it, and to those of the people to whom it is returned. (270)

For some modern readers, terms like *capitalist* and *proprietor who does not labour* may bear a polemical charge that makes it nearly impossible to grasp the ideal of moral stewardship that governs their use in Burke; but he is entirely clear, at any rate, about his abhorrence of British exploitation in India.

There are worse evils than poverty, and the policies of the Company have conjured them up; for example, it promoted alliances among client states that precipitated the bloody revenge of Hyder Ali of Mysore, a victim who "was not of the passive kind" (*Works* 4:258). An authoritative modern history of India relates what happened with bland efficiency: "The hostilities launched by the Nawab at the goading of his creditors drove Haidar Ali to such fierce retaliation that his cavalry galloped within view of the very walls of Fort St. George [Madras] in 1780 and might well have destroyed the British base in the Carnatic had it not been for Hastings's vigorous and timely assistance" (Wolpert 193). Burke's account is very different, summoning a metaphor of natural forces that have been rashly unleashed:

Whilst the authors of all these evils were idly and stupidly gazing on this menacing meteor which blackened all their horizon, it suddenly burst, and poured down the whole of its contents upon the plains of the Carnatic. . . . The miserable inhabitants, flying from their flaming villages, in part were slaughtered; others, without regard to sex, to age, to the respect of rank, or sacredness of function, fathers torn from children, husbands from wives, enveloped in a whirlwind of cavalry, and amidst the goading spears of drivers and the trampling of pursuing horses, were swept into captivity in an unknown and hostile land. (4:260)

The ordinary farmers and villagers of India have been invisible to the Parliament that is reviewing the Company's misdeeds; Burke's goal is to bring them into view. After eighteen months of fighting, a British army traveled for hundreds of miles through the Carnatic, and "through the whole line of their march they did not see one man, not one woman, not one child, not one four-footed beast of any description whatever. One dead, uniform silence reigned over the whole region" (4:262). Lest this should sound like poetic exaggeration, Burke says that he has interviewed reliable witnesses and soberly adds, "With the inconsiderable exceptions of the narrow vicinage of some few forts, I wish to be understood as speaking literally." To drive home the horror of the scene, he adds that "the Carnatic is a country not much inferior in extent to England."

In his elaboration of an Indian reality, Burke's achievement lies in the union of rhetorical energy with a closely woven fabric of explanation:

That debt to the company is the pretext under which all the other debts lurk and cover themselves. That debt forms the foul, putrid mucus in which are engendered the whole brood of creeping ascarides, all the endless involutions, the eternal knot, added to a knot of those inexpugnable tape-worms, which devour the nutriment and eat up the bowels of India. It is necessary, Sir, you should recollect two things: first, that the Nabob's debt to the company carries no interest. In the next place you will observe that whenever the company has occasion to borrow, she has always commanded whatever she thought fit at eight per cent. Carrying in your mind these two facts, attend to the process with regard to the public and private debt, and with what little appearance of decency they play into each other's hands a game of utter perdition to the unhappy natives of India. The Nabob falls into an arrear to the company. The Presidency presses for payment. The Nabob's answer is, I have no money. Good. But there are soucars [money-lenders] who will supply you on the mortgage of your territories. Then steps forward some Paul Benfield [the Nabob's financier, later an M.P.], and from his grateful compassion to the Nabob and his filial regard to the company, he unlocks the treasures of his virtuous industry; and for a consideration of twenty-four or thirty-six per cent on a mortgage of the territorial revenue, becomes security to the company for the Nabob's arrear. (4:282–83)

The metaphor of the ascarides or tapeworms, perhaps inspired by the tape with which official papers were bound up, is sufficiently satirical, especially in the nasty assonance of *putrid mucus*. One inevitably thinks of the homology of money and excrement in Swift and Pope. But in Burke's exposition the metaphor is inseparable from the plain speaking from which it emerges and to which it returns, a straightforward account of manipulated interest rates and the nominal transfer of imaginary debts.

At the end of the *Arcot* speech Burke returns to the theme of his epigraph from Julian, declaring ringingly, "Let who will shrink back, I shall be found at my post" (4:322). Even in the short run, his fight was not in vain. And from a longer perspective it is possible to say that Burke's imagination, more than any other single factor, brought about a change in British attitudes toward India, as Sutherland departs from her usually dry prose to say:

As the torrent of Burke's oratory poured forth in the House, sentiment became a real force which must drive any government to action. For the first time there were heard in the House expressions of regret (to become common among the humanitarians of the nineteenth century) that Europeans had ever set foot on these distant shores and imposed their wills on these alien societies. Of this humanitarianism Burke was certainly the main inspiration, and it is impossible even now to read his words without being stirred by them. (367)

His versions of reality were able, for many decades, to influence those of countless readers, including many in high places.

Perhaps the most striking feature of Burke's account of India is its faithful reliance on documents. Just because India is so strange and so far away, its existence has to be reconstructed from thousands of pieces of paper; and beyond this, Burke seems to entertain a conviction (somewhat analogous to Boswell's) that reality is fluid and murky unless it is continuously transcribed. As it turned out, the later administration of India was to be meticulously recorded on paper, as John Stuart Mill observed in 1852:

> The whole Government of India is carried on in writing. All the orders given, and all the acts of the executive officers, are reported in writing, and the whole of the original correspondence is sent to the Home Government; so that there is no single act done in India, the whole of the reasons for which are not placed on record. This appears to me a greater security for good government than exists in almost any other government in the world, because no other probably has a system of recordation so complete. (De Schweinitz 93–94)

In response to this Victorian optimism, Burke would probably have a good deal to say about the bureaucratic potential for distorting and misusing the written word, but all the same, it is much better than nothing, particularly since far-off India can only be governed by means of messages. In the *Ninth Report* Burke dwells at length on the scanty and contradictory information that Hastings and his colleagues have sent to London, and concludes that "the Company is left without any fixed data upon which they can make a rational disposition of their affairs" (*Works* 11:84–85). And in the 1786 *Articles of Charge of High Crimes and Misdemeanors against Warren Hastings* Burke mentions that the directors of the Company in London had "reason to conceive that for the purpose of concealing corrupt transactions, their servants in India had made unfair, mutilated, and garbled communications of correspondence, and sometimes had wholly withheld the same" (11:382). In Godwin the dark possibility will arise that garbling is not accidental but inevitable—that no documents are ever trustworthy, and that the reality they comprise is an infinite regression of half-truths that never add up to truth. But for Burke, orator on paper and discursive reasoner in the public forum, words can be used against words to liberate something like the truth.

FRANCE: THE ABYSS OF INDIVIDUALISM

By the end of his life Burke saw himself as a scapegoat and prophet, destined to fight international revolution even in death. In the *Letter to a Noble Lord* he exclaims, "Must I be annihilated, lest, like old John

Zisca's, my skin might be made into a drum, to animate Europe to eternal battle against a tyranny that threatens to overwhelm all Europe, and all the human race?" (*Works* 8 : 5). But it would be wrong to suppose that the crisis of the 1790s shocked Burke into a stance of unprecedented reaction. On the contrary, the *Reflections* confirms attitudes that he held throughout his life, crystallizing three issues in particular: the status of the fictions that describe and alter "reality"; the implications of radical individualism for the modern imagination; and the nature and intelligibility of historical process.

These issues are closely intertwined. Older conservatives like Hume and Johnson took human nature to be constant, so that revolutions—which meant, literally, circular movements—simply reflected the tendency of any order to break down and be succeeded by other, similar ones. National and historical differences of course exist, but in the philosophical sense they are accidental. Burke, with a newly historicizing sense of the way societies mutate over time, perceives them as fragile in a way that older conservatives did not. From Johnson's point of view, if America and Britain disagree, the answer is simply for Britain to exert its authority and punish the offenders. From Burke's point of view, loss of consensus, especially when ideologically motivated, can lead to irreversible change. To Gibbon the French Revolution is just one more breakdown of civilized order, a reenactment of events that have always happened and always will. To Burke it is the triumph of an imaginative misprision so fundamental that it may succeed in its avowed aim of altering human nature itself, and this arouses his deepest anxieties.

At the heart of the *Reflections* is the fiction of a perfect fit between individual and world, not only in the present moment but over the whole course of historical time. "Our political system is placed in a just correspondence and symmetry with the order of the world, and with the mode of existence decreed to a permanent body composed of transitory parts; wherein, by the disposition of a stupendous wisdom, moulding together the great mysterious incorporation of the human race, the whole, at one time, is never old, or middle-aged, or young; but in a condition of unchangeable constancy moves on through the varied tenour of perpetual decay, fall, renovation, and progression" (120). The "stupendous wisdom" is that of the Almighty, ensuring that the orders of self, society, and world are mutually translatable. The individual disappears into "the whole" as a tree into the forest, and "the whole" perpetuates itself by an organic process very similar to that of vegetation.

In practical terms, this vision rises out of an extended and hardheaded analysis of the so-called Revolution of 1688, which as Burke says confirmed the hereditary monarchy rather than (as radicals were claiming) affirming a right to get rid of kings and replace them with anyone the people might choose. The proof of the harmonious world order, for Burke, is the continued health of the British constitution that participates in it. But as the emotional rhetoric of the *Reflections* testifies, Burke has to fight fiction with fiction, countering the radicals' version of the 1688 settlement with his own conservative version. In Burke's account, 1688 resolved a crisis created in the 1640s by what modern historians call the English Revolution, but which Burke regards as a rebellion that was never endorsed by the majority of the population and that led to unjustifiable civil war.

The rebellion of the 1640s was certainly ideological in origin, and in the *Thoughts on French Affairs* Burke suggests that the French Revolution resembles it as "a revolution of doctrine and theoretic dogma" of which "a spirit of proselytism makes an essential part" (*Works* 7:13–14). Burke thus recognizes what Michael Walzer has argued in *The Revolution of the Saints*, that a peculiar spirit of commitment, and a totalizing demand for change, are common to militant Calvinists and militant Jacobins. The various religious revolutions, however, shared a common biblical code with the governors they sought to displace, even if the two sides interpreted the Bible in very different ways. The French Revolution was unprecedented in a militant atheism that was at once a cause of, and an index to, its novel status as "a revolution in sentiments, manners, and moral opinions" (*Reflections* 175). "Before this of France," Burke says six years after the *Reflections* in the *Letter to a Noble Lord*, "the annals of all time have not furnished an instance of a *complete* revolution. That Revolution seems to have extended even to the constitution of the mind of man" (*Works* 8:5).

While the events of the 1790s seemed to confirm Burke's fears, as the Revolution degenerated into terror and dictatorship, still later events have legitimized the changes that appalled him, and a nonreligious democracy no longer seems contrary to the order of nature. All the same, one should not dismiss his insight into the breakdown of the consensus that holds civilization together. In *A Letter to a Member of the National Assembly* in 1791 Burke prophesies the course of future wars with great accuracy: "The new school of murder and barbarism set up in Paris, having destroyed (so far as in it lies) all the other manners and principles which have hitherto civilized Europe, will destoy also the mode of civilized war, which, more than any thing else, has distinguished the Christian world" (*Works* 6:43). It may be easy for modern readers to smile at the naiveté of this claim and to dismiss *civilized war* as an oxymoron. Yet Burke is right: in his day total war against a people, not just against its armies, was only beginning to be envisioned. Even in our own day most people believe that certain extremities—poison gas, or nuclear weapons—are unacceptable in war; to this extent the "manners and principles" Burke speaks of are still in existence.

In the struggle between competing ideologies, political experience has become a text that wicked interpreters are trying to rewrite: "I cannot conceive how any man can have brought himself to that pitch of presumption, to consider his country as nothing but *carte blanche,* upon which he may scribble whatever he pleases" (*Reflections* 266). Against the spurious clarity of metaphysical abstraction, Burke opposes his own counter-rhetoric and emphasizes that metaphors are no less metaphoric for being covert. In a deft maneuver which William Dowling analyzes in "Burke and the Age of Chivalry," Burke turns the tables on his opponents by showing that they claim to despise romance but base their own philosophy on extravagances that fully deserve to be called romantic. In a neat stroke of guilt-by-association he links Hume with Rousseau:

Mr. Hume told me that he had from Rousseau himself the secret of his principles of composition. That acute, though eccentric, observer had perceived that to strike and interest the public, the marvelous must be produced; that the marvelous of the heathen mythology had long since lost its effect; that giants, magicians, fairies, and heroes of romance which succeeded had exhausted the portion of credulity which belonged to their age; that now nothing was left to a writer but that species of the marvelous which might still be produced, and with as great an effect as ever, though in another way; that is, the marvelous in life, in manners, in characters, and in extraordinary situations, giving rise to new and unlooked-for strokes in politics and morals. (*Reflections* 283–84)

Johnson claimed that Hume and Rousseau invented paradoxes just to get an effect; in the *Letter to a Member of the National Assembly* Burke says that Rousseau's master passion is a "vanity" that impels him to say anything that will get attention (*Works* 6:32). In the *Reflections* he goes further: the outrageousness of the *philosophes* is founded, as all effective rhetoric must be, on flights of imagination. No one except inexperienced youths, as Johnson says in *Rambler* No. 4, ever took the old romances for guides to conduct. The new romances are pernicious because they alter events.

In the *Reflections* Burke aims, then, to rehabilitate the old consensus by exposing the fictions of the new. His success is measured by the extent to which his own fiction enters history and influences it. As Ronald Paulson has said, "Once Edmund Burke's 'French Revolution' itself had become a referent, for which the revolutionaries and counterrevolutionaries found their own signifiers and signifieds, we reach a point where literature and the process of 'making' have taken over" (5). Burke's famous comparison of the Revolution to a tragedy includes the Humean statement that "our passions instruct our reason" (*Reflections* 175) and that "it is *natural*" for us to be moved. Art draws upon nature, intensifying but not altering it, and certain historical events are so powerful that they affect the mind as tragedy does.

Writing at a safe remove in England, Burke can perceive events in terms of plot and scene, though he also reiterates his claim from the *Philosophical Enquiry* that reality is more potent than art: "Some tears might be drawn from me if such a spectacle were exhibited on the stage. I should be truly ashamed of finding in myself that superficial, theatric sense of painted distress, whilst I could exult over it in real life" (*Reflections* 175). Burke's preoccupation with theatrical metaphors was by no means a product of a peculiarly "literary" imagination, for as Hannah Arendt remarks, the French revolutionaries regularly "preferred to draw their images from the language of the theatre" (106). His opponents, naturally enough, sought to revalue the currency; whereas Burke invokes the emotions appropriate to a cultivated audience at a theater, Paine responds in *The Rights of Man* with imagery of the monarchy as a tawdry pantomime or puppet show.

In each writer, as J. T. Boulton remarks (143–44), the choice of analogy indicates the class of readers whose approval is sought. Paine is perfectly clear about the artful fictionality of the *Reflections*, filled with "tragic paintings" that are "very well calculated for theatrical representation, where facts are manufactured for the sake of show" (Paine 71). Burke, in turn, reappropriates the theatrical metaphor in *A Letter to a Member of the National Assembly*, written a year after the *Reflections*: "Statesmen like your present rulers exist by every thing which is spurious, fictitious, and false; by every thing which takes the man from his house, and sets him on a stage; which makes him up an artificial creature, with painted, theatric sentiments, fit to be seen by the glare of candle-light, and formed to be contemplated at a due distance" (*Works* 6:34). In the combat between fictive systems, each sees itself as real and the other, in Burke's phrase, as "false and theatric" (6:34).

This is a battle not simply about metaphors but about the nature of reality. Both Paine and Burke believe they are arguing about which fiction best corresponds to reality, and both understand that the Revolution reflects a concept of individualism that has challenged the deepest assumptions of the existing order. In the first of the *Letters on a Regicide Peace* (1796) Burke looks back on the now-successful French Revolution as, once again, the product of a new and terrifying ideology. The involuted density of his language is expressive of the complexity of the idea:

Out of the tomb of the murdered monarchy in France has arisen a vast, tremendous, unformed spectre, in a far more terrific guise than any which ever yet have overpowered the imagination, and subdued the fortitude of man. Going straight forward to its end, unappalled by peril, unchecked by remorse, despising all common maxims and all common means, that hideous phantom overpowered those who could not believe it was possible she could at all exist, except on the principles which habit rather than nature had persuaded them were necessary to their own particular welfare, and to their own ordinary modes of action. (*Works* 8: 82–83)

This phantom or specter is ultimately unreal, since it is a product of the imagination rather than of the "ordinary modes of action" that nature inspires. Yet it has had the power to murder the French king and abolish his monarchy. Evidently the new ideology resembles the phantom of Death in *Paradise Lost*, an allegory of nonbeing that exercises power through the complicity of deluded imaginations. As Burke puts it in the *Reflections*, the delegates to the French National Assembly "have a power given to them, like that of the evil principle, to subvert and destroy" (161). The phrase "given to them" implies something like the providential permission which, in the Christian myth, gives Satan his temporary power to pervert good into evil. Pondering the American rebellion, Burke was sympathetic to the force of ideology and argued that what the colonists believed to be happening *was* happening. Pondering the French Revolution, he will make no such concession.

The logic of Burke's tortuous second sentence, then, runs something like this:

1. The specter has achieved its success because people who would otherwise have resisted it did not believe it possible that it could exist. Habit—but not a habit derived from nature—made them adopt principles according to whose lights the specter was not really a specter. (Most English people, including Burke's Whig allies, refused in 1790 to believe that the French Revolution posed any real threat, though opinion rapidly shifted thereafter.)

2. But contrariwise, the specter could not exist unless people (other people? the same people?) believed it possible for it to exist. Once false principles had generated wrong habits, the specter was conjured out of

unbeing into reality; but because it *is* a specter, people fail to realize what that reality actually is. By calling the specter "she," incidentally, Burke participates in a widespread tendency that Neil Hertz has analyzed, which identifies revolution with a female fury or gorgon, a tendency that combines political opposition with fantasies of sexual threat.

Burke's formulation here is the exact inverse of dialectical materialism: he believes that the "ordinary modes of action" would have continued to dictate traditional habits—specifically, deference to the aristocracy and the church—but that seductive ideas have generated new and disastrous habits in their stead. These habits have in turn produced an ideology which, although illusory at bottom, because unconnected with the realities of social existence, is single-minded in its implacable progress toward a programmatic goal, "going straight forward to its end." Life hitherto has been lived according to a kind of proverbial wisdom, "common maxims" reflecting "common means." The new ideology not only attacks those maxims but openly despises them, and it is impervious to moral reproach ("unchecked by remorse"). Put simply, a fiction has become a reality and the consensus is shattered, but Burke and his opponents cannot begin to agree about what the specter represents.

The revolutionaries, according to Burke, "find, on all sides, bounds to their unprincipled ambition in any fixed order of things. But in the fog and haze of confusion all is enlarged, and appears without any limit" (*Reflections* 136). In 1660 and 1668 traditional limits were ratified by a stable social consensus, never seriously threatened even by Jacobitism. But if the Jacobites could not break down the boundaries of British society from above, the Jacobins may succeed in collapsing French society from below: "The levellers therefore only change and pervert the natural order of things; they load the edifice of society, by setting up in the air what the solidity of the structure requires to be on the ground" (*Reflections* 138). The radicals, Burke observes bitterly, "consider our House of Commons as only 'a semblance,' 'a form,' 'a theory,' 'a shadow,' 'a mockery,' perhaps 'a nuisance' " (147). His purpose is to show where the theory-shadow actually lies.

Human nature, for Burke as for Johnson and Hume, cannot really change. What has changed is the fictions by which it understands itself, and the new fictions have liberated an individualism that Burke regards with fascinated fear. In *A Letter to a Member of the National Assembly* he declares that the "great problem" faced by the revolutionaries is "to find a substitute for all the principles which hitherto have been employed to regulate the human will and action" (*Works* 6:31). Burke then

launches into a remarkable attack on Rousseau as the chief villain undermining a social system in which taste, sexual morality, and class hierarchy
are elaborately intertwined. "Taste and elegance" have traditionally rec-
ommended virtue and mitigated vice, but these values are now openly
despised.

Rousseau, a writer of great force and vivacity, is totally destitute of taste in any
sense of the word. Your masters, who are his scholars, conceive that all refinement
has an aristocratic character. The last age had exhausted all its powers in giving
a grace and nobleness to our mutual appetites, and in raising them into a higher
class and order than seemed justly to belong to them. Through Rousseau, your
masters are resolved to destroy these aristocratic prejudices. (6:37)

Aristocracy connotes not just wealth and privilege, but the whole system
of stylized conduct developed by the *ancien régime,* in which human appetites are sublimated into "higher" forms or at least disguised in attractive
ways.

In Burke's nostalgic vision, the final chapter is being written of a chivalric code that "ennobled whatever it touched" and under whose influence—in a formulation that Johnson would probably have repudiated as
self-interested rationalization—"vice itself lost half its evil, by losing all
its grossness" (*Reflections* 170). No doubt Burke betrays a good deal of
personal anxiety here; Kramnick makes a good case for believing that
"repression of dangerous sexual passion becomes a conscious life strategy
for Burke" (139). At any rate, in the *Letter to a Member of the National
Assembly,* Rousseauvian morals (Burke seems to be thinking mainly of
La nouvelle Héloise) lead directly to a collapse of social hierarchy, and
the equation between aristocratic manners and aristocratic privilege is
explicitly made.

When the fence from the gallantry of preceptors is broken down, and your families are no longer protected by decent pride and salutary domestic prejudice, there
is but one step to a frightful corruption. The rulers in the National Assembly
are in good hopes that the females of the first families in France may become
an easy prey to dancing-masters, fiddlers, pattern-drawers, friseurs, and valets de
chambre. . . . By a law they have made these people their equals. By adopting
the sentiments of Rousseau they have made them your rivals. In this manner these
great legislators complete their plan of leveling, and establish their rights of men
on a sure foundation. (*Works* 6:38)

Earlier in the *Letter* Burke makes a very interesting admission: "The
retrograde order of society has something flattering to the dispositions of
mankind. The life of adventurers, gamesters, gipsies, beggars, and rob-
bers is not unpleasant. It requires restraint to keep men from falling into

that habit" (6:12). Burke's relative Will was a daring gamester, and we have seen in Boswell's *London Journal* how appealing the fantasy role of the highwayman was for a young man of good family preparing himself for a conventional career. In Blakean terms this is a society built on repression, and indeed Burke is quite willing to say that if people cannot sufficiently repress themselves, someone else will have to do it for them. "Society cannot exist unless a controlling power upon will and appetite be placed somewhere, and the less of it there is within, the more there must be without" (6:64).

The French Revolution, then, is at once a quasi-religious ideology made more dangerous by translating "enthusiasm" into atheistic fanaticism, and a repetition of the anarchy of individualism that has always developed whenever democracy has been tried, from ancient Greece onward (*Reflections* 228–29). Social order has been overturned in France, whose revolutionary National Assembly is filled with provincial persons "suddenly, and, as it were, by enchantment, snatched from the humblest rank of subordination" (130). Here the language of romance is used to make proximate and contemporary events seem exotic and unreal. Hierarchy has been replaced by an undifferentiated "people" that represents the chaos of mere individuals, giving rise to a dog-eat-dog struggle in which power is bound to reassert itself, but in a world that has foregone the controlling limits of custom. The old fictions used to be so familiar as to seem inseparable from nature itself (or herself); the new ones are so obviously manufactured that they are inherently unstable and can never be the basis for a dependable consensus.

In the *Appeal from the New to the Old Whigs*, maintaining a pretense that the writer is an impartial admirer of "the author [i.e., Burke himself] whose cause I defend" (*Works* 6:208), Burke declares that in the *Reflections* "he proposed to convey to a foreign people, not his own ideas, but the prevalent opinions and sentiments of a nation, renowned for wisdom, and celebrated in all ages for a well understood and well regulated love of freedom" (6:76). Thanks to their wisdom the British people understand what freedom really is and is not, and are willing to allow their freedom to be "regulated." This indeed is consensus, and Burke is confident that his "representation" of it speaks successfully for the whole: "The matter stands exactly as he wishes it. He is . . . happy to have his fidelity in representation recognised by the body of the people" (6:77).

But it has become increasingly obvious that even while he claims to speak for the entire nation, Burke is more of an outsider than ever, having retired from Parliament and existing, as it were, entirely in print. The *Ap-*

peal from the New to the Old Whigs opens on a note of injured merit and bewildered self-pity:

> His political associates . . . tell him he has loaded the stage too long. They conceive it, though an harsh yet a necessary office, in full parliament to declare to the present age, and to as late a posterity as shall take any concern in the proceedings of our day, that by one book [the *Reflections*, which at first struck readers as intemperate] he has disgraced the whole tenor of his life. Thus they dismiss their old partner of the war. (6:73)

The political warrior has been ejected from the public forum where he shone for so long—in the words of Johnson's *Vanity of Human Wishes*, "Superfluous lags the vet'ran on the stage"—and he now has no hope except to "slide down, in silence and obscurity, the slope of his declining days" (6:75).

At the beginning of the first *Letter on a Regicide Peace* Burke says somberly, "I shall not live to behold the unravelling of the intricate plot which saddens and perplexes the awful drama of Providence, now acting on the moral theatre of the world" (8:77–78). What, finally, is the meaning of that drama? And more specifically, if time confers legitimacy on whatever happens, why can it not confer legitimacy on the French Revolution?

Burke's commitment to historical process is implicit in his tireless defenses of "prescription," defined in Johnson's *Dictionary* as "rules produced and authorized by long custom; custom continued till it has the force of law." Prescription can serve Burke as a legitimizing principle because his view of time is essentially retrospective. What *has become* is now, by definition, right; but Burke has less to say about what *will become* —the direction in which Romantic thinkers were soon to carry historicism. As Paul Lucas observes, "If prescription could begin in violence and bad faith, then any historical fact could be legitimated by a wholesome passage of time" (58).

This possibility haunts the celebrated conclusion to Burke's *Thoughts on French Affairs*: "If a great change is to be made in human affairs, the minds of men will be fitted to it, the general opinions and feelings will draw that way. Every fear, every hope, will forward it; and then they, who persist in opposing this mighty current in human affairs, will appear rather to resist the decrees of Providence itself, than the mere designs of men" (*Works* 7:85). Yet surely Burke does not intend the paradox, as one of his interpreters has formulated it, that "principles and procedures Burke had denounced as immoral, impious, and atheistic will become, in the new dispensation, moral, pious, and divine" (Kilcup 407). The burden of the

Thoughts is that France is governed by a "gang of murderers and savages" (79) who seek to ignite revolutions throughout the whole of Europe, and Burke does not expect that God will ever endorse as "pious" the principles of militant atheism. Rather, he is invoking the age-old belief that since nothing happens without the superintendence of Providence, everything in history somehow reflects God's will. But God's will, as preachers had always said, may take the form of rebuke and punishment.

The real point of Burke's doubts about the fate of the Revolution is the status of the specter that has become a (false) reality. If the old consensus has been irreparably shattered and if everyone ends up believing in the new reality, then Burke and his reality are faced with inevitable extinction. But that does not mean that he has changed his mind about the French Revolution or that he accepts anything like a "verdict of history." Rather, Burke finds himself at the logical terminus of a lifetime spent in opposition. The consensus that generates reality has moved on to a place where he refuses to follow it.

Rather than representing a historicist endorsement of the process of change, Burke's late position may be seen as a reversion to an older notion of change as irrational and chaotic, explicable *only* on the assumption that Providence somehow directs it. Apocalyptic imagery, Pocock has observed, was widely invoked in the Renaissance, by representatives of the established power structure just as much as by rebels against it, "because only a dramatised providence seemed capable of explaining secular and particular happenings when their particularity was so marked as to assume the character of sudden change" (*Politics* 84). For Burke—as for Blake, who comes at them from the opposite viewpoint—the events of the 1790s are deeply apocalyptic. Burke's analysis of what has happened is very far from suggesting an intelligible development of tensions in French society. On the contrary, it is profoundly ahistorical, regarding the Revolution as an invasion of the historically sanctioned patriarchal order by evil forces.

Burke's solution thus resembles the one that Pocock describes in late-medieval thinkers: transition and change represent "a disruption of rationality, a move from order to disorder, which could only be dealt with, conceptually or practically, by restoring the order that had existed before" (*Politics* 82). In his last speeches and pamphlets Burke calls incessantly for a military invasion to eject the revolutionaries and return France to its prerevolutionary condition. But if the new ideology were really to take root, such a return would be impossible. Bruce Smith has well said in *Politics and Remembrance* that "the appeal of custom was not the fixed character that Burke knew it not to possess, but the appearance of fixity it so successfully created" (116). The cataclysm of the Revolution demolished the fictions of fixity, and from Burke's point of view it represented crazed destruction that was itself ahistorical. Just as words were being arbitrarily redefined, in contempt for the normal slow process of linguistic evolution, so all of the institutions of life were being altered in "a falsification of man's experience in time, a falsification which constitutes a kind of radical antihistory" (Blakemore 290).

This is the context within which Burke found himself compelled to deal with a crucial fact that Johnson and Hume, writing when the old order still felt secure, tended to overlook: since reality is psychological, new psychologies produce new realities. His own texts can be subjected to modes of interpretation that would have struck him not just as erroneous but as inexplicable: in the *Philosophical Enquiry* and the *Reflections*, Paulson says, Burke "uses the imagery of tumescence to describe the sublime experience" and dramatizes "the experience of the son's revolt, with its implications of sexual release, followed by his feelings of guilt, and the accommodations by which he comes to terms with the father, internalizes him as superego, and himself becomes a father" (69–70). But this account would make perfect sense to Blake. A new imaginative world is being born, and like Blake, Burke knows it.

The fictions of Romanticism embody a change that is conceptual, not just tactical or rhetorical, hinging not on describing the same things differently but on rethinking the way we think. In terms to which T. S. Kuhn has given currency, Burke alone of the major eighteenth-century conservatives finds himself writing at a moment of profound paradigm change, a time when it is not so much that the old answers seem wrong as that the old questions seem misconceived. To give an example, in response to Burke's claims that "liberty" has meaning only as specific liberties in specific contexts, Paine or Godwin would argue that to refuse to consider "liberty" philosophically is to confer a spurious permanence on the specific contexts in which "liberties" currently happen to be found. What Burke despises as mere metaphysics is, for them, the only hope of doing something about the suffering and exploitation that Burke regards as inevitable features of the providential order. But Godwin and Blake also see, as Paine does not, that the old fictions are far stronger than the revolutionaries first believed, implanted by custom in the human imagination in exactly the way that Burke describes. For the new fiction to achieve a similar substantiality and permanence, it is not enough to proclaim the rights of man and to behead the king; some means must be found to internalize it until it too, in its turn, begins to seem indistinguishable from reality itself.

But as Burke's labors on behalf of India should remind us, superseded versions of reality live on in their successors, and although the plan of the present book gives Godwin the last word chronologically, that is not to say that Godwin's reality has greater permanent validity than Burke's. Moreover, the frequent charge that Burke aestheticizes experience, though accurate enough, runs the risk of dismissing his achievement too easily. Another way of thinking about that achievement is to reflect that in our own time, artistic form has seemed to many people an essential weapon in the fight against oppression. In a recent review Helen Vendler remarks that for Czeslaw Milosz sensual, aesthetic, metaphysical, and ethical categories are inseparable, and taken together represent "what we mean by the 'real'" (125). Vendler quotes some lines by Milosz:

> Though the good is weak, beauty is very strong.
> Nonbeing sprawls, everywhere it turns into ash whole expanses of being.
> It masquerades in shapes and colors that imitate existence
> And no one would know it, if they did not know that it was ugly.

At the end of the *Reflections* Burke describes himself as one "in whose breast no anger durable or vehement has ever been kindled, but by what he considered as tyranny" (376). Now that Marxian celebrations of the French Revolution no longer stand unchallenged, it is possible to see that Burke's hatred of tyranny in France, like his hatred of tyranny in British India, is no mere paranoid fantasy. Milosz's lines have a deep resonance with Burke's thought, from the analysis of the aesthetic force of power in the early *Philosophical Enquiry* all the way to Burke's final vision of the suicide of civilization. His deepest insight is that moral ugliness is what finally exposes the ashy specter of nonbeing.

7

Godwin
Resymbolizing the World

TOWARD A NEW CONSENSUS

IN 1793 William Godwin published his *Enquiry concerning Political Justice,* which quickly became a central text for radicals, including (temporarily) the young Wordsworth and Coleridge. In the following year he published a remarkable novel entitled *Things as They Are; or, The Adventures of Caleb Williams* (not retitled *Caleb Williams* until 1831), which addresses the issues with which this book has been concerned—the psychologizing of reality, the relation of the individual to the community, the truth status of fictions—in ways that go far beyond the mainstream literature of the eighteenth century.

By contrast with *Caleb Williams, Political Justice* has been largely neglected by literary scholars, or has been treated as a rationalist dream from which Godwin awoke when he wrote his novel. But far from repudiating *Political Justice,* Godwin reissued it in 1796 and 1798, with extensive revisions that are intended to remove "crude and juvenile remarks" (74) and to clarify its argument, and the third edition of 1798 is the one normally quoted. In fact the two works form an interrelated pair: the theoretical book proposes a new consensus to replace the collapsing eighteenth-century one, while the novel explores the negative energy that the old beliefs continue to possess. *Caleb Williams* is the most psychological of the works considered in this book, carrying the message that "reality" is always shaped by internalized systems of symbolism. Hume's radical deconstruction of the self is conducted within the framework of a secure social order; Godwin's radical attack on the social order produces a deconstruction of the self far more devastating than Hume's, and like Blake's poetic myth yields grim insights into the need for symbols that lies at the heart of human experience.

The old Augustinian world view, which survives in intellectual conservatives like Johnson, recognizes that there are forces in human nature which we cannot control, and ascribes these to original sin. Enlightenment naturalism like Hume's grounds experience in a "nature" that harmoniously directs psychological and cultural behavior. Toward the end of the century there was a rediscovery of unconscious impulses that are neither desired nor controlled by the conscious mind, and a recognition that social change could succeed only if these deep sources of behavior were identified and modified. Godwin, who began life as a Calvinist minister and later turned atheist, moved through all three intellectual categories and continued to hold them in uneasy suspension.

Political Justice was inspired, Godwin says in the preface to the first edition, by "the concussion that the minds of men have suffered" from the American and French Revolutions (67). Godwin's necessitarianism, much more rigorous than Hume's, is very much a response to the unprecedented events of the 1790s, which seem to have produced a new consciousness of what it feels like to be carried along by the historical process. Hannah Arendt quotes Georg Foster referring in 1793 to "the majestic lava stream of the revolution which spares nothing and which nobody can arrest" (49), and she comments that as events overwhelmed the actors who had set them in motion, the politics of liberation paradoxically gave birth to a philosophy of necessity. "Where yesterday—that is in the happy days of Enlightenment—only the despotic power of the monarch had seemed to stand between man and his freedom to act, a much more powerful force had suddenly arisen which compelled men at will, and from which there was no release, neither rebellion nor escape, the force of history and historical necessity" (51).

It became increasingly apparent, moreover, that events cannot be understood in themselves, but only in the stories that get told about them. As Dale Porter observes, "The event observes its past, not as a neutral investigator, but as an agent of creative process: the past becomes *its* past" (69). By a process of imaginative back-formation the French Revolution redefined the past, and just as Burke feared, it gave rise to new stories that canceled out the old ones. So in an important sense Burke and Godwin continue to share a single emphasis, even while taking reversed positions toward it. Both are preoccupied with—even obsessed by—the radical changes that seem to be impending in British society. Burke argues that changes should *not* occur but probably will. Godwin argues that they *should* occur but probably won't.

Writers throughout the eighteenth century, as we have seen, regularly identified as fictions the assumptions that hold society together, but they insisted just as regularly on the naturalness and permanence of those fictions. The purpose of *Political Justice* is to develop the insight that society is a human invention whose rules might well be changed. In writing about "justice" Godwin is not so much asserting an absolute standard of truth (though he often talks that way) as using intellectual abstractions to pry apart the presuppositions of the society he lives in. But it is one thing to recognize the arbitrariness of rules and another to get them changed. William James remarks, "The aim of a football team is not merely to get the ball to a certain goal (if that were so, they would simply get up on some dark night and place it there), but to get it there by a fixed machinery of conditions" (*Pragmatism* 80). Hume and Burke insist that the game and its rules are prior to the wishes of any individual player. Godwin focuses on the individual and demands that society change the rules, or even the game.

The fundamental premise of *Political Justice* is that government is not merely negative, as standard Enlightenment theory had it, but "insinuates itself into our personal dispositions, and insensibly communicates its own spirit to our private transactions" (81). The eighteenth-century consensus, in Godwin's view, far from reflecting a happy synonymity of social needs, is a self-serving manipulation of the majority by the minority: "The rich are . . . directly or indirectly the legislators of the state; and of consequence are perpetually reducing oppression into a system, and depriving the poor of that little commonage of nature which might otherwise still have remained to them. The opinions of individuals, and of consequence their desires, for desire is nothing but opinion maturing for action, will always be in a great degree regulated by the opinions of the community" (92). Government and economics rest on a psychological foundation in which desire itself becomes a tool of oppression.

According to Burke "the heart owns, and the understanding ratifies" the drapery of the moral imagination (*Reflections* 171). Godwin's aim is to show that "the heart" is a very unreliable guide. He emphasizes reason in *Political Justice* just because eighteenth-century conservatism had denigrated it, lining up "feeling" on the side of the status quo. "We must bring everything to the standard of reason," Godwin therefore declares; "nothing must be sustained because it is ancient, because we have been accustomed to regard it as sacred, or because it has been unusual to bring its validity into question" (139). The rejection of the ancient and sacred implicitly rebukes Johnson and Burke, and the rejection of what is normally unquestioned rebukes Hume as well.

In a provocative thought experiment, Godwin asks the reader to imagine a burning building from which only one person can be saved: Archbishop Fénelon (author of the antimonarchical *Télémaque*) or Fénelon's valet. Godwin holds it to be self-evident that "that life ought to be preserved which will be most conducive to the general good." Even if the valet were one's own father or brother, "this would not alter the truth of the proposition. . . . What magic is there in the pronoun 'my' that should justify us in overturning the decisions of impartial truth?" (169–70). In Godwin's austere position—often satirized in the next generation, when Romanticism turned conservative and "feeling" regained primacy—it is our duty to "put ourselves in the place of an impartial spectator . . . beholding us from an elevated station, and uninfluenced by our prejudices" (174). In other words, Godwin strives to view himself as Gibbon views the distant past, surrendering to the force of "omnipotent" and "irresistible" truth (143).

This truth, however, remains more problematic and qualified than Godwin's exalted language might make one think. Unlike the Romantic poets, he is a thoroughgoing empiricist: "The human mind, so far as we are acquainted with it, is nothing else but a faculty of perception. All our knowledge, all our ideas, everything we possess as intelligent beings, comes from impression" (146). The clause "so far as we are acquainted with it" is a fine touch: if there were more to our minds than this, there would be no way to know it.

At many points Godwin recognizes that truth is not "something having an independent and separate existence" outside of "the mind of him who utters or hears it" (117). But he also holds that some "propositions" seem true so clearly, and for so long a period of time, that we feel safe in relying on them:

It cannot be denied that there are some propositions which are believed for a time and afterwards refuted; and others, such as most of the theorems of mathematics, and many of those of natural philosophy, respecting which there is no probability that they ever will be refuted. . . . Taken in this sense, truth is immutable. He that speaks of its immutability does nothing more than predict with greater or less probability, and say, "This is what I believe, and what all reasonable beings, till they shall fall short of me in their degree of information, will continue to believe." (117)

Godwin thus endorses the pragmatist notion of consensus common to most of the writers we have been considering. So long as everyone in the community believes that a given proposition will never be refuted, it is *in that sense* true.

In contrast to eighteenth-century tradition, Godwin's crucial move is to propose a new consensus to replace the one that Hume and Johnson took as given. This alternative consensus is based in the movement known as Rational Dissent, whose members tended to view human beings as "essentially reasonable and socially responsive and responsible" (Philp 129), and provided "a social network in which [Godwin's] ideas and values found confirmation and, perhaps more important, a vocabulary for expression and a set of shared conventions and assumptions from which to work" (Philp 224). The hope, then, is that the majority will be persuaded to adopt the consensus now held, strongly and communally, by a small minority. Godwin approvingly quotes Hume as saying that "government is founded in opinion" (*Political Justice* 148), but holds that what Blake called the "mind-forged manacles" will be removed with surprising ease if the prevailing assumptions are challenged: "In reality the chains fall off of themselves when the magic of opinion is dissolved" (149).

The special peculiarity of the Dissenting consensus, with its roots in inner-light pietism, is its basis in individual commitment rather than collective ethos. Whereas Johnson and Burke regard society as larger than the sum of its parts, a collectivity of opinions adding up to something more stable than the infinite variations of individuals, Godwin insists that it is nothing more than an abstraction. "The acts which go under the name of the society are really the acts now of one single person and now of another" (558). This is a nominalism more uncompromising than anything in Hume, for whom the uniformity of human nature guarantees the congruence of opinion within any given society. And of course the radically individual basis of the new consensus makes its establishment far from likely anytime soon. One should not forget that Godwin's utopian vision is set in a remote future, and that his vision of present conditions is disillusioned in the extreme. More than once he cites Swift with approval, and his account of history is much more Swiftian than Gibbonian:

The whole history of the human species, taken in one point of view, appears a vast abortion. . . . Contemplate the physiognomy of the species. Observe the traces of stupidity, of low cunning, of rooted insolence, of withered hope, and narrow self-ishness. . . . Recollect the horrors of war, that last invention of deliberate profligacy for the misery of man. Think of the variety of wounds, the multiplication of anguish, the desolation of countries, towns destroyed, harvests flaming, inhabitants perishing by thousands of hunger and cold. (402)

Godwin did not foresee the even more dreadful consequences of total war, but unlike many of the *philosophes*, he would not have found them surprising.

There is a double movement, then, in Godwin's thought: an affirmation that human beings can change, and a recognition that they do not change easily. In opposition to traditional British conservatism he embraces the Enlightenment ideology of progress—"Man is perfectible, or in other words susceptible of perpetual improvement" (140)—and *Political Justice* is sustained by a belief in the malleability of human nature: arguments should be based not on "men as we now find them" but on "men as they may hereafter be made" (490). In Godwin's thought the Humean self is an invitation to change, not conformity:

Ideas are to the mind nearly what atoms are to the body. The whole mass is in a perpetual flux; nothing is stable and permanent; after the lapse of a given period not a single particle probably remains the same. Who knows not that in the course of a human life the character of the individual frequently undergoes two or three revolutions of its fundamental stamina? . . . There is scarcely such a thing in character and principles as an irremediable error. (104)

Education therefore lies at the heart of Godwin's social vision, as it does of Rousseau's. "Children are a sort of raw material put into our hands, a ductile and yielding substance, which, if we do not ultimately mould in conformity to our wishes, it is because we throw away the power committed to us" (112).

Godwin's position is thus the logical culmination of the individualism that eighteenth-century conservatism feared. As Robert Paul Wolff puts it (in Kantian terms) in *In Defense of Anarchism*, "The autonomous man, insofar as he is autonomous, is not subject to the will of another. He may do what another tells him, but not *because* he has been told to do it. He is therefore, in the political sense of the word, *free*" (14). All of the writers we have been considering would deny that this sort of autonomy and freedom are possible. Etymologically *autonomy* is a law unto oneself, or as Johnson defines it, "living according to one's mind and prescription." Godwin envisions a society of free individuals who act as law to themselves while using reason to ensure cooperation rather than competition. Johnson, in contrast, sees *anarchy* as the abolition of law, not its fulfillment: "Want of government; a state in which every man is unaccountable; a state without magistracy" (*Dictionary*).

To see society in this way is to recognize that authority and power are not synonymous, though Johnson seems to imply as much when he says that "where obedience is not compelled, there is no government" (*Political Writings* 448), just as Burke does in the assertion that "liberty, when men act in bodies, is *power*" (*Reflections* 91). Godwin, very differently, would endorse Wolff's distinction: "Authority is the right to command, and correlatively, the right to be obeyed. It must be distinguished from power, which is the ability to compel compliance, either through the use or the threat of force. When I turn over my wallet to a thief who is holding me at gunpoint, I do so because the fate with which he threatens me is worse than the loss of money which I am made to suffer" (Wolff 4). Burke's doctrine of prescription is an admission that if the thief can get control of a state at gunpoint, future generations of "subjects" will be obligated to obey his descendants; power mutates insensibly into authority. Likewise Hume says, with no ambiguity or qualification, that "that power, which at first was founded only on injustice and violence, becomes in time legal and obligatory" (*Treatise* 566). But Godwin declares that any authority *in which one does not share* is only a mask for power, an institutionalized form of armed robbery.

At the heart of *Political Justice*, therefore, is a recognition of the fictions on which society is based, together with a rejection of the view that such fictions have positive effects. Burke's "salutary prejudices" (Godwin quotes him directly) are sustained by "illusions" and by an empty pageantry of symbolism: "To be drawn in a coach of state by eight milk-white horses is the highest of all human claims to our veneration" (*Political Justice* 443). At the literal level, this produces a king-has-no-clothes hypocrisy, as Godwin observes with satiric reductiveness:

In the [Gordon] riots in the year 1780, the mace of the House of Lords was proposed to be sent into the passages, by the terror of its appearance to quiet the confusion, but it was observed that if the mace should be rudely detained by the rioters, the whole would be thrown into anarchy. Business would be at a stand; their insignia, and with their insignia, their legislative and deliberative functions would be gone. Who can expect firmness and energy in a country where everything is made to depend, not upon justice, public interest and reason, but upon a piece of gilded wood? (444–45)

At a less playful level, Godwin explores the willed deceptions of a society that chooses to treat fictions as truths, for instance the maxim that the king can do no wrong, which was originally intended to protect the continuity of the monarchy by punishing the king's advisers but never the king himself:

Having first invented this fiction, it becomes the business of such constitutions, as nearly as possible, to realize it. A ministry must be regularly formed; they must concert together; and the measures they execute must originate in their own discretion. The king must be reduced, as nearly as possible, to a cypher. So far as he fails to be completely so, the constitution must be imperfect. (455–56)

But of course kings are men, not fictions, and no sane man will consent to "have no opinion, but be the vacant and colourless mirror by which [the ministers'] is reflected." It is therefore "among the most egregious and palpable of all political mistakes to imagine that we can reduce a human being to this neutrality and torpor" (456). If a country has a king, he will *be* a king, and—as was perfectly obvious in eighteenth-century Britain— the power struggle between king and parliament threatens the very compromise which the fiction of "the king can do no wrong" was intended to sustain.

Godwin believes that the breakdown of the old consensus has advanced too far for defensive maneuvers to save it. By openly acknowledging the role of fictions, Burke and his allies have committed themselves to a cover-up that simultaneously uncovers: "At the same time that he tells us we should cherish the mistake as mistake, and the prejudice as prejudice, he is himself lifting the veil, and destroying his own system. . . . The moment they begin to write books to persuade us that we ought to be willing to be deceived, it may well be suspected that their system is upon the decline" (504). In particular, Burke's "age of chivalry" is a moribund fiction whose lack of connection with reality makes it increasingly unconvincing even as a shibboleth:

The feudal system was a ferocious monster, devouring, wherever it came, all that the friend of humanity regards with attachment and love. The system of titles appears under a different form. The monster is at length destroyed, and they who followed in his train, and fattened upon the carcases of those he slew, have stuffed his skin, and, by exhibiting it, hope still to terrify mankind into patience and pusillanimity. (476)

Burke sees the French Revolution as a phantom; in Godwin's view the real phantom is the feudal or chivalric tradition, which has survived as a symbol of power long after the world that gave rise to it has vanished.

The special tragedy of Burke, in Godwin's opinion, is that he has allowed himself to be seduced by his own fictions. In a footnote that pays warm tribute to Burke's talents—"in subtlety of discrimination, in magnitude of conception, in sagacity and profoundness of judgment, he was never surpassed"—Godwin shrewdly suggests that Burke's notorious financial troubles, far from being accidental blemishes in his brilliant career, are symptoms of a fundamental misapprehension:

His principal defect consisted in this, that the false estimate as to the things entitled to our deference and admiration, which could alone render the aristocracy with whom he lived unjust to his worth, in some degree infected his own mind. He therefore sought wealth and plunged in expense, instead of cultivating the simplicity of independence; and he entangled himself with a petty combination of political men, instead of reserving his illustrious talents unwarped for the advancement of intellect and the service of mankind. (788–89)

Burke's own friends, Johnson and Goldsmith for instance, complained similarly of his extravagance and his identification with party, but failed to appreciate the depth of his compulsion to play the role of a landed magnate. In Godwin's analysis, Burke's self-destructive behavior is a consequence of actually believing in the social fictions he has helped to propagate.

In this world of illusion, human beings conceal their true feelings from themselves and from each other, so that they become "mere phantoms of men" (205). The individual surrenders to the pressure of the group, sincerity is perverted by role-playing, and "such characters as ours are the mere shadows of men, with a specious outside perhaps, but destitute of substance and soul. When shall we arrive at the land of realities, where men shall be known for what they are, by energy of thought and intrepidity of action!" (601).

Godwin's brand of utilitarianism combines radical individualism with a collectivist ideal. On the one hand, "society is nothing more than an aggregation of individuals" (176), each of whom must make judgments on the basis of dispassionate reason. On the other hand, "morality is that system of conduct which is determined by a consideration of the greatest general good" (165–66), and the primacy of "public utility" (166) is an unquestioned axiom: "Each man is but the part of a great system, and all that he has is so much wealth to be put to the account of the general stock" (178). For all his anarchism, Godwin's commitment to a social standard of the good is deeply expressive of eighteenth-century values, whether Enlightened or traditional, and he pleads for gradual improvement rather than social cataclysm.

Godwinian anarchism is not, in fact, an invitation to anarchy, but a plea for the very reverse: a gradual improvement of society that may someday permit the state to wither away. In the meantime, "the wise and just man, being unable, as yet, to introduce the form of society which his understanding approves, will contribute to the support of so much coercion as is necessary to exclude what is worse, anarchy" (667). The ideal society would reflect the rational wishes of every one of its members, which means that any revolution led by a minority is bound to be destructive. As Godwin explains in characteristically gnarled syntax, "Government, in particular, is founded in opinion; nor can any attempt to govern men otherwise than in conformity to their own conceptions be expected to prove salutary" (250). It is difficult to govern men in conformity to their conceptions, but at any rate they should not be governed *otherwise;* or rather, since in most societies they are indeed governed otherwise, no one should *expect* the results to be salutary. Here Godwin is in full agreement with Burke. "Revolution is engendered by an indignation against tyranny, yet is itself ever more pregnant with tyranny" (269).

Godwin's system is of course a product of its time, and internalizes traditional values in ways that Godwin himself could not have perceived, claiming to deduce values rationally that are in fact deeply embedded cultural presuppositions. As Hilary Putnam says, "Utilitarianism is an attempt to make a series of ideas which have deep and complex roots in our culture—values of equality, liberal values of choice, and values of fraternity and happiness—seem simple and non-arbitrary" (60). And as Godwin became increasingly conservative in the first decades of the nineteenth century, admirers of Burke might well have recalled an observation in the *Reflections*: "Almost all the high-bred republicans of my time have, after a short space, become the most decided, thorough-paced courtiers; they soon left the business of a tedious, moderate, but practical resistance to those of us whom, in the pride and intoxication of their theories, they have slighted as not much better than Tories" (154–55). Disappointed utopianism can turn more radically conservative than dogged reformism ever does.

CALEB WILLIAMS:
THE PRISON HOUSE OF SYMBOLS

Of all the writers we have examined, Godwin might be thought to be the least likely to have attempted a work of fiction. In part, he seems to have undertaken *Caleb Williams* (as Johnson did *Rasselas*) in order to make money. But he soon found himself writing, as he remembered years afterward, "in a state of excitement" (*Caleb Williams* 338), and what resulted was not a polemical tract but a troubled meditation on the way fictions operate in life, embodying the insights of *Political Justice* in a world of psychological experience rather than of metaphysical abstraction. The successive editions of *Political Justice* continue to proclaim, in an almost Puritanical way, the incompatibility of fiction with individual truth:

Shall we have theatrical exhibitions? This seems to include an absurd and vicious cooperation. It may be doubted whether men will hereafter come forward in any mode formally to repeat words and ideas that are not their own. . . . All formal repetition of other men's ideas seems to be a scheme for imprisoning, for so long a time, the operations of our own mind. It borders perhaps, in this respect, upon a breach of sincerity. (*Political Justice* 760)

This rather prim suspicion finds an ominous counterpart in *Caleb Williams*, a fiction that comes close to showing that social fictions are at once unavoidable and destructive, and that the only thing worse than believing them is to stop believing them.

In conception Godwin's novel is highly programmatic. Social privilege is personified in Ferdinando Falkland, a local magnate of immense charm who has "imbibed the love of chivalry and romance" from Italian poets, is profoundly motivated by "sentiments of birth and honour" (*Caleb Williams* 10), and (as Burke would put it) feels even the least stain to be a mortal wound. Unluckily Falkland finds himself in conflict with a gross and tyrannical squire named Tyrrel, and his grim secret, which Caleb eventually uncovers, is that after a public quarrel he stabbed Tyrrel to death. Godwin's message is that Falkland is a prisoner of the system, in which his own virtues destroy him by compelling him to avenge the stain on his honor, and then to preserve his secret by ruthless behavior—allowing innocent men to be executed for his own crime—that is morally no better than Tyrrel's was. Caleb, who has risen from humble origins to the position of a servant in Falkland's household, is trapped in his turn by discovering the secret, joined now to his master in a permanent bond of guilt.

Godwin implicitly agrees with Burke that the social graces embodied by Falkland (and by a poet named Mr. Clare) represent a valuable ideal; in *Political Justice* he remarks that "the pleasures of a savage, or, which is much the same thing, of a brute, are feeble indeed compared with those of the man of civilization and refinement" (133). But in the present system of civilization these advantages are purchased at an unacceptable cost. The crux of Godwin's quarrel with Burke lies in the affective element in the *Reflections*, as for example when Burke protests, "On the principles of this mechanic philosophy, our institutions can never be embodied, if I may use the expression, in persons; so as to create in us love, veneration, admiration, or attachment" (172). Godwin wants institutions to be answerable solely to reason, and as an anarchist he wants as few of them as possible. Caleb's veneration of Falkland amounts to a paralyzing disability, and represents the mechanism by which the old order sustains itself even when its secret crimes are found out. During the Hastings trial Burke told the House of Lords that Britain should not have sent "obscure people" to govern India, for although "oppression and robbery are at all times evils, they are more bearable when exercised by persons whom we have been habituated to regard with awe, and to whom mankind for ages have been accustomed to bow" (*Works* 15:404).

In *Caleb Williams* the balance between fact and fiction tips over: Godwin sees that if experience is fictive and if consensus breaks down, then fiction is *nothing but* fiction. Hume psychologizes reality but assumes that nature encourages each person to feel and believe in similar ways. Godwin likewise psychologizes reality, but believes (like Rousseau) that culture has taken the place of nature, insinuating beliefs and values that are pernicious and nevertheless are felt to be normal. *Political Justice* seeks to displace one ideology by another; *Caleb Williams* explores the ways in which, for many if not most people, the old ideology continues to represent "things as they are." If reality exists in the imagination, the Burke/Falkland reality *is real* for most of Godwin's contemporaries.

In Rousseau's famous challenge in *The Social Contract*, "Man is born free and we find him everywhere in chains." Caleb says similarly of a temporary escape from Falkland, "I thought with unspeakable loathing of those errors, in consequence of which every man is fated to be more or less the tyrant or the slave. I was astonished at the folly of my species, that they did not rise up as one man, and shake off chains so ignominious and misery so unsupportable" (*CW* 156). But when Caleb echoes Rousseau's "born free" later on, it is in bitter recognition of an individualism that cannot find happiness in society or out of it:

I was born free: I was born healthy, vigorous and active. . . . The free spirit and the firm heart with which I commenced, one circumstance was sufficient to blast. I was ignorant of the power which the institutions of society give to one man over others; I had fallen unwarily into the hands of a person, who held it as his fondest wish, to oppress and destroy me. . . . In every human countenance I feared to find the countenance of an enemy. . . . I was shut up a deserted, solitary wretch in the midst of my species. (255)

The dilemma is profound: one must choose bondage within society or else be hunted like an animal outside it. "The soul yearns," Godwin writes eloquently in *Political Justice*, "for the society of its like. . . . Who can tell the sufferings of him who is condemned to uninterrupted solitude?" (677). Or as Caleb exclaims, "Solitude, separation, banishment! These are words often in the mouths of human beings; but few men, except myself, have felt the full latitude of their meaning" (*CW* 303).

Even before Caleb's persecution begins, the institutionalized inequality of eighteenth-century society has sunk into his imagination and crippled it. Johnson, who certainly harbored no contempt for working people, makes clear why servants were widely distrusted: they existed as a sort of fifth column inside the family (in Johnson's *Dictionary* the word "family" still meant "those who live in the same house; household"): "No condition is more hateful or despicable, than his who has put himself in the power of his servant. . . . It is seldom known that authority, thus acquired, is possessed without insolence, or that the master is not forced to confess, by his tameness or forbearance, that he has enslaved himself by some foolish confidence" (*Rambler* No. 68). What is new in Godwin is a recognition that the master-servant relationship is equally deforming from the opposite direction. "Observe the servants that follow a rich man's train, watchful of his looks, anticipating his commands, not daring to reply to his insolence, all their time and their efforts under the direction of his caprice" (*PJ* 726). It is to avoid this mutual degradation that the elder Hawkins, to Tyrrel's amazement, refuses to allow his teenaged son to enter service: "The poorest neger, as a man may say, has some point that he will not part with. I will lose all that I have, and go to day-labour, and my son too, if needs must; but I will not make a gentleman's servant of him" (*CW* 71).

Burke sees society as a family with the king as its father, God's viceregent on earth. Caleb's imagination is haunted by the same equation, father = king = God, and a major goal of *Caleb Williams* is to discredit these equivalences. In Godwin's writings as in Blake's myth, the institution of the family does not work, and neither do the social institutions that claim to replicate it. That the orphaned Caleb chooses Falkland as a father is obvious from the start. But the role of son does not come easily: "I was but ill prepared for the servile submission Mr. Falkland demanded. In early life I had been accustomed to be much my own master" (*CW* 143). Caleb inverts the normal progression from childhood submission to adult independence. Meanwhile he tries to establish filial relationships with a whole series of people: Falkland's steward Collins, his friend Forester, the thieves' captain Raymond, the venal watchmaker Spurrel, Mrs. Marney the kindly landlady, and finally (in additions made in the third edition of 1797) Laura Denison whom he explicitly calls "mother." Oppressed by guilt, Caleb seeks above all a parent who can forgive him, and every one of these candidates fails to do so.

Godwin's profound analysis of the role of law, both in *Political Justice* and in *Caleb Williams*, reflects a recognition that in this kind of world the legal system is an instrument not of justice but of privilege. As a laborer cynically says—referring to a garbled version of Caleb's story concerning "the notorious housebreaker, Kit Williams"—"When two squires lay their heads together, they do not much matter law, you know; or else they twist the law to their own ends, I cannot exactly say which; but it is much at one, when the poor fellow's breath is out of his body" (*CW* 235–36). In the terms of Douglas Hay's analysis in "Property, Authority and the Criminal Law," Godwin's abstract concept of justice represents a debunking critique of a paternalist system that sustains itself by public displays of leniency as well as punishment. "Where authority is embodied in direct personal relationships, men will often accept power, even enormous despotic power, when it comes from the 'good King,' the father of his people, who tempers justice with mercy" (39). While the legal code was growing increasingly draconian, frequent pardons served to reinforce a patriarchal system in which justice was a gift rather than a right. This point was of course not lost on Godwin: "In England the criminal law is administered with greater impartiality [than in France] so far as regards the trial itself; but the number of capital offences, and of consequence the frequency of pardons, open a wide door to favour and abuse" (*PJ* 94). Coercion is disguised under the false colors of mercy and forgiveness, so that "a system of pardons is a system of unmitigated slavery" (699).

The fictions, then, must be stripped away. "Government," Godwin says in *Political Justice*, "is nothing but regulated force; force is its appropriate claim upon your attention" (242). And again, "Law is merely relative to the exercise of political force, and must perish when the necessity for that force ceases, if the influence of truth do not still sooner extirpate it from the practice of mankind" (695). In a brilliant chapter on the institution of law, Godwin observes that the most enlightened governments are precisely the ones with the densest proliferation of statutes, since they accept the impossible ideal of foreseeing everything in perfect fairness. The result is prophetic of Dickens and Kafka: "Time and industry, even were they infinite, would not suffice. It is a labyrinth without end; it is a mass of contradictions that cannot be disentangled" (687). But since life apart from society and its values is impossible—Godwin agrees in this with Burke—it is useless to drop out, since you can never drop far enough. Anarchy must be conceived of as replacing the present order rather than merely opposing it from the outside.

As has often been noted, crime plays an important role in much eighteenth-century fiction. If the novel is the genre that most fully represents society, then crime is the antisocial activity that tests society's limits and exposes its deceptions. As Blake epigrammatically puts it in *The Marriage of Heaven and Hell*, "Prisons are built with stones of Law, Brothels with bricks of Religion." Having caused his niece Emily's death in *Caleb Williams*, Tyrrel defiantly declares, "I did nothing but what the law allows" (*CW* 91).

Against the social order that makes such tyranny possible, a rebel named Mr. Raymond is a philosophical anarchist who leads his band of theives against a society founded on property and repression. "We, who are thieves without a license, are at open war with another set of men, who are thieves according to the law" (*CW* 216). In conservative satires like Gay's *Beggar's Opera* this sort of insight operates from higher to lower but not the other way around: the prime minister is shown to be no better than a highwayman, but without really challenging the moral authority of a system that has exalted Walpole while hanging Macheath and Wild. And *The Beggar's Opera* notoriously transforms criminality into costume-drama romance; Boswell among his prostitutes likes to think of himself as Macheath. It is interesting, incidentally, that there is no "romantic" element in *Caleb Williams*; sex is both a metaphor for oppression and an instance of it. The world of Godwin's novel oscillates between the extreme poles of the isolated self and the social machine, without the intermediary refuge, so dear to Victorian fiction, of the loving couple and their family.

Mr. Raymond's anarchism goes all the way, and rejects the rule of law outright: "Either be the friend of law, or its adversary. Depend upon it that wherever there are laws at all, there will be laws against such people as you and me. Either therefore we all of us deserve the vengeance of the law, or law is not the proper instrument of correcting the misdeeds of mankind" (223). But it is impossible to live outside the social order, as Caleb eventually makes Raymond see, for the reason that Hume gives in the *Inquiry concerning the Principles of Morals*:

Suppose . . . that it should be a virtuous man's fate to fall into the society of ruffians, remote from the protection of laws and government, what conduct must he embrace in that melancholy situation? He sees such a desperate rapaciousness prevail, such a disregard to equity, such contempt of order, such stupid blindness to future consequences, as must immediately have the most tragical conclusion and must terminate in destruction to the greater number and in a total dissolution of society to the rest. (18)

Or as Johnson says in the *Idler*, "There is no crime more infamous than the violation of truth. It is apparent that men can be social beings no longer than they believe each other. When speech is employed only as the vehicle of falsehood, every man must disunite himself from others, inhabit his own cave, and seek prey only for himself" (No. 20). Raymond's cave dwellers literalize this insight. There can be no society outside society; Raymond presides over a pseudosociety that is more like a gang of thugs than like Robin Hood's merry men, and its cruelest member, Gines, eventually returns to the world and becomes an instrument of Falkland's oppression.

The ideal of *Political Justice* is a radical individualism; the practical reality of *Caleb Williams* is a social world from which exclusion means immediate danger and eventual despair. An individual, if sufficiently reflective, might hope to understand his or her own heart, but in Godwin's view we are even more hidden from each other than Hume tends to suggest. In *Political Justice* he observes that "there is no species of evidence that can adequately inform us" of another person's motives (649). And when he reflects at length on the nature of evidence in a chapter concerning judicial punishment, he evokes a murky world that is very different from the sunlit space of idealized Reason:

The veracity of witnesses will, to an impartial spectator, be a subject of continual doubt. . . . How much will every word and every action come distorted by the medium through which it is transmitted? . . . I am found near to the body of a man newly murdered. I come out of his apartment with a bloody knife in my hand, or with blood upon my clothes. If under these circumstances, and unexpectedly charged with murder, I falter in my speech, or betray perturbation in my countenance, this is an additional proof. Who does not know that there is not a man in England, however blameless a life he may lead, who is secure that he shall not end it at the gallows? (655–56)

The denouement of Fielding's *Tom Jones* turns on just such a series of circumstantial evidence, but in Fielding's cheery comedy it is artistically inevitable that Tom should be snatched from the gallows. *Caleb Williams* replays this theme in a grimmer key.

Justice is to Caleb what honor is to Falkland: an abstract yet loved principle around which the whole of life must be organized. But Caleb's quest for justice is agonizing because it carries two very different symbolic meanings, a fact which he only gradually recognizes. In the sense emphasized in *Political Justice* it is a theoretical question of social equity, "a rule of conduct originating in the connection of one percipient being with another" (169). But in another sense, which descends from Protestant theology rather than from political theory, it is an emotional question of justification before God, which is to say, in the internal forum of one's conscience. And it is there that Caleb is unable to feel himself justified; like Falkland he has internalized an ideology that finally destroys him.

In ferreting out Falkland's secret crime, Caleb is driven not so much by abstract principle as by "an infantine and unreasonable curiosity" (*CW* 144) that seeks what it can never find, in an endless behaviorist regression: "The mind is urged by a perpetual stimulus; it seems as if it were continually approaching to the end of its race; and, as the insatiable desire of satisfaction is its principle of conduct, so it promises itself in that satisfaction an unknown gratification" (122). In a gothic episode in which Falkland's house—rather like Archbishop Fénelon's in *Political Justice*—bursts into flames, "some mysterious fatality" (131) brings Caleb to the library, and he is about to force open a trunk which he believes to contain evidence when Falkland apprehends him. "My offence," Caleb concludes, "had merely been a mistaken thirst of knowledge," but unlike Adam and Eve's it was such "as to admit neither of forgiveness nor remission" (133). Forgiveness will indeed be the final burden of *Caleb Williams*, but meanwhile Caleb is plunged into "death-dealing despair" (134).

As Rudolf Storch argues, a Freudian interpretation easily suggests itself: Caleb's "infantine curiosity" impels him to expose the "father's" secret, and this transgression is at once exhilarating and paralyzing. A political allegory is also attractive, in which Caleb reenacts Godwin's own assault in *Political Justice* on the traditional social order with its hidden basis in oppression. But one comes closest to Godwin's imaginative conception, I believe, if one sees the story as religious symbolism with the belief taken out, guilt and justification corroding a psychic world that has lost any correlative in a realm of ultimate meaning.

Very like the Blake of the 1790s, Godwin uses religious symbols with full awareness of their traditional misuse, and like Blake he seeks to identify the sources of destructive symbols within the human mind. It is therefore reductive to declare, as Marilyn Butler does, "For Godwin to have written a religious novel, even a novel unwittingly subverted by a religious consciousness, is incompatible with his role in radical politics" (241). *Caleb Williams* is not a religious novel, but there is nothing unwitting about its use of religious symbolism. Godwin's critique of "things as they are" includes a critique of religious consciousness, and of the fictions of reality which he sees it as sustaining, at a deeper symbolic level than any that Hume or Gibbon recognize.

A taboo, Paul Ricoeur says in *The Symbolism of Evil*, is "a punishment anticipated and forestalled emotionally in an interdiction" (33), and Godwin comes to see that taboo and punishment persist even when the God who authorized them has been abolished. The paradoxes of freedom, that great Enlightenment theme, are deeply entangled here. On the one hand, Caleb is in bondage to irresistible stimuli and feels helplessly driven. On the other hand, he believes that he cannot be guilty unless he has somehow abused his freedom, and he knows that he does feel guilty. The plot of *Caleb Williams* enacts the phenomenon of which Freud speaks in *The Ego and the Id*: "In many criminals, especially youthful ones, it is possible to detect a very powerful sense of guilt which existed before the crime, and is therefore not its result but its motive. It is as if it was a relief to be able to fasten this unconscious sense of guilt on to something real and immediate" (42). Guilt remains as the internalization of punishment even when the punishing authority is cast into question. To feel guilty is to be guilty; to be guilty is to deserve punishment and, in a sense, to seek it, as Caleb indicates very early: "For God's sake, sir, turn me out of your house. Punish me in some way or other, that I may forgive myself" (*CW* 119). Ricoeur comments that "the metaphor of the tribunal . . . invades all registers of the consciousness of guilt" (108). This is as true of *Caleb Williams* as of Kafka's *Trial*, and Caleb, like Joseph K., behaves with unexpected self-condemnation when the tribunal is finally at hand.

Seeking sources of inspiration, Godwin says that he "turned over the pages of a tremendous compilation, entitled 'God's Revenge against Murder,' where the beam of the eye of Omniscience was represented as perpetually pursuing the guilty, and laying open his most hidden retreats to the light of day" (*CW* 340). The title page of that work (by John Reynolds) cites Psalm 9:16, "The Lord is known in executing judgment, and the wicked is snared in the works of his own hand," and all of the tales are designed to show that "his Divine Majesty hath infinite more ways to punish murther, than man hath to commit it" (Reynolds 209). In *Caleb Williams*, however, it is Falkland the persecutor God who has committed murder and Caleb the victim who is innocent, even though "it was like what has been described of the eye of omniscience pursuing the guilty sinner" (*CW* 305).

The God of the Puritans has departed, and solitude turns to isolation as Caleb learns that no divine approval will reward his heroic alienation. "I endeavoured to sustain myself by the sense of my integrity, but the voice of no man upon earth echoed to the voice of my conscience. 'I called aloud; but there was none to answer; there was none that regarded'" (308). It has not been noticed that the allusion is brilliantly ironic: the priests of Baal call upon their God but receive no answer.

And it came to pass at noon, that Elijah mocked them, and said, Cry aloud: for he is a god; either he is talking, or he is pursuing, or he is in a journey, or peradventure he sleepeth, and must be awaked. And they cried aloud, and cut themselves after their manner with knives and lancets, till the blood gushed out upon them. And it came to pass, when midday was past, and they prophesied until the time of the offering of the evening sacrifice, that there was neither voice, nor any to answer, nor any that regarded. (1 Kings 18.27–29)

Caleb lacerates himself as the priests of Baal once did, but it is now Jehovah who has fallen asleep or gone away. The religious symbols on which Johnson and Burke build their consensus, and to which Hume and Gibbon are ready to pay at least lip service, are exposed as obsolete.

But just as in Blake's myth, it is one thing to expose a false symbol and another to learn to live without it. At several moments of crisis Falkland appears "without the smallest notice, and as if he had dropped . . . from the clouds" (149): when a brutal farmer is about to rape Emily, when Emily is trapped in a burning house, when Falkland's own house is on fire and Caleb is forcing the trunk, and when Caleb has accidentally met Mr. Forester at an inn. Falkland himself is fond of drawing the analogy.

Why do you trifle with me? You little suspect the extent of my power. At this moment you are enclosed with the snares of my vengeance, unseen by you, and at the instant that you flatter yourself you are already beyond their reach, they will close upon you. You might as well think of escaping from the power of the omnipresent God, as from mine! If you could touch so much as my finger, you should expiate it in hours and months and years of a torment of which as yet you have not the remotest idea! (144)

As the story unfolds Caleb is indeed unable to escape: "Did his power reach through all space, and his eye penetrate every concealment? Was he like that mysterious being, to protect us from whose fierce revenge mountains and hills we are told might fall on us in vain?" (240).

Having literalized the religious symbol in the plot of *Caleb Williams*, Godwin makes Caleb acknowledge its psychological reality. "In my case it was not a subject of reasoning or of faith; I could derive no comfort either directly from the unbelief which, upon religious subjects, some men avow to their own minds, or secretly from the remoteness and incomprehensibility of the conception; it was an affair of sense; I felt the fangs of the tyger striking deep into my heart" (240). "It was an affair of sense": Godwin has embedded the religious metaphor in the empiricist world of the novel. Cut loose from theological and metaphysical contexts, the symbolism of guilt and punishment is now free-floating and endlessly inescapable.

Falkland himself, in an extraordinary passage, describes his tyranny over Caleb as the secret benevolence of the Calvinist deity, whose apparent cruelties are but a Jobian test: "I had my eye upon you in all your wanderings. . . . I meditated to do you good. For that reason I was willing to prove you" (281). Soon afterward the servant Thomas confirms the analogy, representing Falkland as a Christlike "lamb" who has protected a "reprobate" Caleb from the rigors of the Law (286). But there is no ignoring the fact that Falkland is a murderer, "an overseer, vigilant from conscious guilt" (138), and that his treatment of Caleb is motivated by the need to protect his guilty secret.

The symbolism of Christianity is merged here with that of Greek tragedy, in what Ricoeur calls "the mystery of iniquity of the wicked god"

(222). *Caleb Williams* is filled with suggestions that Falkland is diabolical as well as divine, a remorseless persecutor as well as an all-seeing
father. "This Falkland haunts me like a demon," Tyrrel complains (31);
and again, "That man is a legion of devils to me" (54). At the moment
when Caleb reveals his suspicions, Falkland confronts him with "somewhat frightful, I had almost said diabolical, in his countenance" (120). By
the end of the novel his "hunting me round the world" seems to Caleb not
godlike but "fiend-like" (274), and Falkland's inner torment is explicitly
compared to "the imaginary hell, which the great enemy of mankind is
represented as carrying every where about with him" (284).

Considered simply as novelistic characters, Caleb and Falkland are
victims together of the mind-forged manacles. "I was his prisoner: and
what a prisoner! All my actions observed; all my gestures marked. I could
move neither to the right nor the left, but the eye of my keeper was upon
me. He watched me; and his vigilance was a sickness to my heart" (143).
Caleb watches Falkland with a reciprocal vigilance. The solution to this
mutual torment must be mutual forgiveness. In the original manuscript
ending of the novel, Caleb's final accusation of Falkland is once again dis-
believed, and the last pages are the incoherent jottings of a man who has
been reduced to subhuman thingness: "I wonder which is the man, I or
my chair? . . . All day long I do nothing—am a stone—a GRAVE-STONE!
—an obelisk to tell you, HERE LIES WHAT WAS ONCE A MAN!" (334). In the
ending which Godwin published, Caleb's accusation provokes Falkland to
confess his guilt at last, and Caleb in turn abandons his position: "I came
hither to curse, but I remain to bless. I came to accuse, but am compelled
to applaud. I proclaim to all the world that Mr. Falkland is a man worthy
of affection and kindness, and that I am myself the basest and most odious
of mankind!" (323). Godwin may seem to be saying that Caleb is unable
to escape the servile attitudes of his culture. But on a larger view, Falkland too is a prisoner of that culture, and the novel's pessimistic ending
discloses the difficulty of trying to think one's way beyond "things as they
are."

Both Caleb and Falkland feel guilty and need punishment; no wonder
then that they are symbiotically entwined, like the Siamese "twin-births"
to which society is compared (303). "Williams," Falkland cries, "you have
conquered! I see too late the greatness and elevation of your mind" (324).
But this sharing of emotion takes on a complicated twist if one reflects
that Caleb's passionate fixation on Falkland is the product of socially
conditioned emotions that bind servant to master in mutual paralysis. "I
began these memoirs," Caleb says, "with the idea of vindicating my char-

acter. I have now no character that I wish to vindicate" (326). Falkland, protecting his reputation by deceit and oppression, preserves the simulacrum of his character at the cost of its reality, while Caleb ends up with neither. And this is a consequence not simply of his final collapse, but of the crippling doubleness to which he is condemned.

For Boswell, role-playing is an improvisatory game; for Caleb it is at once a shield against detection and an abdication of self.

My life was all a lie. I had a counterfeit character to support. I had counterfeit manners to assume. My gait, my gestures, my accents were all of them to be studied. I was not free to indulge, no not one, honest sally of the soul. (256)

Caleb's enemies invent false accounts of him which well-meaning people like Collins and Laura accept as true. But beyond that, Caleb comes to see that there remains no true "character" of which these are misrepresentations, and his story ends with nothing but a hole where a man used to be. That is the abyss that lurks beneath the urbane ironies of Hume's theory of the self: under the flux of perceptions may be nothing at all, unless the surrounding social context permits one to build it up again.

Berger and Luckmann describe the life of society as a drama whose actors must play their parts correctly: "The judging individual is not acting 'on his own,' but *qua* judge. . . . The realization of the drama depends upon the reiterated performance of its prescribed roles by living actors" (75). Falkland plays the role of the Good Squire, at first with ease because it fits his desired self-image comfortably, later with anguish because he knows that his dreadful secret makes a mockery of it. Caleb loses the role of the Good Servant, and tries to refuse the role of the Bad Servant which society seeks to force upon him. He also resists other possible roles (such as merry Kit Williams the prison breaker) and aspires to be simply *himself*. But outside of a fantasy world like that of *Robinson Crusoe*, there can be no such thing as a self apart from society, and Caleb's final submission comes as a deep psychological relief. At last he reassumes his role and knows who he is—this time, the Bad but Repentant Servant.

To quote Berger and Luckmann again, deviations from socially defined reality are perceived "as moral depravity, mental disease, or just plain ignorance" (66). It cannot be surprising that Caleb, after everyone he meets has confirmed the diagnosis of his own deviance, should give up the fight and acknowledge its appropriateness. In the final courtroom scene Godwin emphasizes the sympathy felt by all, a triumph of eighteenth-century sensibility: "Every one that heard me was melted into tears. They could not resist the ardour with which I praised the great qualities of

Falkland; they manifested their sympathy in the tokens of my penitence" (323–24). Within the frame of the story, actors and spectators experience one kind of enlightenment in this recognition scene with its attendant pity and fear. Outside the story, the reader is intended to experience enlightenment of a different kind.

Insofar as *Caleb Williams* is a tragedy, it corresponds to the pattern of *Oedipus* or *Hamlet*: the obsessive pursuit of the guilty secret, the horror of exposing it together with the irresistible compulsion to do so. But the aim of a political philosophy like Godwin's is to rise above tragedy, indeed to demystify it as a massive misconception. Raymond Williams observes, "The idea of tragedy, in its ordinary form, excludes especially that tragic experience which is social, and the idea of revolution, again in its ordinary form, excludes especially that social experience which is tragic" (*Modern Tragedy* 64). Falkland has committed a crime, but against a totally vicious person of whom the world is well rid. What good could it possibly do to bring him to "justice"? No wonder the victory turns sour the moment it is achieved—and no wonder Godwin revised the original ending of the novel in which Caleb retained his moral superiority by never winning his courtroom victory.

Caleb at the end is a victim (or a symptom) of the structure of eighteenth-century English society. In the trials of that period, prosecution followed the lead of a private accuser rather than of the state, so that a charge would be dropped if the victim chose not to press it. In accusing Falkland, Caleb literally becomes, in the words of a contemporary French observer quoted by Douglas Hay, "the arbitrator of the culprit's fate" (41). In Adam Smith's *Theory of Moral Sentiments*, a murderer feels distress most painfully because he has cut himself off from sympathy, the fellow feeling of human beings who instead regard him with abhorrence. Caleb experiences that abhorrence although he is not a murderer, and since everyone treats him as a criminal he begins to feel that he must be one. Falkland, meanwhile, *is* a criminal, but is treated with respect since nobody knows it, and in the end Caleb cannot fight free of the internalized attitudes that shape his experience. The point of institutionalized punishment, in John Bender's account of Adam Smith, is that "it draws the criminal back from the abyss of irrevocable solitude into a demarcated isolation that punishes while protecting consciousness from the horror of its own dissolution" (224–25). Caleb punishes himself and enters into that horror.

Perhaps this is a way of saying that *Caleb Williams* has left the eighteenth century behind and has become a Romantic novel. Robert Kiely, surveying it in that context, sees a characteristic split between the subjective individual and a society that is perceived not as an integrated whole, but rather as a hostile collection of other individuals who oppose the authentic self. Godwin's political and sociological program therefore becomes blurred, because the questions his novel poses are finally "questions about individuals" rather than about institutions (89). Pursuing an ideal of total truth, Caleb achieves an isolation so total that he loses his reason; even while rebelling against the social order, he has continued to internalize its deepest values. When these are decisively challenged, he has nothing left with which to make sense of the world. It turns out that it was opposition that kept him going, for as Kiely observes, "the struggle against a clearly defined antithesis had kept alive in him a firm concept of a 'real' self" (95), and the loss of that structuring opposition results —very much as in Blake's myth—in a fragmentation and collapse of the self. All the same, Godwin believes that social change is possible, and this is because the empiricist self is almost infinitely alterable. Instead of despairing when his ideal "character" has been demolished, Caleb should look forward to acquiring a new and better one.

More than any other literary form, the modern novel is haunted by temporal change. As Fredric Jameson says, "The novel exists as a form when we are thrown into the minds and experiences of characters for whom the future, for whom destiny, has not yet taken shape, who grope and invent their own destinies, living blindly within the entanglement of the author's unforeseeable actions and under the menace of history's unforeseeable development" (200). Just so does Caleb exclaim, on recounting a moment of particular bewilderment, "Great God! What is man? Is he thus blind to the future, thus totally unsuspecting of what is to occur in the next moment of his existence?" (279). In Godwin's determinist universe, one can grasp the connections between events only when they have receded into an irrecoverable past. Behind everything lurks the murder of Tyrrel long ago, but the events within the narrative are successively deposited in the same region of fixity. "It is too late to look back" (136), Falkland tells Caleb at the moment of confessing the crime. "It was too late," Caleb reflects at the moment of exposing Falkland in court. "The mistake I had committed was now gone past all power to recall" (320).

Narrative, by definition, is post facto, and the past which it uncovers can never change. "In its implications," Freud says in a much-quoted remark, "the distortions of a text resemble a murder: the difficulty is not in perpetrating the deed, but in getting rid of its traces" (*Moses and Monotheism* 43). It can be argued that by transforming bewildering experience into connected narrative, Caleb becomes a type of the artist who achieves a conquest of imagination overs absurdity, and that his final collapse is a premonition of modernism—"a man of no character, hunger artist, and chameleon poet," as W. B. Carnochan describes him (*Confinement* 134). But this is not an achievement that Caleb himself intends or understands. On the contrary, his narrative folds in and collapses as the pressure of reality catches up with it (Caleb's reality, that is, which is Godwin's fiction).

By this time in the story, plenty of alternative versions of Caleb's story have accumulated, including the apocryphal *Wonderful and Surprising History of Caleb Williams* (301):

I addressed myself to our hostess, a buxom, bluff, good humoured widow, and asked what sort of a man this Kit Williams might be? She replied that, as she was informed, he was as handsome, likely a lad, as any in four counties round; and that she loved him for his cleverness, by which he outwitted all the keepers they could set over him, and made his way through stone walls as if they were so many cobwebs. (237)

As Eric Rothstein comments, Caleb finds himself "socially altered into a literary object" (231). He is now the picaresque hero of a lower-class romance in the Newgate genre. But this sort of fiction actually serves the larger purposes of the social order. It is part of the campaign to expose Caleb even in his most obscure retreats—Laura rejects him after seeing it—and it carries the munificent reward of one hundred pounds for anyone who will turn Caleb in. At an alehouse he listens in horror to some laborers who act as "historians and commentators" of his story: one of them expresses reluctance to make money by "bringing a Christian creature to the gallows," and another retorts, "Poh, that is all my granny! Some folks must be hanged to keep the wheels of our state folks a-going" (236).

For a long time Caleb hopes to defeat calumny "by a plain, unvarnished tale" (160), but one lesson of *Caleb Williams* is that every tale needs varnishing. And in a world of competing stories, it is not obvious that telling the truth is the best policy. The upright but stern Squire Forester warns Caleb when Falkland has accused him of theft, "Make the best story you can for yourself; true, if truth, as I hope, will serve your purpose; but, if not, the most plausible and ingenious you can invent. That is what self-defence requires from every man where, as it always happens to a man upon his trial, he has the whole world against him, and has his own battle to fight against the world" (162–63). It is even possible to be believed in vain. At the end of *Tom Jones*, the truth comes out and puts everything to rights; at the end of *Caleb Williams*, the truth comes out and completes Caleb's destruction.

The shift at the end from retrospective to present-tense narration has striking consequences. Up until then the book has been presented *as* a book, the explanatory tale that will refute competing tales and salvage Caleb's reputation. Caleb's understanding of the past is shaped by analogy with prior texts—the Bible, romances, crime narratives—and he aspires to complete a text of his own that can make permanent sense of what has happened, "writing a past that defers its meaning to texts before it and a text that is yet to appear" (Hogle 270). But a thoroughgoing deconstructive reading would miss the difference between Caleb's world of collapsing texts and Godwin's determination to suggest a real world—the world of "presence" so repugnant to deconstruction—that stands outside of all texts, including the text of *Caleb Williams*.

Caleb Williams is not only a novel about the difficulty of finding truth, or about the self-deceptions that lead a person like Caleb to mistake the truth about himself. Beyond that, it is about the intractable patterns of human nature that keep people from making use of truth even if they know it. Hayden White speaks of the modernist suspicion that "narrative in general, from the folktale to the novel, from the annals to the fully realized 'history,' has to do with the topics of law, legality, legitimacy, or, more generally, *authority*" ("Value of Narrativity" 13). *Caleb Williams* offers itself as a narrative against law and authority, but in the end it reveals the extent to which narrative legitimation of the sacred and of law is so deeply rooted in human consciousness that it is impossible to live without it.

So even if *Caleb Williams* is intended as a programmatic companion to *Political Justice*, it ends up far more pessimistic than the theoretical work; the effort of imagining a story gets Godwin inside the complexity of social experience, in which "things as they are" come to seem all but inevitable even to a radical critic. And although Godwin had set out to debunk Burke's code of aristocracy and "prejudice," it turned out that Burke and successors like Coleridge foretold the immediate future. Godwin soon became the discredited prophet of a defeated radical tradition, and conservatism seemed persuasive again before the century was out. Most writers continued to endorse orthodox religion or at least orthodox morality, exploring the motivation of individuals while accepting the social order as a given state of affairs.

Underlying this acceptance was a double theodicy in which the order of society was presumed to mirror that of the universe, cosmos and *nomos* in harmony once again. The fiction of harmony could not last forever, but Victorian culture made it last for a long time. And it did so by protecting the social order not only from Godwin's kind of critique, but from the skeptical conservatism of his predecessors as well. Threatened by a breakdown of their world, many Victorian thinkers were deeply suspicious of skepticism, whereas the conservative thinkers of the eighteenth century, more confident of the integrity of their world, could afford to give skepticism a surprisingly free rein.

Moreover, even if Hume accepted the political order and Johnson the religious order as well, it would be wrong to suppose that they pulled their punches or that their skepticism had no consequences. Their texts are haunted, sometimes unconsciously but often very consciously, by the fear that there is no such thing as a unitary self and no such thing as a reliably "real" world—or at least no reliable way of representing it to oneself and to others. They thus occupy an important stage in the process of development that has led, through Marx and Nietzsche and Freud and Foucault, to the endless nest of puzzles that constitutes modern intellectual life. Their problems continue to be, in many ways, our problems, as is obvious when theorists in every field, from historiography to nuclear physics, tell us that fact and reality are imaginative constructs. It is of course true that the modern world, insofar as the thinkers of the eighteenth century are able to foresee it, is precisely what their writings are designed to hold at bay. But it is also true that their subtle union of conservative affirmation and skeptical doubt makes them unusually open to the contradictions that haunt the study of psychology and society—contradictions which later and more dogmatic thinkers have not always faced as clear-sightedly as they.

Works Cited

Index

Works Cited

Abrams, M. H. *The Mirror and the Lamp: Romantic Theory and the Critical Tradition*. New York: Oxford University Press, 1953.

Adams, William. *Essay on Mr. Hume's Essay on Miracles*. London, 1751.

Aikin, John. *An Essay on the Application of Natural History to Poetry* (1777). Rpt. New York: Garland, 1970.

Alkon, Paul K. "Boswellian Time," *Studies in Burke and His Time* 14 (1973): 239–56.

Arendt, Hannah. *On Revolution*. Harmondsworth: Penguin, 1973.

Auden, W. H. "Young Boswell." *New Yorker*, 25 November 1950: 146–48.

Auerbach, Erich. *Mimesis: The Representation of Reality in Western Literature*. Trans. Willard R. Trask. Princeton: Princeton University Press, 1953.

Augustine. *The City of God*. Trans. Henry Bettenson. Harmondsworth: Penguin, 1972.

Bagehot, Walter. *Literary Studies*. 2 vols. London: Dent, Everyman's Library, n.d.

Bakhtin, M. M. *The Dialogic Imagination: Four Essays*. Trans. Caryl Emerson and Michael Holquist. Austin: University of Texas Press, 1981.

Barrell, John. *English Literature in History 1730–1780: An Equal, Wide Survey*. New York: St. Martin's, 1983.

Bate, Walter Jackson. *The Achievement of Samuel Johnson*. New York: Oxford University Press, 1961.

Bate, Walter Jackson. *Samuel Johnson*. New York: Harcourt Brace Jovanovich, 1977.

Beattie, James. *An Essay on Truth*. In *Essays*. Edinburgh, 1776.

Becker, Carl. *The Heavenly City of the Eighteenth-Century Philosophers*. New Haven: Yale University Press, 1932.

Bender, John. *Imagining the Penitentiary: Fiction and the Architecture of Mind in Eighteenth-Century England*. Chicago: University of Chicago Press, 1987.

Berger, Peter L. *Invitation to Sociology: A Humanistic Perspective*. New York: Doubleday Anchor Books, 1963.

Berger, Peter L., and Thomas Luckmann. *The Social Construction of Reality*. New York: Doubleday Anchor Books, 1967.

Blakemore, Steven. "Burke and the Fall of Language: The French Revolution as Linguistic Event," *Eighteenth-Century Studies* 17 (1984): 284–307.

Bloch, Marc. *The Historian's Craft.* Trans. Peter Putnam. New York: Vintage Books, 1953.

Bogel, Fredric. "Johnson and the Role of Authority." In *The New Eighteenth Century: Theory, Politics, English Literature,* ed. Felicity Nussbaum and Laura Brown, 189–209. New York: Methuen, 1987.

Bogel, Fredric. *Literature and Insubstantiality in Later Eighteenth-Century England.* Princeton: Princeton University Press, 1984.

Boswell, James. *Boswell in Extremes.* Ed. C. M. Weis and F. A. Pottle. New York: McGraw-Hill, 1970.

Boswell, James. *Boswell's London Journal 1762–1763.* Ed. Frederick A. Pottle. New York: McGraw-Hill, 1950.

Boswell, James. *Boswell on the Grand Tour: Germany and Switzerland, 1764.* Ed. Frederick A. Pottle. New York: McGraw-Hill, 1953.

Boswell, James. *The Correspondence and Other Papers of James Boswell Relating to the Making of the "Life of Johnson".* Ed. Marshall Waingrow. London: Heinemann, 1969.

Boswell, James. *The Hypochondriack.* Ed. Margery Bailey. 2 vols. Stanford: Stanford University Press, 1928.

Boswell, James. *Journal of a Tour to the Hebrides with Samuel Johnson.* Ed. Frederick A. Pottle. New York: McGraw-Hill, 1961. [Cited in this book as *Journal.*]

Boswell, James. *A Journal of A Tour to the Hebrides, with Samuel Johnson LL.D.* Printed as Vol. 5 of *Boswell's Life of Johnson,* ed. G. B. Hill, rev. L. F. Powell. Oxford: Clarendon, 1964. [Cited in this book as *Tour.*]

Boswell, James. *Life of Johnson.* Ed. G. B. Hill. Rev. L. F. Powell. 6 vols. Oxford: Clarendon Press, 1934–50.

Boswell, James. *Private Papers of James Boswell.* Ed. Geoffrey Scott and F. A. Pottle. 18 vols. New York: privately printed, 1928–34.

Boulton, James T. *The Language of Politics in the Age of Wilkes and Burke.* London: Routledge & Kegan Paul, 1963.

Brady, Frank. *James Boswell: The Later Years, 1769–1795.* New York: McGraw Hill, 1984.

Braudel, Fernand. *On History.* Trans. Sarah Matthews. Chicago: University of Chicago Press, 1980.

Braudy, Leo. *Narrative Form in History and Fiction.* Princeton: Princeton University Press, 1970.

Brooks, Peter. *Reading for the Plot: Design and Intention in Narrative.* New York: Knopf, 1984.

Brown, Peter. *The Making of Late Antiquity.* Cambridge: Harvard University Press, 1978.

Browning, Robert. *The Emperor Julian.* Berkeley: University of California Press, 1976.

Brownley, Martine Watson. "Gibbon's Artistic and Historical Scope in the *Decline and Fall,*" *Journal of the History of Ideas* 42 (1981): 629–42.

Burke, Edmund. *A Notebook of Edmund Burke: Poems, Characters, Essays and Other Sketches in the Hands of Edmund and William Burke.* Ed. H. V. F. Somerset. Cambridge: Cambridge University Press, 1957.

Burke, Edmund. *A Philosophical Enquiry into the Origin of Our Ideas of the Sublime and Beautiful.* Ed. J. T. Boulton. Notre Dame: University of Notre Dame Press, 1958.

Burke, Edmund. *Reflections on the Revolution in France.* Ed. Conor Cruise O'Brien. Harmondsworth: Penguin, 1969.

Burke, Edmund. *The Works of the Right Honourable Edmund Burke.* 16 vols. London: Rivington, 1826.

Burke, Peter. "Tradition and Experience: The Idea of Decline from Bruni to Gibbon." In *Edward Gibbon and the Decline and Fall of the Roman Empire,* ed. G. W. Bowersock, John Clive, and Stephen R. Graubard. Cambridge: Harvard University Press, 1977.

Burrow, J. W. *Gibbon.* Oxford: Oxford University Press, 1985.

Butler, Marilyn. "Godwin, Burke, and *Caleb Williams,*" *Essays in Criticism* 32 (1982): 237–57.

Byrd, Max. "Johnson's Spiritual Anxiety," *Modern Philology* 78 (1981): 368–78.

Capaldi, Nicholas. "Hume as Social Scientist," *Review of Metaphysics* 32 (1978): 99–123.

Capaldi, Nicholas. "Hume's Theory of the Passions." In *Hume: A Re-evaluation,* Ed. Donald W. Livingston and James T. King, 172–90. New York: Fordham University Press, 1976.

Capitan, William H. "Part X of Hume's *Dialogues.*" In *Hume: A Collection of Critical Essays,* ed. V. C. Chappell, 383–95. New York: Doubleday Anchor Books, 1966.

Carlyle, Thomas. *The Works of Thomas Carlyle.* Ed. H. D. Traill. New York: Scribner's, 1896–1901.

Carnochan, W. B. *Confinement and Flight: An Essay on English Literature of the Eighteenth Century.* Berkeley: University of California Press, 1977.

Carnochan, W. B. *Gibbon's Solitude: The Inward World of the Historian.* Stanford: Stanford University Press, 1987.

Cassirer, Ernst. *The Philosophy of the Enlightenment* (1932). Trans. Fritz C. A. Koelln and James P. Pettegrove. Princeton: Princeton University Press, 1951.

Cavell, Stanley. "Politics as Opposed to What?" In *The Politics of Interpretation,* ed. W. J. T. Mitchell, 181–202. Chicago: University of Chicago Press, 1983.

Chapin, Chester. "Samuel Johnson and the Scottish Common Sense School," *The Eighteenth Century* 20 (1979): 50–64.

Chapman, Gerald W. *Edmund Burke: The Practical Imagination.* Cambridge: Harvard University Press, 1967.

Christensen, Jerome. *Practicing Enlightenment: Hume and the Formation of a Literary Career.* Madison: University of Wisconsin Press, 1987.

Clark, J. C. D. *English Society, 1688–1832: Ideology, Social Structure and Political Practice during the Ancien Régime.* Cambridge: Cambridge University Press, 1985.

Cohen, Ralph. "The Rationale of Hume's Literary Inquiries." In *David Hume: Many-Sided Genius,* ed. Kenneth R. Merrill and Robert W. Shahan. Norman: University of Oklahoma Press, 1976.

Cone, Carl B. *Burke and the Nature of Politics.* 2 vols. Lexington: University of Kentucky Press, 1957 and 1964.

Curley, Thomas M. *Samuel Johnson and the Age of Travel.* Athens: University of Georgia Press, 1976.

Curtis, Lewis P. "Gibbon's Paradise Lost." In *The Age of Johnson: Essays Presented to Chauncey Brewster Tinker,* ed. Frederick W. Hilles. New Haven: Yale University Press, 1949.

Danto, Arthur C. *Analytical Philosophy of History.* Cambridge: Cambridge University Press, 1965.

Darwin, Charles. *The Life and Letters of Charles Darwin,* ed. Francis Darwin, 2 vols. New York: Appleton, 1896.

Derham, William. *Physico-Theology; or, A Demonstration of the Being and Attributes of God, from His Works of Creation.* 2d ed. London, 1714.

De Schweinitz, Karl Jr. *The Rise and Fall of British India: Imperialism as Inequality.* London: Methuen, 1983.

Dewey, John. *Experience and Nature.* La Salle, Ill.: Open Court, 1929.

Dickinson, H. T. "The Politics of Edward Gibbon," *Literature and History* 8 (1978): 175–96.

Diderot, Denis. *Oeuvres philosophiques de Diderot,* ed. Paul Vernière. Paris: Garnier, 1964.

Dowling, William C. *The Boswellian Hero.* Athens: University of Georgia Press, 1979.

Dowling, William C. "Burke and the Age of Chivalry." *Yearbook of English Studies* 12 (1982), 109–24.

Empson, William. *Seven Types of Ambiguity.* New York: Meridian Books, 1955.

Epstein, William H. "*Bios* and *Logos*: Boswell's *Life of Johnson* and Recent Literary Theory," *South Atlantic Quarterly* 82 (1983): 246–55.

Faulkner, John E. "Edmund Burke's Early Conception of Poetry and Rhetoric," *Studies in Burke and His Time* 12 (1970–71): 1747–63.

Febvre, Lucien. *A New Kind of History.* Trans. K. Folca. New York: Harper Torchbooks, 1973.

Fielding, Henry. *The Journal of a Voyage to Lisbon.* Vol. 16 in *The Works of Henry Fielding,* ed. W. E. Henley. New York: Barnes and Noble, 1967.

Fish, Stanley. *Is There a Text in This Class? The Authority of Interpretive Communities.* Cambridge: Harvard University Press, 1980.

Fisher, James. Introduction and notes to Gilbert White, *The Natural History of Selborne.* London: Cresset Press, 1960.

Forbes, Duncan. *Hume's Philosophical Politics.* Cambridge: Cambridge University Press, 1975.

Fothergill, Robert. *Private Chronicles: A Study of English Diaries.* London: Oxford University Press, 1974.

Fried, Michael. *Absorption and Theatricality: Painting and Beholder in the Age of Diderot.* Berkeley: University of California Press, 1980.

Freud, Sigmund. *The Ego and the Id.* Trans. Joan Riviere. Rev. James Strachey (New York: Norton, 1960).

Freud, Sigmund. *Moses and Monotheism.* Vol. 23 in *The Standard Edition of the Complete Works of Sigmund Freud,* trans. James Strachey. London: Hogarth Press, 1964.

Frye, Northrop. "Towards Defining an Age of Sensibility." In *Eighteenth-Century*

English Literature: Modern Essays in Criticism, ed. James L. Clifford, 311–18. New York: Oxford University Press, 1959.

Gadamer, Hans-Georg. *Philosophical Hermeneutics*. Trans. David E. Linge. Berkeley: University of California Press, 1976.

Gay, Peter. *The Enlightenment: An Interpretation*. Vol. 1: *The Rise of Modern Paganism*. New York: Knopf, 1966.

Gay, Peter. *Style in History*. London: Jonathan Cape, 1974.

Geertz, Clifford. *The Interpretation of Cultures*. New York: Basic Books, 1973.

Gibbon, Edward. *The Autobiographies of Edward Gibbon*. Ed. John Murray. New York, 1907.

Gibbon, Edward. *The English Essays of Edward Gibbon*. Ed. Patricia B. Craddock. Oxford: Clarendon Press, 1972.

Gibbon, Edward. *The History of the Decline and Fall of the Roman Empire*. Ed. J. B. Bury. 7 vols. London: Methuen, 1909–14.

Gibbon, Edward. *Memoirs of My Life*. Ed. Betty Radice (Harmondsworth: Penguin Books, 1984.

Gillispie, Charles C. *The Edge of Objectivity*. Princeton: Princeton University Press, 1960.

Gilmore, Myron. "Introduction." *Edward Gibbon and the Decline and Fall of the Roman Empire*, ed. G. W. Bowersock, John Clive, and Stephen R. Graubard. Cambridge: Harvard University Press, 1977.

Godwin, William. *Caleb Williams*. Ed. David McCracken. London: Oxford University Press, 1970.

Godwin, William. *Enquiry concerning Political Justice*. Ed. Isaac Kramnick. Harmondsworth: Penguin Books, 1976.

Gombrich, E. H. *Art and Illusion: A Study in the Psychology of Pictorial Representation*. Princeton: Princeton University Press, 1961.

Gossman, Lionel. *The Empire Unpossess'd: An Essay on Gibbon's "Decline and Fall"*. Cambridge: Cambridge University Press, 1981.

Gossman, Lionel. "History and Literature: Reproduction or Signification." In *The Writing of History: Literary Form and Historical Understanding*, ed. Robert H. Canary and Henry Kozicki, 3–39. Madison: University of Wisconsin Press, 1978.

Gould, Stephen Jay, and Rosamond Wolff Purcell. *Illuminations: A Bestiary*. New York: Norton, 1986.

Grave, S. A. *The Scottish Philosophy of Common Sense*. Oxford: Clarendon, 1960.

Greene, Donald J. *The Politics of Samuel Johnson*. New Haven: Yale University Press, 1960.

Gunn, Giles. *The Culture of Criticism and the Criticism of Culture*. New York: Oxford University Press, 1987.

Hacking, Ian. *The Emergence of Probability: A Philosophical Study of Early Ideas about Probability, Induction and Statistical Inference*. Cambridge: Cambridge University Press, 1975.

Hallett, H. F. "Dr. Johnson's Refutation of Bishop Berkeley," *Mind* 56 (1947): 132–47.

Hay, Douglas. "Property, Authority and the Criminal Law." In *Albion's Fatal*

Tree: Crime and Society in Eighteenth-Century England, ed. Hay et al., 17–63. New York: Pantheon Books, 1975.

Heller, Erich. *In the Age of Prose: Literary and Philosophical Essays*. Cambridge: Cambridge University Press, 1984.

Hertz, Neil. "Medusa's Head: Male Hysteria under Political Pressure," *Representations* 4 (1983): 27–54.

Hiley, David R. "The Deep Challenge of Pyrrhonian Scepticism," *Journal of the History of Philosophy* 25 (1987): 185–213.

Hill, G. B., ed. *Johnsonian Miscellanies*. 2 vols. Oxford: Clarendon Press, 1897.

Hogle, Jerrold E. "The Texture of the Self in Godwin's *Things as They Are*," *Boundary 2: A Journal of Postmodern Literature* 7 (1979): 261–81.

Holroyd, Michael. *Lytton Strachey: A Critical Biography*. 2 vols. New York: Holt, Rinehart and Winston, 1968.

Holt-White, Rashleigh, ed. *The Life and Letters of Gilbert White of Selborne*. 2 vols. London: Murray, 1901.

Hume, David. *Dialogues Concerning Natural Religion*. Ed. Norman Kemp Smith. Indianapolis: Bobbs-Merrill, 1947.

Hume, David. *Essays, Moral, Political, and Literary*. Ed. Eugene F. Miller. Indianapolis: Liberty Classics, 1987.

Hume, David. *The History of England*. 6 vols. Boston: Little, Brown, 1854.

Hume, David. *An Inquiry concerning Human Understanding, with a Supplement: An Abstract of A Treatise of Human Nature*. Ed. Charles W. Hendel. Indianapolis: Bobbs-Merrill, 1955.

Hume, David. *An Inquiry concerning the Principles of Morals*. Ed. Charles W. Hendel. Indianapolis: Bobbs-Merrill, 1957.

Hume, David. *The Letters of David Hume*. Ed. J. Y. T. Greig. 2 vols. Oxford: Clarendon Press, 1932.

Hume, David. *The Natural History of Religion*. Ed. H. E. Root. Stanford: Stanford University Press, 1957.

Hume, David. *New Letters of David Hume*. Ed. Raymond Klibansky and Ernest C. Mossner. Oxford: Clarendon Press, 1954.

Hume, David. *A Treatise of Human Nature*. Ed. L. A. Selby-Bigge. Rev. P. H. Nidditch. Oxford: Clarendon Press, 1978.

Innes, Joanna. "Jonathan Clark, Social History, and England's 'Ancient Régime,'" *Past and Present* 115 (1987): 165–200.

James, William. *Pragmatism*. Cleveland: Meridian Books, 1955.

James, William. *The Principles of Psychology*. Cambridge: Harvard University Press, 1981.

Jameson, Fredric, "Sartre's Literary Criticism." In *Modern French Criticism from Proust and Valéry to Structuralism*, ed. John K. Simon. Chicago: University of Chicago Press, 1972.

Janes, Regina. "Edmund Burke's Indian Idyll," *Studies in Eighteenth-Century Culture* 9 (1979): 3–13.

Johnson, Samuel. *A Dictionary of the English Language*. 2 vols. London, 1755. Facsimile reprint, New York: Arno Press, 1979.

Johnson, Samuel. *The History of Rasselas, Prince of Abyssinia*. In *The Oxford Authors: Samuel Johnson*, ed. Donald J. Greene, 335–418. Oxford: Oxford University Press, 1984.

Johnson, Samuel. *The Idler and The Adventurer*. Ed. W. J. Bate, John M. Bullitt, and L. F. Powell. New Haven: Yale University Press, 1963.

Johnson, Samuel. *Johnson on Shakespeare*. Ed. Arthur Sherbo. Vols. 7 and 8 of the Yale Edition of the Works of Samuel Johnson. New Haven: Yale University Press, 1968.

Johnson, Samuel. *A Journey to the Western Islands of Scotland*. Ed. Mary Lascelles. New Haven: Yale University Press, 1971.

Johnson, Samuel. *The Letters of Samuel Johnson*. Ed. R. W. Chapman. 3 vols. Oxford: Clarendon Press, 1952.

Johnson, Samuel. *Lives of the English Poets*. Ed. G. B. Hill. 3 vols. Oxford: Clarendon Press, 1905.

Johnson, Samuel. *Political Writings*. Ed. Donald J. Greene. New Haven: Yale University Press, 1977.

Johnson, Samuel. *Preface* to *A Dictionary of the English Language*. In *The Oxford Authors: Samuel Johnson*, ed. Donald J. Greene, 307–28. Oxford: Oxford University Press, 1984.

Johnson, Samuel. *Preface* to edition of Shakespeare. In *Johnson on Shakespeare*. Ed. Arthur Sherbo. Vol. 7 of the Yale Edition of the Works of Samuel Johnson. New Haven: Yale University Press, 1968.

Johnson, Samuel. *The Rambler*. Ed. W. J. Bate and Albrecht B. Strauss. 3 vols. New Haven: Yale University Press, 1969.

Johnson, Samuel. *The Vision of Theodore, the Hermit of Teneriffe*. In *The Oxford Authors: Samuel Johnson*, ed. Donald J. Greene, 165–74. Oxford: Oxford University Press, 1984.

Jordan, David P. *Gibbon and His Roman Empire*. Urbana: University of Illinois Press, 1971.

Julian. *The Works of the Emperor Julian*. Ed. and trans. Wilmer Cave Wright. Loeb Classical Library. 3 vols. Cambridge: Harvard University Press, 1923.

Keast, William R. "The Element of Art in Gibbon's *History*," *English Literary History* 23 (1956): 153–62.

Keith, W. J. *The Rural Tradition: A Study of the Non-Fiction Prose Writers of the English Countryside*. Toronto: University of Toronto Press, 1974.

Kernan, Alvin. *Printing Technology, Letters, and Samuel Johnson*. Princeton: Princeton University Press, 1987.

Kiely, Robert. *The Romantic Novel in England* (Cambridge: Harvard University Press, 1972.

Kilcup, Rodney W. "Burke's Historicism," *Journal of Modern History* 49 (1977): 394–410.

Kivy, Peter. "Voltaire, Hume, and the Problem of Evil," *Philosophy and Literature* 3 (1979): 211–24.

Knapp, Steven, and Walter Benn Michaels. "Against Theory." In *Against Theory: Literary Studies and the New Pragmatism*, ed. W. J. T. Mitchell, 11–30. Chicago: University of Chicago Press, 1985.

Knoblauch, Cyril H. "Coherence Betrayed: Samuel Johnson and the 'Prose of the World,'" *Boundary* 2 7 (1979): 235–60.

Kramnick, Isaac. *The Rage of Edmund Burke: Portrait of an Ambivalent Conservative*. New York: Basic Books, 1977.

Kuhn, Thomas S. *The Structure of Scientific Revolutions*. Chicago: University of Chicago Press, 1962.

Kundera, Milan. *The Book of Laughter and Forgetting*. Trans. Michael Henry Heim. Harmondsworth: Penguin Books, 1981.

LaCapra, Dominick. *History and Criticism*. Ithaca: Cornell University Press, 1985.

LaCapra, Dominick. *Rethinking Intellectual History: Texts, Contexts, Language*. Ithaca: Cornell University Press, 1983.

Land, Stephen K. *From Signs to Propositions: The Concept of Form in Eighteenth-Century Semantic Theory*. London: Longman, 1974.

Lanham, Richard. *The Motives of Eloquence: Literary Rhetoric in the Renaissance*. New Haven: Yale University Press, 1976.

Lewis, C. S. *English Literature in the Sixteenth Century*. Oxford: Clarendon Press, 1954.

Livingston, Donald W. *Hume's Philosophy of Common Life*. Chicago: University of Chicago Press, 1984.

Locke, John. *An Essay concerning Human Understanding*. Ed. A. C. Fraser. 2 vols. New York: Dover, 1959.

Lossky, Andrew. "Introduction: Gibbon and the Enlightenment." In *The Transformation of the Roman World: Gibbon's Problem after Two Centuries*, ed. Lynn White, Jr. Berkeley: University of California Press, 1966.

Lowell, James Russell. *My Study Windows*. London: Scott, 1887.

Lucas, Paul. "On Edmund Burke's Doctrine of Prescription; or, An Appeal from the New to the Old Lawyers," *Historical Journal* 11 (1968): 35–63.

Macpherson, C. B. *Burke*. Oxford: Oxford University Press, 1980.

Mabey, Richard. *Gilbert White: A Biography of the Author of "The Natural History of Selborne"*. London: Century Hutchinson, 1986.

Maddox, Lucy B. "Gilbert White and the Politics of Natural History," *Eighteenth-Century Life* 10 (1986): 45–57.

Mandel, Barrett John. "The Problem of Narration in Edward Gibbon's *Autobiography*," *Studies in Philology* 67 (1970): 550–64.

Manuel, Frank. "Edward Gibbon: Historien-Philosophe." In *Edward Gibbon and the Decline and Fall of the Roman Empire*, ed. G. W. Bowersock, John Clive, and Stephen R. Graubard. Cambridge: Harvard University Press, 1977.

Marshall, David. "Adam Smith and the Theatricality of Moral Sentiments," *Critical Inquiry* 10 (1984): 592–613.

Marshall, Dorothy. *English People in the Eighteenth Century*. London: Longmans, Green, 1956.

Mink, Louis O. "Narrative Form as a Cognitive Instrument." In *The Writing of History: Literary Form and Historical Understanding*, ed. Robert H. Canary and Henry Kozicki, 129–49. Madison: University of Wisconsin Press, 1978.

Montesquieu, Charles-Louis de Secondat, Baron de. *The Persian Letters*. Trans. George R. Healy. Indianapolis: Bobbs-Merrill, 1964.

Mossner, Ernest Campbell. *The Life of David Hume*. 2d ed. Oxford: Clarendon Press, 1980.

Mulso, John. *The Letters to Gilbert White of Selborne from . . . John Mulso*. Ed. Rashleigh Holt-White. London: Porter, 1907.

Nietzsche, Friedrich. *Beyond Good and Evil.* Trans. Helen Zimmern. In *The Philosophy of Nietzsche.* New York: Modern Library, 1954.

Norton, David Fate. *David Hume: Common-Sense Moralist, Sceptical Metaphysician.* Princeton: Princeton University Press, 1982.

Noxon, James. "Remembering and Imagining the Past." In *Hume: A Re-Evaluation,* ed. Donald W. Livingston and James T. King, 270–95. New York: Fordham University Press, 1976.

Nussbaum, Felicity A. "Father and Son in Boswell's *London Journal,*" *Philological Quarterly* 57 (1978): 383–97.

Ober, William B., M.D. *Boswell's Clap and Other Essays.* Carbondale: Southern Illinois University Press, 1979.

O'Gorman, Frank. *Edmund Burke: His Political Philosophy.* Bloomington: Indiana University Press, 1973.

Paine, Thomas. *The Rights of Man.* Ed. Henry Collins. Harmondsworth: Penguin, 1969.

Paley, William. *Natural Theology: Selections.* Ed. Frederick Ferré. Indianapolis: Bobbs-Merrill, 1963.

Passmore, John. *Hume's Intentions.* 3d ed. London: Duckworth, 1980.

Patey, Douglas Lane. "Johnson's Refutation of Berkeley: Kicking the Stone Again," *Journal of the History of Ideas* 47 (1986): 139–45.

Patey, Douglas Lane. *Probability and Literary Form: Philosophic Theory and Literary Practice in the Augustan Age.* Cambridge: Cambridge University Press, 1984.

Paulson, Ronald. *Representations of Revolution, 1789–1820.* New Haven: Yale University Press, 1983.

Penelhum, Terence. *Hume.* New York: St. Martin's Press, 1975.

Penelhum, Terence. "Natural Belief and Religious Belief in Hume's Philosophy," *Philosophical Quarterly* 33 (1983): 166–81.

Phillipson, Nicholas. "Hume as Moralist: A Social Historian's Perspective." In *Philosophers of the Enlightenment,* ed. S. C. Brown, 140–61. Brighton: Harvester Press, 1979.

Philp, Mark. *Godwin's Political Justice.* London: Duckworth, 1986.

Pocock, J. G. A. "Gibbon and the Shepherds: The Stages of Society in the *Decline and Fall,*" *History of European Ideas* 2 (1981): 193–202.

Pocock, J. G. A. *The Machiavellian Moment: Florentine Political Thought and the Atlantic Republican Tradition.* Princeton: Princeton University Press, 1975.

Pocock, J. G. A. *Politics, Language and Time: Essays on Political Thought and History.* New York: Atheneum, 1973.

Pocock, J. G. A. *Virtue, Commerce, and History: Essays on Political Thought and History, Chiefly in the Eighteenth Century.* Cambridge: Cambridge University Press, 1985.

Porter, Dale H. *The Emergence of the Past: A Theory of Historical Explanation.* Chicago: University of Chicago Press, 1981.

Porter, Roy. *English Society in the Eighteenth Century.* Harmondsworth: Penguin, 1982.

Pottle, Frederick A. *James Boswell: The Earlier Years, 1740–1769.* New York: McGraw-Hill, 1966.

Putnam, Hilary. *The Many Faces of Realism*. La Salle, Ill.: Open Court, 1987.

Ray, John. *The Wisdom of God Manifested in the Works of the Creation*. 12th ed. London, 1759.

Reichard, Hugo. "Boswell's Johnson, the Hero Made by a Committee," *PMLA* 95 (1980): 225–33.

Reid, Christopher. *Edmund Burke and the Practice of Political Writing*. Dublin and London: Gill & Macmillan and St. Martin's Press, 1985.

Reid, Thomas. *An Inquiry into the Human Mind*. Ed. Timothy Duggan. Chicago: University of Chicago Press, 1970.

Reynolds, John. *The Triumph of God's Revenge Against the Crying and Execrable Sin of (Wilful and Premeditated) Murther, With His Miraculous Discoveries, and Severe Punishment Thereof, in Thirty Several Tragical Histories . . . Very Necessary to Restrain and Deter Us from that Bloody Sin which in These our Days Makes so Ample and Large a Progression*. 5th ed. London, 1670.

Reynolds, Joshua. *Discourses on Art*. Ed. Stephen O. Mitchell. Indianapolis: Bobbs-Merrill, 1965.

Richetti, John J. *Philosophical Writing: Locke, Berkeley, Hume*. Cambridge: Harvard University Press, 1983.

Ricoeur, Paul. *The Symbolism of Evil*. Trans. Emerson Buchanan. Boston: Beacon, 1969.

Rorty, Richard. *Philosophy and the Mirror of Nature*. Princeton: Princeton University Press, 1979.

Rorty, Richard. "Texts and Lumps," *New Literary History* 17 (1985): 1–16.

Rothstein, Eric. *Systems of Order and Inquiry in Later Eighteenth-Century Fiction*. Berkeley: University of California Press, 1975.

Rota, Gian-Carlo. Introduction to Philip J. Davis and Reuben Hersh, *The Mathematical Experience*. Boston: Houghton Mifflin, 1981.

Rousseau, Jean-Jacques. *The Confessions*. Trans. J. M. Cohen. Harmondsworth: Penguin, 1954.

Rousseau, Jean-Jacques. *The Social Contract and Discourse on the Origin and Foundation of Inequality among Mankind*. Trans. Lester G. Crocker. New York: Washington Square, 1967.

Sachs, Arieh. *Passionate Intelligence: Imagination and Reason in the Work of Samuel Johnson*. Baltimore: Johns Hopkins University Press, 1967.

Said, Edward W. *Beginnings: Intention and Method*. Baltimore: Johns Hopkins University Press, 1975.

Scholes, Robert. "Language, Narrative, and Anti-Narrative." In *On Narrative*, ed. W. J. T. Mitchell, 200–208. Chicago: University of Chicago Press, 1981.

Sen, Sunil Kumar, ed. *Edmund Burke on Indian Economy*. Calcutta: Progressive Publishers, 1969.

Sextus Empiricus. *Outlines of Pyrrhonism*. Trans. R. G. Bury. Cambridge: Harvard University Press, 1933.

Sibbes, Richard. *The Soul's Conflict*. In vol. 1 of *Complete Works*, ed. Alexander Grosart. Edinburgh, 1862.

Siebert, Donald T. "Hume on Idolatry and Incarnation," *Journal of the History of Ideas* 45 (1984): 379–96.

Sitter, John. *Literary Loneliness in Mid-Eighteenth-Century England*. Ithaca: Cornell University Press, 1982.

Smith, Barbara Herrnstein. *On the Margins of Discourse: The Relation of Literature to Language*. Chicago: University of Chicago Press, 1978.

Smith, Bruce James. *Politics and Remembrance: Republican Themes in Machiavelli, Burke, and Tocqueville*. Princeton: Princeton University Press, 1985.

South, Robert. *Sermons*. London, 1737.

Spacks, Patricia Meyer. *Imagining a Self: Autobiography and Novel in Eighteenth-Century England*. Cambridge: Harvard University Press, 1976.

Sprat, Thomas. *The History of the Royal Society*. London, 1667.

Starobinski, Jean. *Jean-Jacques Rousseau: la Transparence et l'obstacle*. Paris: Plon, 1957.

Stephen, Leslie. *History of English Thought in the Eighteenth Century*. 2 vols. 1876. Rpt. New York: Harcourt, Brace and World, 1962.

Stephen, Leslie. "Johnsoniana." In *Studies of a Biographer*, 1:105–46. London: Duckworth, 1898.

Storch, Rudolf E. "Metaphors of Private Guilt and Social Rebellion in Godwin's *Caleb Williams*," *ELH* 34 (1967): 188–207.

Strachey, Lytton. *Portraits in Miniature and Other Essays*. New York: Harcourt, Brace, 1931.

Sutherland, Lucy S. *The East India Company in Eighteenth-Century Politics*. Oxford: Clarendon Press, 1952.

Tacitus. *The Annals of Imperial Rome*. Trans. Michael Grant. Harmondsworth: Penguin, 1977.

Trevelyan, George Macaulay. *Clio, A Muse, and Other Essays*. London: Longmans Green, 1930.

Trilling, Lionel. "Why We Read Jane Austen," *Times Literary Supplement*, 5 March 1976: 250–52.

Trowbridge, Hoyt. *From Dryden to Jane Austen: Essays on English Critics and Writers, 1660–1818*. Albuquerque: University of New Mexico Press, 1977.

Updike, John. "Through the Mid-Life Crisis with James Boswell, Esq." In *Hugging the Shore: Essays and Criticism*. New York: Knopf, 1983.

Vance, John A. "Johnson and Hume: Of Like Historical Minds," *Studies in Eighteenth-Century Culture* 15 (1986): 241–56.

Van Tassel, Mary M. "Johnson's Elephant: The Reader of *The Rambler*," *SEL* 28 (1988): 461–69.

Vendler, Helen. "Sentences Hammered in Metal." *New Yorker*, 24 October 1988: 122–30.

Vidal, Gore. *Julian*. New York: Vintage Books, 1977.

Voitle, Robert. *Samuel Johnson the Moralist*. Cambridge: Harvard University Press, 1961.

Voltaire. *Candide*. Trans. John Butt. Harmondsworth: Penguin Books, 1976.

Walker, Robert G. "Johnson and the 'Age of Evidences,'" *Huntington Library Quarterly* 44 (1980): 27–41.

Walzer, Michael. *The Revolution of the Saints: A Study in the Origins of Radical Politics*. New York: Atheneum, 1968.

Works Cited

Warburton, William. Commentary on the *Essay on Man*. Vol. 3 of the *Works* of Alexander Pope. London, 1751.

Watson, Richard. *An Apology for Christianity, in a Series of Letters Addressed to Edward Gibbon, Esq.* 2d ed. Cambridge, 1778.

White, Gilbert. *Antiquities of Selborne*. In *The Natural History and Antiquities of Selborne*, ed. A. W. Pollard. London: Macmillan, 1900.

White, Gilbert. *Gilbert White's Journals*. Ed. Walter Johnson. 1931. Rpt. London: Routledge & Kegan Paul, 1970.

White, Gilbert. *The Natural History of Selborne*. Ed. Richard Mabey. Harmondsworth: Penguin, 1977.

White, Hayden. "The Question of Narrative in Contemporary Historical Theory," *History and Theory* 23 (1984): 1–33.

White, Hayden. *Tropics of Discourse: Essays in Cultural Criticism*. Baltimore: Johns Hopkins University Press, 1978.

White, Hayden. "The Value of Narrativity in the Representation of Reality." In *On Narrative*, ed. W. J. T. Mitchell, 1–23. Chicago: University of Chicago Press, 1981.

Wilkins, Burleigh Taylor. *The Problem of Burke's Political Philosophy*. Oxford: Clarendon Press, 1967.

Williams, Raymond. *The Country and the City*. London: Chatto & Windus, 1973.

Williams, Raymond. *Modern Tragedy*. Stanford: Stanford University Press, 1966.

Williams, Raymond. *Politics and Letters*. London: NLB, 1979.

Wind, Edgar. *Pagan Mysteries in the Renaissance*. Harmondsworth: Penguin, 1967.

Winks, Robin W. "Hume and Gibbon: A View from a Vantage," *Dalhousie Review* 41 (1962): 496–504.

Wolff, Robert Paul. *In Defense of Anarchism*. New York: Harper & Row, 1976.

Wollstonecraft, Mary. *A Vindication of the Rights of Woman*. Ed. Carol H. Poston. New York: Norton, 1975.

Wolpert, Stanley. *A New History of India*. New York: Oxford University Press, 1977.

Woodman, Tony. "Self-Imitation and the Substance of History." In *Creative Imitation and Latin Literature*, ed. David West and Tony Woodman, 143–55. Cambridge: Cambridge University Press, 1979.

Woolf, Virginia. "The Historian and 'the Gibbon.'" In *The Death of the Moth and Other Essays*. London: Hogarth Press, 1942.

Woolf, Virginia. "White's Selborne." In *Collected Essays*, 3:122–26. New York: Harcourt, Brace & World, 1967.

Yolton, John W. *Perceptual Acquaintance from Descartes to Reid*. Minneapolis: University of Minnesota Press, 1984.

Young, G. M. *Gibbon*. London: Rupert Hart-Davis, 1948.

Index

Index